n imprint
Building, 11 York Road, London, SE1 7NX
on Avenue, New York, NY 10017-6550

version of *Celebrating Common Prayer* was compiled by:

liffe, Bishop of Salisbury, Chairman of the
mmission of the Church of England and erstwhile Chairman
ory Panel for *Celebrating Common Prayer*.

Tristam SSF, General Secretary of the
aint Francis, Member of the Liturgical Commission
f *Celebrating Common Prayer*.

ography:
pean Province of the Society of Saint Francis 1994

ry for Liturgy SSF
ary
TER, Dorset DT2 7BE, UK

se a stamped, addressed envelope.

hed 1994; reprinted 1995; 1996; 1998; 2000

57351-4

gements, see pages 314 & 315.

peset in Palatino 8 point by the Society of St Francis.
em by Sister Regina OSB.

bound in Great Britain by The Bath Press, Bath

Celebrating Common P

The Pocket Version

MOWBRAY

Mowbray
A Continu
The Towe
370 Lexin

· **Compilers**
This pock

David Sta
Liturgical
of the Adv

and **Broth**
Society of
and Edito

Text and t
© The Eu

All rights
reproduce
including
retrieval s
should be

The Secre
Hilfield F
DORCHE

Please enc

First publ

ISBN 0-26

Acknowle

Computer
Cover em

Printed an

CONTENTS

Preface

A word of explanation about why this book has been produced and how it differs from the full version of *Celebrating Common Prayer* is probably in order.

Many who use and enjoy celebrating the Office from *Celebrating Common Prayer* have said that, particularly when they are travelling, the book plus a Bible is simply too heavy and cumbersome. So we have included a selection of short bible readings which follow the same daily and weekly pattern as the psalms; so you do not need to carry a separate Bible.

Another regular question is that if all the psalms are not listed to be used, why include them? The answer is that some users do make full use of the whole Psalter, and there is a table for this in the full edition. However, we acknowledge that for those using the proposed selection of psalms in this version, it is much easier if they are printed where they are used.

As we have brought out this new pocket version, it seems sensible to make some improvements, but these are relatively minor and translations of spoken texts are no different from those found in the full edition of *Celebrating Common Prayer*. The simplest change is the renaming of each Day/Season as Form 1 through 7, which we hope will reduce any confusion. The section previously called 'After the Office' is now renamed 'Occasional Services', as we feel these can stand on their own if so desired, and not just as a conclusion to a full Office. In addition, refrains have been omitted and the responsory shortened to a simple versicle and response.

We have simplified 'The Christian Year' in two ways: major feasts of the Church are indicated in **bold** type in the Calendar but it is left to the user how to mark other festivals and commemorations. Nor have we included collects for all the Sundays through the year: we felt that those provided in the context of the Office were adequate. As a result, we have managed to integrate the seasons with the saintly holy days, which should make things less complicated.

We hope you enjoy this book and that it will enhance the celebration of your own prayer life and that of the Church.

✠ **David Sarum**   **Tristam SSF**

Introduction

The Worshipping Group Whether you are an individual
(travelling, at home or in a place of worship), a small group,
a parish at prayer or a religious community, the first decision
you have to make is what your regular pattern of worship is to
be.

What to Pray What you choose will depend on the circumstances
and the time available. Some will want to use the whole
provision. Some people will simply say one Office each day, at
a time of day which is most suitable to work and leisure
patterns. Others will say Morning and Evening Prayer daily and
may also take part in a daily Eucharist. The Office may be
said by a person alone or by two people or as a group or
community prayer; it may be said or sung. It may be led by
anyone and does not need an ordained minister present for its
celebration.

Where to Look Next, you need to know where to find what it is
you have chosen to use. Each of the Offices is set out in full
for each day of the week: in Ordinary Time or 'green' seasons,
simply turn to the appropriate day, for example, *Morning
Prayer, Monday*, and you will find the whole Office set out in
order. The psalms and scripture readings are printed in the
text of the Office in a seven-week cycle. To discover which
week to use, refer to the table on page 307; using the date,
you can find out where you are in 'The Christian Year'.
Alternatively, refer to the Calendar on pages 7 to 22.

Special Seasons When you are in a special season of the
Christian Year, the Office is **not** used according to all the
days of the week but that of one particular day, which has the
seasonal flavour, using the sevenfold pattern of psalms and
readings for each day of the week. In this way, the pattern of
the Christian Year is reinforced by the repetition each week of
psalms, canticles, readings and prayers particularly suited to
that season. So in Advent, Tuesday's Office is used; in
Christmastide, Wednesday's; in Epiphanytide, Thursday's; in
Lent and Passiontide, Friday's; in Eastertide, Sunday's; in
Pentecost, Monday's; and in the Kingdom season in November,
Saturday's.

The Shape of the Office   Even though the Office is flexible, however much or little the Office is used the basic framework should remain clear.   In essence, the Office has three main parts: The Introduction, The Word of God and The Prayers.   The Introduction begins by addressing prayer to God and an acclamation.   The Word of God includes psalms and a canticle, a bible reading and concludes with a gospel canticle.   The Prayers include intercession, summarised by a collect, and culminates in the Lord's Prayer.

Deciding Where   The Notes, page 5, give some suggestions for how to tailor the Office to the situation, but the following points may be helpful.

A group may find it more helpful to sit in a semicircle in an appropriate size space, around a lectern holding the Bible, rather than behind each other in pews in the main body of the church.   Another focus, in addition to or occasionally in place of the lectern – such as a cross, a candle, a seasonal icon or some other Christian symbol – may be found helpful.

Those praying alone should find a quiet place, if possible, but even in the midst of noise, such as on a train journey, the Office will help to create its own atmosphere.

Deciding How   The way in which the Office is celebrated helps or hinders the prayer of the worshipping group.   Singing, however simply, helps unite the prayer (though this is not recommended on a train journey!); a regular pace also assists this unity and helps to focus the worship on God and not on the words for their own sake.

Being Ready   Preparation beforehand helps, particularly if there is more than one person praying. The Officiant or leader will need to prepare the intercessions, possibly using material from page 245 to 260, or from other sources. If one of the sections from 'The Occasional Services' (pages 261 to 282) is to be used, others present should be told first. At Evening Prayer, if the Blessing of the Light is to be used, a suitable candle needs to be prepared ready for lighting during the singing of the Song of Light. If all are to hold candles, these need to be distributed beforehand. If incense is to be used, a small brazier (a censer or thurible, or a simple pot) with hot coals (charcoal already prepared is the easiest to cope with) needs to be made ready in a suitable place so that incense may be put on. This all ensures that worship can be offered by a well-prepared and confident praying community.

Beginning the Office   The person leading the Office begins with an invitation and acclamation to which everybody responds.

How to Recite   Whether singing or speaking, there are different ways in which psalms and canticles can be treated. Some of the psalms, such as the more personal and penitential ones, are perhaps best spoken by a single voice. Others may be recited antiphonally (different individuals or groups taking alternate verses). Other psalms may be recited together: this is particularly appropriate for the canticles. The asterisk at the half-way point indicates that a short pause is appropriate.

Psalm Prayer   Instead of the *Gloria Patri* at the end of the psalms, a prayer is provided for each psalm in order to articulate the fact that the community's prayer is in Christ.

Bible Reading   The reading might be read from the lectern Bible, if in a place of worship; at the conclusion of the reading, the **Response** is said after a brief pause, which may be followed by a period of silence. The easiest way of concluding this silence is for the Officiant to rise.

The Gospel Canticle follows and is best recited together, preferably standing if, so far in the Office, sitting has been the norm.

The Prayers   After the gospel canticle, the Officiant introduces the prayers of intercession. This may take several forms: short litanies as printed in the text, or additional ones on pages 249 to 257, may be suitable or a series of biddings. A regular pattern helps trigger the response. At the end of the Prayers, the Officiant concludes with the Collect, the Lord's Prayer and a final versicle and response.

Ending the Office   After the Office, if any corporate movement is to take place, to the font for example, the Officiant should have already explained this before the service.

Notes

A GENERAL

1 **The Psalms** Use the psalms as printed in the Office.
If another psalm is desired, that for *Week 1/Sundays* can be
used each day before that already provided for the day.
Any alternative table of psalms may be used, but note that
the whole Psalter is not included in this book.
The week for the psalms is on pages 8, 9 & 10.

2 **Canticles** The canticles may be replaced by hymns.

3 **Litanies** Alternative litanies are on pages 249 to 257.
The Great Litany, page 249, is especially suitable on Ash
Wednesday, on Fridays in Lent and on the Commemoration
of the Faithful Departed (2 November).

4 **Silences** Appropriate places for silence are: after the
psalm; after the reading (though, when the Response is
used, the silence should follow that); before the Collect;
and before the confession at Night Prayer.

5 **Scripture Readings** The Lectionary is designed especially
for when travelling. Other regular lectionaries or patterns
of reading should be used when a Bible is available.

6 **The Collect** Where a collect ends with 'Christ our
Lord/Saviour/Redeemer . . .' the longer ending may be
added: 'who is alive and reigns with you and the Holy
Spirit, one God, now and for ever. Amen.'

7 **The Lord's Prayer** The tradition from the early Church is
that the Lord's Prayer should be prayed three times a day.

B EVENING PRAYER

Blessing of the Light A light, which may be the Paschal
Candle, is brought in, or a candle may simply be lit. From
Easter to Pentecost, the Paschal Candle may be burning in
its customary place. Incense may be burnt.

C NIGHT PRAYER

1 **Blessing of the Light** On suitable occasions, Night
Prayer may begin with 'The Blessing of the Light' and the
burning of incense.

2 **Preparation** In the Preparation section, all that precedes
'O God, make speed to save us' may be omitted.

D SEASONS OF THE YEAR

1 **Advent** Advent begins at Evening Prayer on the eve of
Advent Sunday and ends before Evening Prayer on
Christmas Eve. During this season, Form 3 is used.

2 **Christmas** Christmas begins at Evening Prayer on
Christmas Eve. Christmas ends before Evening Prayer on
5 January. During this season, Form 4 is used.

3 **Epiphany** Epiphanytide begins at Evening Prayer on the
eve of the Epiphany (5 January) and ends either at Night
Prayer on the feast of the Presentation (2 February) or, if
that feast is being kept on the Sunday following, at Night
Prayer on that day. During this season, Form 5 is used.

4 **Lent** Lent begins at Morning Prayer on Ash Wednesday
and before the Vigil of Easter. During this season, Form 6
is used. 'Alleluia' is not said again until Easter Day.

5 **Eastertide** Easter begins with the Vigil of Easter and ends
after Night Prayer on the feast of Pentecost. During this
period, Form 1 is used.

6 **Pentecost** Pentecost begins with Morning Prayer on the
Friday after Ascension Day and ends with Night Prayer on
the feast of Pentecost. During this period, Form 2 is used.

7 **The Kingdom Season** The Kingdom season begins at
Evening Prayer on the eve of All Saints' Day and ends
before Evening Prayer on the eve of Advent Sunday.
During this season, Form 7 is used.

8 **Ordinary Time** Ordinary Time (sometimes called the
'green' season) extends from the day after the feast of the
Presentation until Night Prayer on Shrove Tuesday; and
from the day after the feast of Pentecost to Evening
Prayer on the eve of All Saints' Day. During these times,
the Office follows the regular Form 1 to Form 7 order.
The *Week* for the psalms can be found on pages 8, 9 and 10.

The Calendar

Holy days in the Christian year have been given a description which help to suggest how the day should be kept:
principal holy days & festivals (printed in bold typeface);
lesser festivals (printed in ordinary roman typeface);
commemorations (printed in a smaller roman typeface).
All Sundays are festivals, though different seasons are given a different emphasis: e.g. Advent and Lent are times of preparation and penitence; Christmas and Easter are periods of rejoicing in the incarnation of our Lord and his redemption of the world.

This Calendar gives some new occasions for celebrating those who 'excite us to holiness', and some new dates for old ones, in line with proposals from the Liturgical Commission.

When it is desired to keep a saint's day as more than a commemoration, special readings, responses and collects can be found in *The Christian Year*, pages 283 to 306, either for the individual feast or in an appropriate 'common' category.

Some additional local commemorations are suggested in a smaller typeface below the ordinary text each month.

DAYS OF SPECIAL OBSERVANCE
The following days are considered special and thought should be given as to how they are kept, in whatever way is appropriate to the local situation:

Christmas Eve and Easter Eve are days of preparation and vigil.

Ash Wednesday, the days of Holy Week and the Commemoration of the Faithful Departed (2 November) are days of special devotion.

The days after Christmas until 6 January, and the days of Easter Week, are days of special thanksgiving.

The nine days after Ascension Day until Pentecost are days of prayer and preparation to celebrate the outpouring of the Spirit.

Ember Days, Rogation Days and Harvest Thanksgivings are observed at the Eucharist.

THE SEASONS

ADVENT – Use Form 3
1st Sunday of Advent
2nd Sunday of Advent
3rd Sunday of Advent
From 17 December (O Sapientia) begin
the eight days of prayer before Christmas
4th Sunday of Advent
Eve and Vigil of Christmas

CHRISTMASTIDE – Use Form 4
Christmas Day – *25 December*
1st Sunday of Christmas – The Holy Family
2nd Sunday of Christmas

EPIPHANYTIDE – Use Form 5
Epiphany of Christ – *6 January*
Baptism of Christ – *1st Sunday of the Epiphany*
2nd Sunday of the Epiphany
3rd Sunday of the Epiphany
4th Sunday of the Epiphany
Presentation of Christ – Candlemas – *2 February*

PRE-LENT – Use the Office according to the day of the week
Fifth Sunday before Lent – *Week 3*
Fourth Sunday before Lent – *Week 4*
Third Sunday before Lent – *Week 5*
Second Sunday before Lent – *Week 6*
Sunday next before Lent – *Week 7*

LENT – Use Form 6
Ash Wednesday
1st Sunday of Lent
2nd Sunday of Lent
3rd Sunday of Lent
4th Sunday of Lent – *Mothering Sunday*
5th Sunday of Lent *(Passiontide begins)*

Palm Sunday
Monday of Holy Week
Tuesday of Holy Week
Wednesday of Holy Week
Maundy Thursday
Good Friday
Eve and Vigil of Easter

EASTERTIDE – Use Form 1
Easter Day
Monday of Easter Week
Tuesday of Easter Week
Wednesday of Easter Week
Thursday of Easter Week
Friday of Easter Week
Saturday of Easter Week
2nd Sunday of Easter
3rd Sunday of Easter
4th Sunday of Easter
5th Sunday of Easter
6th Sunday of Easter
Ascension Day

From Friday after Ascension begin the nine days of prayer before Pentecost. Use Form 2 through this period and on the Day of Pentecost.
7th Sunday of Easter
Pentecost (Whit Sunday)

AFTER PENTECOST
Weekdays after the Day of Pentecost – *Week 7*
Use the Office according to the day of the week
Trinity Sunday – *1st Sunday after Pentecost – Week 1*
Day of Thanksgiving for the Eucharist – **Corpus Christi**
    – *Thursday after Pentecost 1*
2nd Sunday after Pentecost – *Week 2*
3rd Sunday after Pentecost – *Week 3*
4th Sunday after Pentecost – *Week 4*
5th Sunday after Pentecost – *Week 5*
6th Sunday after Pentecost – *Week 6*

7th Sunday after Pentecost – *Week 7*
8th Sunday after Pentecost – *Week 1*
9th Sunday after Pentecost – *Week 2*
10th Sunday after Pentecost – *Week 3*
11th Sunday after Pentecost – *Week 4*
12th Sunday after Pentecost – *Week 5*
13th Sunday after Pentecost – *Week 6*
14th Sunday after Pentecost – *Week 7*
15th Sunday after Pentecost – *Week 1*
16th Sunday after Pentecost – *Week 2*
17th Sunday after Pentecost – *Week 3*
18th Sunday after Pentecost – *Week 4*
19th Sunday after Pentecost – *Week 5*
20th Sunday after Pentecost – *Week 6*
21st Sunday after Pentecost – *Week 7*
22nd Sunday after Pentecost – *Week 1*
Last Sunday after Pentecost – *Week 2*

Dedication Festival – *Last Sunday of October*

THE KINGDOM – Use Form 7
All Saints' Day – *1 November*
1st Sunday of the Kingdom – *All Saints' Sunday*
2nd Sunday of the Kingdom – *Remembrance Sunday*
3rd Sunday of the Kingdom
4th Sunday of the Kingdom – *The Sunday next before Advent
which may be observed as the feast of*
The Kingship of Christ

THE HOLY DAYS

JANUARY

PRINCIPAL HOLY DAYS & FESTIVALS
1 The Naming & Circumcision of Jesus
6 The Epiphany
25 The Conversion of Paul

LESSER FESTIVALS
2 Basil the Great & Gregory Nazianzen, Bishops,
     Teachers, 379 & 389
13 Hilary, Bishop of Poitiers, Teacher, 367
17 Antony of Egypt, Abbot, 356
18-25 Week of Prayer for Christian Unity
21 Agnes, Child-Martyr at Rome, 304
26 Timothy & Titus, Companions of Paul
28 Thomas Aquinas, Priest, Teacher, 1274
30 Charles, King & Martyr, 1649

COMMEMORATIONS
2 Mary Ward, Founder of the Institute of the BVM, 1645
2 Seraphim, Monk of Sarov, Mystic, Staretz, 1833
3 Gladys Aylward, Missionary in China, 1970
11 Mary Slessor, Missionary in West Africa, 1915
12 Benedict Biscop, Abbot of Wearmouth, Scholar, 689
13 Kentigern (Mungo), Missionary Bishop
     in Strathclyde & Cumbria, 603
13 George Fox, Founder of the Society of Friends (the Quakers), 1691
14 Richard Meux Benson, Founder of the Society of St John
     the Evangelist, 1915
19 Wulfstan, Bishop of Worcester, 1095
22 Vincent of Saragossa, Deacon, first Martyr of Spain, 304
23 Charles Gore, Bishop, Teacher,
     Founder of the Community of the Resurrection, 1932
24 Francis de Sales, Bishop of Geneva, Teacher, 1622
26 Dorothy Kerin, Founder of the Burrswood Healing Community, 1963
31 John Bosco, Priest, Founder of the Salesian Teaching Order, 1888

FEBRUARY

PRINCIPAL HOLY DAYS & FESTIVALS
2   **The Presentation of Christ in the Temple (Candlemas)**

LESSER FESTIVALS
3   Anskar, Archbishop of Hamburg,
    Missionary to Denmark & Sweden, 865
14 Cyril & Methodius, Missionaries to the Slavs, 869 & 885
17 Janani Luŵum, Archbishop of Uganda, Martyr, 1977
23 Polycarp, Bishop of Smyrna, Martyr, c.155
27 George Herbert, Priest, Poet, 1633

COMMEMORATIONS
1   Brigid, Abbess of Kildare, c.525
4   Gilbert of Sempringham, Founder of the Gilbertine Order, 1189
10 Scholastica, Abbess of Plombariola, c.543
14 Valentine, Martyr at Rome, 269
15 Thomas Bray, Priest, Missionary, Founder of SPCK, 1730
20 Cecile Isherwood, Founder of the Community of the Resurrection,
    Grahamstown, South Africa, 1906

MARCH

APRIL

MAY

PRINCIPAL HOLY DAYS & FESTIVALS

1 **Philip & James, Apostles**
14 **Matthias the Apostle**
31 **The Visit of the Blessèd Virgin Mary to Elizabeth**

LESSER FESTIVALS

2 Athanasius, Bishop of Alexandria, Teacher, 373
4 Saints & Martyrs of the English Reformation Era
8 Julian of Norwich, Mystic, Teacher, c.1417
19 Dunstan, Archbishop of Canterbury, 988
24 John & Charles Wesley, Priests, Poets, Teachers,
     1792 & 1788
25 The Venerable Bede, Priest, Monk of Jarrow, Historian, 735
26 Augustine, first Archbishop of Canterbury, 605
30 Josephine Butler, Social Reformer, 1906

COMMEMORATIONS

15 Charles Williams, Spiritual Writer, 1945
16 Caroline Chisholm, Social Reformer, 1877
21 Helena, Protector of the Faith, 330
23 Petroc, Abbot of Padstow, 6th century
25 Aldhelm, Abbot of Malmesbury, Bishop of Sherborne, 709
28 Lanfranc, Prior of Le Bec, Archbishop of Canterbury, 1089
30 Joan of Arc, Visionary, 1431

JUNE

PRINCIPAL HOLY DAYS & FESTIVALS

11 **Barnabas the Apostle**
24 **The Birth of John the Baptist**
29 **Peter & Paul, Apostles**

LESSER FESTIVALS

1 Justin, Martyr at Rome, c.165
5 Boniface (Wynfrith) of Crediton, Archbishop of Mainz,
     Apostle of Germany, Martyr, 754
9 Columba, Abbot of Iona, Missionary, 597
15 Evelyn Underhill, Mystical Writer, 1941
16 Richard of Chichester, Bishop, 1253
22 Alban, first Martyr of Britain, c.209
23 Etheldreda, Abbess of Ely, c.678
28 Irenæus, Bishop of Lyons, Teacher, Martyr, c.200

COMMEMORATIONS

1 Angela de' Merici, Founder of the Institute of St Ursula, 1540
3 Martyrs of Uganda, 1886 & 1978
3 John XXIII, Bishop of Rome, Inspirer of Renewal, 1963
6 Ini Kopuria, Founder of the Melanesian Brotherhood, 1945
9 Ephrem of Syria, Deacon, Hymnographer, Teacher, 373
14 Richard Baxter, Priest, Hymnographer, Teacher, 1691
17 Samuel & Henrietta Barnett, Social Reformers, 1913 & 1936
18 Bernard Mizeki, Apostle to the Mashona, 1896
19 Sundar Singh of India, Evangelist, Teacher, Sadhu, 1929

JULY

PRINCIPAL HOLY DAYS & FESTIVALS

3 **Thomas the Apostle**
22 **Mary Magdalen, Apostle to the Apostles**
25 **James the Apostle**

LESSER FESTIVALS

6 Thomas More, Scholar & Martyr
   & John Fisher, Bishop & Martyr, 1535
11 Benedict of Nursia, Father of Western Monasticism, c.550
14 John Keble, Priest, Poet, Tractarian, 1866
15 Bonaventure, Franciscan Friar, Bishop, Peacemaker, 1274
19 Gregory, Bishop of Nyssa, & his sister Macrina,
   Teachers, c.394 & c.379
29 William Wilberforce, Social Reformer, 1833

COMMEMORATIONS

15 Swithun, Bishop of Winchester, c.862
16 Osmund, Bishop of Salisbury, 1099
23 Bridget of Sweden, Abbess of Vadstena, 1373
26 Anne & Joachim, Parents of the Blessèd Virgin Mary
27 Brooke Foss Westcott, Bishop of Durham, Teacher, 1901
31 Ignatius of Loyola, Founder of the Society of Jesus, 1556

AUGUST

SEPTEMBER

PRINCIPAL HOLY DAYS & FESTIVALS
14 **Holy Cross Day**
21 **Matthew , Apostle & Evangelist**
29 **Michael & All Angels**

LESSER FESTIVALS
3 Gregory the Great, Bishop of Rome, Teacher, 604
4 Cuthbert, Bishop of Lindisfarne, Missionary, 687
8 The Birth of the Blessèd Virgin Mary
13 John Chrysostom, Bishop of Constantinople, Teacher, 407
16 Cyprian, Bishop of Carthage, Martyr, 258
17 Hildegard, Abbess of Bingen, Visionary, 1179
20 John Coleridge Patteson, First Bishop of Melanesia,
     & his Companions, Martyrs, 1871
25 Lancelot Andrewes, Bishop of Winchester,
     Spiritual Writer, 1626
27 Vincent de Paul, Founder of the Congregation
     of the Mission (Lazarists), 1660

COMMEMORATIONS
1 Giles of Provence, Hermit, c.710
2 Martyrs of Papua New Guinea, 1942
4 Birinus, Bishop of Dorchester (Oxon), Apostle of Wessex, 650
6 Allen Gardiner, founder of the South American Missionary
     Society, 1851
6 Albert Schweitzer, Teacher, Physician, Missionary, 1965
7 Douglas Downes, Founder of the Society of Saint Francis, 1957
16 Ninian, Bishop of Galloway, Apostle to the Picts, c.432
16 Edward Bouverie Pusey, Priest, Tractarian, 1882
19 Theodore of Tarsus, Archbishop of Canterbury, 690
25 Sergius of Radonezh, Russian Monastic Reformer, Teacher, 1392

OCTOBER

PRINCIPAL HOLY DAYS & FESTIVALS
18 **Luke the Evangelist**
28 **Simon & Jude, Apostles**

LESSER FESTIVALS
4 Francis of Assisi, Friar, Deacon, Founder of the
   Friars Minor, 1226
6 William Tyndale, Translator of the Scriptures, Martyr, 1536
10 Paulinus, Bishop of York, Missionary, 644
13 Edward the Confessor, 1066
15 Teresa of Avila, Mystic, Teacher, 1582
16 Thomas Cranmer, 1556, Nicholas Ridley & Hugh Latimer,
   1555, Bishops & Martyrs
19 Henry Martyn, Translator of the Scriptures,
   Missionary in India & Persia, 1812
17 Ignatius, Bishop of Antioch, Martyr, c.107
26 Chad & Cedd, Bishops, Religious, Missionaries, 672 & 664
27 Alfred the Great, King of the West Saxons, Scholar, 899

COMMEMORATIONS
1 Remigius, Bishop of Rheims, Apostle of the Franks, 533
1 Thérèse of Lisieux, Carmelite Nun, Spiritual Writer, 1897
3 George Kennedy Bell, Bishop of Chichester, Ecumenist,
   Peacemaker, 1958
8 Robert Grosseteste, Bishop of Lincoln, Philosopher, Scientist, 1253
9 Denys, Bishop of Paris, & his Companions, Martyrs, 258
11 Ethelburga, Abbess of Barking, 675
12 Wilfrid, Abbot of Ripon, Bishop of York, Missionary, 709
12 Elizabeth Fry, Prison Reformer, 1845
25 Crispin & Crispinian, Martyrs at Rome, c.285
29 James Hannington, Bishop of Eastern Equatorial Africa,
   Martyr in Uganda, 1885
30 Martin Luther, Teacher, Reformer, 1546

NOVEMBER

PRINCIPAL HOLY DAYS & FESTIVALS

1 **All Saints' Day**
30 **Andrew the Apostle**, Patron of Scotland

LESSER FESTIVALS

2 Commemoration of the Faithful Departed (All Souls' Day)
3 Richard Hooker, Priest, Anglican Apologist, Teacher, 1600
6 William Temple, Archbishop of Canterbury,
      Teacher, 1944
7 Willibrord of York, Archbishop of Utrecht,
      Apostle of Frisia, 739
8 Saints & Martyrs of England
11 Martin, Monk, Bishop of Tours, c.397
13 Charles Simeon, Priest, Teacher, 1836
16 Margaret of Scotland, Philanthropist,
      Reformer of the Church, 1093
17 Hugh, Carthusian Monk, Bishop of Lincoln, 1200
19 Hilda, Abbess of Whitby, 680
20 Edmund, King of the East Angles, Martyr, 870
21 Edward King, Bishop of Lincoln, Teacher, 1910

COMMEMORATIONS

3 Martin of Porres, Dominican Friar, 1639
14 Samuel Seabury, First Anglican Bishop in North America, 1784
16 Edmund Rich of Abingdon, Archbishop of Canterbury, 1240
19 Elizabeth, Princess of Hungary, Philanthropist, 1231
20 Mechtild, Béguine of Magdeburg, Mystic, Prophet, 1280
20 Priscilla Lydia Sellon, a Restorer of the Religious Life
      in the Church of England, 1876
22 Cecilia, Martyr at Rome, c.230
22 Clive Staples Lewis, Spiritual Writer, 1963
23 Clement, Bishop of Rome, Martyr, c.100
25 Katharine of Alexandria, 4th century
29 Day of Intercession & Thanksgiving for the Missionary
      Work of the Church

DECEMBER

PRINCIPAL HOLY DAYS & FESTIVALS

25 **Christmas Day**
26 **Stephen, Deacon, First Martyr**
27 **John, Apostle & Evangelist**
28 **Holy Innocents**

LESSER FESTIVALS

6 Nicholas, Bishop of Myra, c.326
8 Conception of the Blessèd Virgin Mary
13 Lucy, Martyr at Syracuse, 304
14 John of the Cross, Mystic, Poet, Teacher, 1591
24 Christmas Eve
29 Thomas Becket, Archbishop of Canterbury, Martyr, 1170

COMMEMORATIONS

1 Charles de Foucauld, Hermit, Servant of the Poor, 1916
3 Francis Xavier, Apostle of the Indies, Missionary, 1552
4 Nicholas Ferrar, Deacon, Founder of the Little Gidding
   Community, 1637
7 Ambrose, Bishop of Milan, Teacher, 397
10 Thomas Merton, Monk, Spiritual Writer, 1968
11 Ethel Tompkinson, Missionary in India, 1967
17 *O Sapientia*
31 John Wyclif, Reformer, 1384

The Lord's Prayer

As our Saviour taught us,
so we pray:

Our Father in heaven,
hallowed be your name,
your kingdom come,
your will be done,
on earth as in heaven.
Give us today our daily bread.
Forgive us our sins
as we forgive those
 who sin against us.
Save us from the time of trial
and deliver us from evil.
For the kingdom, the power,
 and the glory are yours
now and for ever. Amen.

Let us pray with confidence
as our Saviour has taught us:

Our Father, who art in heaven,
hallowed be thy name;
thy kingdom come;
thy will be done;
on earth as it is in heaven.
Give us this day our daily bread.
and forgive us our trespasses,
as we forgive those
who trespass against us.
And lead us not into temptation;
but deliver us from evil.
For thine is the kingdom,
the power, and the glory,
for ever and ever. Amen.

Morning Prayer – Form 1
Sunday and daily in Eastertide

THE PREPARATION

O Lord, open our lips;
And our mouth shall proclaim your praise.

Blessèd are you, Lord our God, redeemer and king of all;
to you be glory and praise for ever!
From the waters of chaos you drew forth the world,
and in your great love, fashioned us in your image.
Now, through the deep waters of death
you have brought your people to new birth
by raising your Son to life in triumph.
May we, the firstfruits of your new creation,
rejoice in this new day you have made;
may Christ your light ever dawn in our hearts
as we offer you our sacrifice of thanks and praise,
Father, Son and Holy Spirit:
Blessèd be God for ever!

THE WORD OF GOD
Week 1 & Sundays in Eastertide – Psalm 100

1 Be joyful in the Lord, all you lands;*
    serve the Lord with gladness
        and come before his presence with a song.

2 Know this: The Lord himself is God;*
    he himself has made us and we are his;
        we are his people and the sheep of his pasture.

3 Enter his gates with thanksgiving;
        go into his courts with praise;*
    give thanks to him and call upon his name.

4 For the Lord is good; his mercy is everlasting;*
    and his faithfulness endures from age to age.

*As we enter your courts of light, O Lord,
may we rejoice in your power to save
and praise your faithfulness, day by day;
through Jesus Christ our Lord.* **Amen.**   18

Week 2 & Mondays in Eastertide – Psalm 118

1 Give thanks to the Lord, for he is good;*
  his mercy endures for ever.

2 Let Israel now proclaim,*
  'His mercy endures for ever.'

3 Let the house of Aaron now proclaim,*
  'His mercy endures for ever.'

4 Let those who fear the Lord now proclaim,*
  'His mercy endures for ever.'

5 I called to the Lord in my distress;*
  the Lord answered by setting me free.

6 The Lord is at my side, therefore I will not fear;*
  what can anyone do to me?

7 The Lord is at my side to help me;*
  I will triumph over those who hate me.

8 It is better to rely on the Lord*
  than to put any trust in flesh.

9 It is better to rely on the Lord*
  than to put any trust in rulers.

10 All the ungodly encompass me;*
   in the name of the Lord I will repel them.

11 They hem me in, they hem me in on every side;*
   in the name of the Lord I will repel them.

12 They swarm about me like bees;
     they blaze like a fire of thorns;*
   in the name of the Lord I will repel them.

13 I was pressed so hard that I almost fell,*
   but the Lord came to my help.

14 The Lord is my strength and my song,*
   and he has become my salvation.

15 There is a sound of exultation and victory*
   in the tents of the righteous:

16 'The right hand of the Lord has triumphed!*
   the right hand of the Lord is exalted!
     the right hand of the Lord has triumphed!'

17 I shall not die, but live,*
   and declare the works of the Lord.

18 The Lord has punished me sorely,*
   but he did not hand me over to death.

19 Open for me the gates of righteousness;*
   I will enter them; I will offer thanks to the Lord.

20 'This is the gate of the Lord;*
   whoever is righteous may enter.'

21 I will give thanks to you, for you answered me*
   and have become my salvation.

22 The same stone which the builders rejected*
   has become the chief corner-stone.

23 This is the Lord's doing,*
   and it is marvellous in our eyes.

24 On this day the Lord has acted;*
   we will rejoice and be glad in it.

25 Hosanna, Lord, hosanna!*
   Lord, send us now success.

26 Blessèd is he who comes in the name of the Lord;*
   we bless you from the house of the Lord.

27 God is the Lord; he has shined upon us;*
   form a procession with branches
      up to the horns of the altar.

28 'You are my God and I will thank you;*
   you are my God and I will exalt you.'

29 Give thanks to the Lord, for he is good;*
   his mercy endures for ever.

   *This day, O Lord, you have made your own,
   and have raised us up on the Corner-stone of our salvation:
   open to us the gates of righteousness
   that we may enter and give thanks to your Name;
   through Jesus Christ our Lord.* **Amen.**   14

Week 3 & Tuesdays in Eastertide — from Psalm 135

1 Alleluia! Praise the name of the Lord;*
   give praise, you servants of the Lord,

2 You who stand in the house of the Lord,*
   in the courts of the house of our God.

3 Praise the Lord, for the Lord is good;*
   sing praises to his name, for it is lovely.

4 For the Lord has chosen Jacob for himself*
   and Israel for his own possession.

5 For I know that the Lord is great,*
   and that our Lord is above all gods.

6 The Lord does whatever pleases him,
     in heaven and on earth,*
   in the seas and all the deeps.

7 He brings up rain clouds from the ends of the earth;*
   he sends out lightning with the rain,
     and brings the winds out of his storehouse.

8 It was he who struck down the first-born of Egypt,*
   the first-born both of human and beast.

9 He sent signs and wonders
     into the midst of you, O Egypt,*
   against Pharaoh and all his servants.

10 He overthrew many nations*
   and put mighty kings to death:

12 He gave their land to be an inheritance,*
   an inheritance for Israel his people.

13 O Lord, your name is everlasting;*
   your renown, O Lord, endures from age to age.

14 For the Lord gives his people justice*
   and shows compassion to his servants.

   *We praise you, gracious God,
   and we bless your holy Name
   because you have taken pity on your servants,
   you have preserved us from falsehood and deceit,
   you have given us a rich heritage
   and made us your own possession;
   in Jesus Christ our Lord.* **Amen.**   16

Week 4 & Wednesdays in Eastertide – from Psalm 139

1   Lord, you have searched me out and known me;*
    you know my sitting down and my rising up;
      you discern my thoughts from afar.

2   You trace my journeys and my resting-places*
    and are acquainted with all my ways.

3   Indeed, there is not a word on my lips,*
    but you, O Lord, know it altogether.

4   You press upon me behind and before*
    and lay your hand upon me.

5   Such knowledge is too wonderful for me;*
    it is so high that I cannot attain to it.

6   Where can I go then from your Spirit?*
    where can I flee from your presence?

7   If I climb up to heaven, you are there;*
    if I make the grave my bed, you are there also.

8   If I take the wings of the morning*
    and dwell in the uttermost parts of the sea,

9   Even there your hand will lead me*
    and your right hand hold me fast.

10 If I say, 'Surely the darkness will cover me,*
    and the light around me turn to night',

11 Darkness is not dark to you;
    the night is as bright as the day;*
    darkness and light to you are both alike.

12 For you yourself created my inmost parts;*
    you knit me together in my mother's womb.

13 I will thank you because I am marvellously made;*
    your works are wonderful and I know it well.

14 My body was not hidden from you,*
    while I was being made in secret
    and woven in the depths of the earth.

15 Your eyes beheld my limbs, yet unfinished in the womb;
    all of them were written in your book;*
    they were fashioned day by day,
      when as yet there was none of them.

16 How deep I find your thoughts, O God!*
    how great is the sum of them!

17 If I were to count them,
        they would be more in number than the sand;*
    to count them all,
        my life span would need to be like yours.

18 Search me out, O God, and know my heart;*
    try me and know my restless thoughts.

19 Look well whether there be any wickedness in me*
    and lead me in the way that is everlasting.

*Word of God,
who created and fashioned us,
who know us and search us out,
who abide with us through light and dark:
help us to know your presence in this life
and, in the life to come, still to be with you;
where you are alive and reign,
God, for ever and ever.* **Amen.**   16

Week 5 & Thursdays in Eastertide — from Psalm 33

1 Rejoice in the Lord, you righteous;*
    it is good for the just to sing praises.

2 For the word of the Lord is right,*
    and all his works are sure.

3 He loves righteousness and justice;*
    the loving-kindness of the Lord fills the whole earth.

4 By the word of the Lord were the heavens made,*
    by the breath of his mouth all the heavenly hosts.

5 He gathers up the waters of the ocean
        as in a water-skin*
    and stores up the depths of the sea.

6 Let all the earth fear the Lord;*
    let all who dwell in the world stand in awe of him.

7 For he spoke and it came to pass;*
    he commanded and it stood fast.

8 The Lord brings the will of the nations to naught;*
　 he thwarts the designs of the peoples.

9 But the Lord's will stands fast for ever,*
　 and the designs of his heart from age to age.

10 Happy is the nation whose God is the Lord!*
　 happy the people he has chosen to be his own!

11 The Lord looks down from heaven,*
　 and beholds all the people in the world.

12 From where he sits enthroned he turns his gaze*
　 on all who dwell on the earth.

13 He fashions all the hearts of them*
　 and understands all their works.

14 Behold, the eye of the Lord
　　 is upon those who fear him,*
　 on those who wait upon his love,

15 To pluck their lives from death,*
　 and to feed them in time of famine.

16 Our soul waits for the Lord;*
　 he is our help and our shield.

17 Indeed, our heart rejoices in him,*
　 for in his holy name we put our trust.

18 Let your loving-kindness, O Lord, be upon us,*
　 as we have put our trust in you.

Feed your people, O Lord,
with your holy Word
and free us from the temptations
which lead us away from you
that, being filled with your mercy,
we may be admitted to your holy presence;
through Jesus Christ our Lord. **Amen.**　　　　7

1   I will exalt you, O Lord,
        because you have lifted me up*
    and have not let my enemies triumph over me.

2   O Lord my God, I cried out to you,*
    and you restored me to health.

3   You brought me up, O Lord, from the dead;*
    you restored my life as I was going down to the grave.

4   Sing to the Lord, you servants of his;*
    give thanks for the remembrance of his holiness.

5   For his wrath endures but the twinkling of an eye,*
    his favour for a lifetime.

6   Weeping may spend the night,*
    but joy comes in the morning.

7   While I felt secure, I said,
        'I shall never be disturbed.*
    You, Lord, with your favour,
        made me as strong as the mountains.'

8   Then you hid your face,*
    and I was filled with fear.

9   I cried to you, O Lord;*
    I pleaded with the Lord, saying,

10   'What profit is there in my blood,
        if I go down to the Pit?*
    will the dust praise you or declare your faithfulness?

11   'Hear, O Lord, and have mercy upon me;*
    O Lord, be my helper.'

12   You have turned my wailing into dancing;*
    you have put off my sackcloth and clothed me with joy;

13   Therefore my heart sings to you without ceasing;*
    O Lord my God, I will give you thanks for ever.

Hear our prayers, Lord Christ, and have mercy upon us;
turn our heaviness into joy
and clothe us with gladness and salvation
that we may give thanks to you for ever. **Amen.**   7

Week 7 & Saturdays in Eastertide — from Psalm 66

1   Be joyful in God, all you lands;*
    sing the glory of his name;
      sing the glory of his praise.

2   'All the earth bows down before you,*
    sings to you, sings out your name.'

3   Come now and see the works of God,*
    how wonderful he is in his doing towards all people.

4   He turned the sea into dry land,
      so that they went through the water on foot,*
    and there we rejoiced in him.

5   In his might he rules for ever;
      his eyes keep watch over the nations;*
    let no rebel rise up against him.

6   Bless our God, you peoples;*
    make the voice of his praise to be heard;

7   Who holds our souls in life,*
    and will not allow our feet to slip.

8   For you, O God, have proved us;*
    you have tried us just as silver is tried.

9   You brought us into the snare;*
    you laid heavy burdens upon our backs.

10   You let enemies ride over our heads;
      we went through fire and water;*
    but you brought us out into a place of refreshment.

11   Come and listen, all you who fear God,*
    and I will tell you what he has done for me.

12   I called out to him with my mouth,*
    and his praise was on my tongue.

13   If I had found evil in my heart,*
    the Lord would not have heard me;

14   But in truth God has heard me;*
    he has attended to the voice of my prayer.

15   Blessèd be God, who has not rejected my prayer,*
    nor withheld his love from me.

How generous is your goodness, O God,
how great is your salvation,
how faithful is your love!
Help us to trust in you in trial,
to praise you in deliverance
and to rejoice before you with overflowing hearts;
through Jesus Christ our Lord. **Amen.**   19

THE OLD TESTAMENT CANTICLE
Either: A SONG OF GOD'S REIGN

1   Blessèd be God, who lives for ever,*
    whose reign endures throughout all ages.

2   Declare God's praise before the nations,*
    you who are the children of Israel.

3   For if our God has scattered you among them,*
    there too has he shown you his greatness.

4   Exalt him in the sight of the living,*
    because he is our God and our Father for ever.

5   Though God punishes you for your wickedness,*
    mercy will be shown to you all.

6   God will gather you from every nation,*
    from wherever you have been scattered.

7   When you turn to the Lord
        with all your heart and soul,*
    God will hide his face from you no more.

8   See what the Lord has done for you*
    and give thanks with a loud voice.

9   Praise the Lord of righteousness*
    and exalt the King of the ages.   *Tobit 13. 1-6*

    Glory to the Father, and to the Son,
        and to the Holy Spirit:*
    as it was in the beginning, is now,
        and shall be for ever. Amen.

A SONG OF CREATION – BENEDICITE (page 242) is a particularly
appropriate alternative Canticle on Sundays.

Or: THE SONG OF MOSES & MIRIAM

1   I will sing to the Lord, who has triumphed gloriously;*
    the horse and his rider have been thrown into the sea.

2   The Lord is my strength and my song*
    and has become my salvation.

3   This is my God whom I will praise*
    the God of my forebears whom I will exalt.

4   The Lord fights for his people,*
    the Lord is his name.

5   Your right hand, O Lord, is glorious in power:*
    your right hand, O Lord, shatters the enemy.

6   At the blast of your nostrils, the sea covered them;*
    they sank as lead in the mighty waters.

7   In your unfailing love, O Lord,*
    you lead the people whom you have redeemed,

8   And by your invincible strength*
    you will guide them to your holy dwelling.

9   You will bring them in and plant them, O Lord,*
    in the sanctuary which your hands have established.

                                              From Exodus 15

**Glory to the Father, and to the Son,
    and to the Holy Spirit:***
**as it was in the beginning, is now,
    and shall be for ever. Amen.**

*The EASTER ANTHEMS (page 241), and
A SONG OF SOLOMON (page 237) are particularly appropriate
alternative Canticles in Eastertide.*

THE SCRIPTURE READING
Week 1 & Sundays in Eastertide
In the beginning, God created the heavens and the earth. The
earth was without form and void and darkness was on face of the
deep, and the Spirit of God was moving over the face of the
waters. And God said, 'Let there be light'; and there was light.
And God saw that the light was good.   *Genesis 1. 1-3*

Week 2 & Mondays in Eastertide

We know that Christ, being raised from the dead, will never die again; death no longer has dominion over him. The death he died, he died to sin, once for all; but the life he lives, he lives to God. So you also must consider yourselves dead to sin and alive to God in Jesus Christ. *Romans 6. 9-11*

Week 3 & Tuesdays in Eastertide

When you have come into the land that the Lord your God is giving you as an inheritance to possess, and you possess it, and settle in it, you shall take some of the first of all the fruit of the ground, which you harvest from the land that the Lord your God is giving you, and you shall put it in a basket and go to the place that the Lord your God will choose as a dwelling for his name. You shall go to the priest who is in office at that time and say to him, 'Today I declare to the Lord your God that I have come into the land that the Lord swore to our ancestors to give us. So now I bring the first of the fruit of the ground that you, O Lord, have given me.' You shall set it down before the Lord your God and bow down before the Lord. *Deuteronomy 26. 1-3, 10*

Week 4 & Wednesdays in Eastertide

Then God spoke all these words: I am the Lord your God, who brought you out of the land of Egypt, out of the house of slavery; you shall have no other gods before me. You shall not make for yourself an idol, whether in the form of anything that is in heaven above, or that is on the earth beneath, or that is in the water under the earth. You shall not bow down to them or worship them; for I the Lord your God am a jealous God, punishing children for the iniquity of parents, to the third and fourth generation of those who reject me, but showing steadfast love to the thousandth generation of those who love me and keep my commandments. *Exodus 20. 1-6*

Week 5 & Thursdays in Eastertide

If you have been raised with Christ, seek the things that are
above, where Christ is, seated at the right hand of God. Set
your minds on things that are above, not on things that are on
the earth. For you have died, and your life is hid with Christ
in God. When Christ who is your life is revealed, then you also
will be revealed with him in glory. *Colossians 3. 1-4*

Week 6 & Fridays in Eastertide

I handed on to you as of first importance what I in turn had
received: that Christ died for our sins in accordance with the
scriptures, and that he was buried, and that he was raised on the
third day in accordance with the scriptures. Christ has been
raised from the dead, the first fruits of those who have fallen
asleep. For as by a man came death, by a man has come also the
resurrection of the dead. For as in Adam all die, so also in
Christ shall all be made alive. *1 Corinthians 15. 3-4, 20-22*

Week 7 & Saturdays in Eastertide

The Lord said to Job, 'Who is this that darkens counsel by words
without knowledge? Gird up your loins like a man, I will
question you and you shall declare to me. Where were you when I
laid the foundation of the earth? Who laid its cornerstone when
the morning stars sang together and all the children of God
shouted for joy? Have you entered into the springs of the sea or
walked in the recesses of the deep? Have the gates of death been
revealed to you or have you seen the gates of deep darkness?
Have you comprehended the expanse of the earth? Declare, if you
know all this.' *Job 38. 1-4a, 6b-7, 16-18*

*   *   *

This RESPONSE to the reading may be used:
Awake, O sleeper, and arise from the dead
And Christ shall give you light.

THE GOSPEL CANTICLE: THE BENEDICTUS

1 Blessèd are you, Lord, the God of Israel,*
   you have come to your people and set them free.

2 You have raised up for us a mighty Saviour,*
   born of the house of your servant, David.

3 Through your holy prophets, you promised of old*
   to save us from our enemies,
      from the hands of all who hate us,

4 To show mercy to our forebears,*
   and to remember your holy covenant.

5 This was the oath you swore to our father, Abraham,*
   to set us free from the hands of our enemies,

6 Free to worship you without fear,*
   holy and righteous before you,
      all the days of our life.

7 And you, child,
      shall be called the prophet of the Most High,*
   for you will go before the Lord to prepare the way,

8 To give God's people knowledge of salvation*
   by the forgiveness of their sins.

9 In the tender compassion of our God*
   the dawn from on high shall break upon us,

10 To shine on those who dwell in darkness
      and the shadow of death,*
   and to guide our feet into the way of peace.   *Luke 1. 68-79*

   Glory to the Father, and to the Son,
      and to the Holy Spirit:*
   as it was in the beginning, is now,
      and shall be for ever. Amen.

THE PRAYERS

Intercession and thanksgiving are offered in free prayer or in silence, ending with the following:

One thing we ask of you, O Lord, one thing we seek:
that we may dwell in your house all the days of our life.
Lord, have mercy.

Let your loving-kindness, O Lord, be upon us,
as we have put our trust in you.
Christ, have mercy.

Rise up and help us, O God our Saviour,
and save us for the sake of your steadfast love.
Lord, have mercy.

Ride on and conquer in the cause of truth,
and for the sake of justice.
Christ, have mercy.

Let the heavens declare the rightness of your cause,
and may your praises reach to the world's end.
Lord, have mercy.

THE COLLECT for Sundays:

Almighty and everlasting God,
we thank you that you have brought us safely
to the beginning of this day.
Keep us from falling into sin
or running into danger,
order us in all our doings
and guide us to do always
what is righteous in your sight;
through Jesus Christ our Lord . . .   1)

Or for Eastertide:

Lord of all life and power,
who through the mighty resurrection of your Son
overcame the old order of sin and death
to make all things new in him:
grant that we, being dead to sin
and alive to you in Jesus Christ,
may reign with him in glory;
to whom with you and the Holy Spirit,
be praise and honour, glory and might,
now and in all eternity. **Amen.**   3

THE LORD'S PRAYER may be said.

Let us bless the Lord.
Thanks be to God.

Evening Prayer – Form 1

Sunday and daily in Eastertide

THE BLESSING OF THE LIGHT

You, O Lord, are my lamp; you turn our darkness into light.

The light and peace of Jesus Christ be with you all
And also with you.

Let us give thanks to the Lord our God
Who is worthy of all thanksgiving and praise.

Blessèd are you, Sovereign God,
our light and our salvation;
to you be glory and praise for ever!
You led your people to freedom
by a pillar of cloud by day and a pillar of fire by night.
May we who walk in the light of your presence
acclaim your Christ, rising victorious,
as he banishes all darkness from our hearts and minds,
and praise you, Father, Son and Holy Spirit:
Blessèd be God for ever!

A SONG OF THE LIGHT

1   O gladsome light, O grace
    Of God the Father's face,
    The eternal splendour wearing;
    Celestial, holy, blest,
    Our Saviour Jesus Christ,
    Joyful in your appearing.

2   As day fades into night,
    We see the evening light,
    Our hymn of praise outpouring:
    Father of might unknown,
    Christ, his incarnate Son,
    and Holy Spirit, adoring.

3   To you of right belongs
    All praise of holy songs,
    O Son of God, Lifegiver;
    You, therefore, O Most High,
    The world will glorify,
    And shall exalt for ever.

THE WORD OF GOD

Week 1 & Sundays in Eastertide — From Psalm 104

1   Bless the Lord, O my soul;*
O Lord my God, how excellent is your greatness!
    you are clothed with majesty and splendour.

2   You wrap yourself with light as with a cloak*
and spread out the heavens like a curtain.

3   You lay the beams of your chambers
    in the waters above;*
you make the clouds your chariot;
    you ride on the wings of the wind.

4   You make the winds your messengers*
and flames of fire your servants.

5   You have set the earth upon its foundations,*
so that it never shall move at any time.

6   You set the limits that they should not pass;*
they shall not again cover the earth.

7   You send the springs into the valleys;*
they flow between the mountains.

8   All the beasts of the field drink their fill from them,*
and the wild asses quench their thirst.

9   Beside them the birds of the air make their nests*
and sing among the branches.

10   You water the mountains from your dwelling on high;*
the earth is fully satisfied by the fruit of your works.

11   You make grass grow for flocks and herds*
and plants to serve us all;

12   That they may bring forth food from the earth,*
and wine to gladden our hearts,

13   Oil to make a cheerful countenance,*
and bread to strengthen the heart.

14   You appointed the moon to mark the seasons,*
and the sun knows the time of its setting.

15   You make darkness that it may be night,*
in which all the beasts of the forest prowl.

16 The labourer goes forth to work*
and to toil until the evening.

17 O Lord, how manifold are your works!*
in wisdom you have made them all;
    the earth is full of your creatures.

18 Yonder is the great and wide sea
    with its living things too many to number,*
creatures both small and great.

19 All of them look to you*
to give them their food in due season.

20 You give it to them, they gather it;*
you open your hand and they are filled with good things.

21 You hide your face and they are terrified;*
you take away their breath
    and they die and return to their dust.

22 You send forth your Spirit and they are created;*
and so you renew the face of the earth.

23 May the glory of the Lord endure for ever;*
may the Lord rejoice in all his works.

24 I will sing to the Lord as long as I live;*
I will praise my God while I have my being.

25 May these words of mine please him;*
I will rejoice in the Lord.

26 Bless the Lord, O my soul.*
O praise the Lord!

*O Holy Spirit and giver of life,
who from the beginning
    wrought beauty and peace in all creation;
renew the face of the earth
that we may glorify the Author and Maker of all
and rejoice in the promise of redemption
in Christ our Lord.* **Amen.**   29

1 Not to us, O Lord, not to us,
     but to your name give glory;*
   because of your love and because of your faithfulness.

2 Why should the heathen say,*
   'Where then is their God?'

3 Our God is in heaven;*
   whatever he wills to do he does.

4 Their idols are silver and gold,*
   the work of human hands.

5 They have mouths, but they cannot speak;*
   eyes have they, but they cannot see;

6 Those who make them are like them,*
   and so are all who put their trust in them.

7 You who fear the Lord, trust in the Lord;*
   he is their help and their shield.

8 The Lord has been mindful of us and he will bless us;*
   he will bless the house of Israel;
     he will bless the house of Aaron;

9 He will bless those who fear the Lord,*
   both small and great together.

10 May the Lord increase you more and more,*
    you and your children after you.

11 May you be blessed by the Lord,*
    the maker of heaven and earth.

12 The heaven of heavens is the Lord's,*
    but he entrusted the earth to its peoples.

13 The dead do not praise the Lord,*
    nor all those who go down into silence;

14 But we will bless the Lord,*
    from this time forth for evermore. Alleluia!

   *O Lord of life, who made us in your image
   and taught us to offer ourselves to you
   as a living sacrifice:
   fill us with your lifegiving Spirit
   that in the renewal of our minds
   we may be dead to sin and live to you
   in Jesus Christ our Lord.* **Amen.**   14

Week 3 & Tuesdays in Eastertide – from Psalm 105

1 Give thanks to the Lord and call upon his name;*
   make known his deeds among the peoples.

2 Remember the marvels he has done,*
   his wonders and the judgements of his mouth.

3 Israel came into Egypt,*
   and Jacob became a sojourner in the land of Ham.

4 The Lord made his people exceedingly fruitful;*
   he made them stronger than their enemies;

5 Whose heart he turned, so that they hated his people,*
   and dealt unjustly with his servants.

6 He sent Moses his servant,*
   and Aaron whom he had chosen.

7 They worked his signs among them,*
   and portents in the land of Ham.

8 He sent darkness and it grew dark;*
   but the Egyptians rebelled against his words.

9 He turned their waters into blood*
   and caused their fish to die.

10 Their land was overrun by frogs,*
   in the very chambers of their kings.

11 He spoke and there came swarms of insects*
   and gnats within all their borders.

12 He gave them hailstones instead of rain,*
   and flames of fire throughout their land.

13 He blasted their vines and their fig trees*
   and shattered every tree in their country.

14 He spoke and the locust came,*
   and young locusts without number,

15 Which ate up all the green plants in their land*
   and devoured the fruit of their soil.

16 He struck down the first-born of their land,*
   the first-fruits of all their strength.

17 He led out his people with silver and gold;*
   in all their tribes there was not one that stumbled.

18 Egypt was glad of their going,*
   because they were afraid of them.

19 He spread out a cloud for a covering*
   and a fire to give light in the night season.

20 They asked and quails appeared,*
   and he satisfied them with bread from heaven.

21 He opened the rock and water flowed,*
   so the river ran in the dry places.

22 For God remembered his holy word*
   and Abraham his servant.

23 So he led forth his people with gladness,*
   his chosen with shouts of joy.

24 He gave his people the lands of the nations,*
   and they took the fruit of others' toil,

25 That they might keep his statutes*
   and observe his laws.
      Alleluia!

   *O God of Abraham, Isaac and Jacob,
   you redeemed us from the slavery of sin
   for freedom as your children:
   feed us on our way with the bread of heaven
   and quench our thirst with living water;
   through Jesus Christ our Lord.* **Amen.**   14

Week 4 & Wednesdays in Eastertide – Psalm 114

1   Alleluia!
     When Israel came out of Egypt,*
    the house of Jacob from a people of strange speech,

2   Judah became God's sanctuary*
    and Israel his dominion.

3   The sea beheld it and fled;*
    Jordan turned and went back.

4   The mountains skipped like rams,*
    and the little hills like young sheep.

5   What ailed you, O sea, that you fled?*
    O Jordan, that you turned back?

6   You mountains, that you skipped like rams?*
    you little hills like young sheep?

7   Tremble, O earth, at the presence of the Lord,*
    at the presence of the God of Jacob,

8   Who turned the hard rock into a pool of water*
    and flintstone into a flowing spring.

*All creation trembles before you, Lord God,
for you have plumbed the deep waters of death
and have brought us forth as new-born into your sanctuary:
may your presence go before us to guide us
    into your kingdom;
through Jesus Christ our Lord.* **Amen.**   14

Week 5 & Thursdays in Eastertide – from Psalm 136

1   Give thanks to the Lord, for he is good,
    give thanks to the God of gods,*
    give thanks to the Lord of lords,
    for his mercy endures for ever;

2 Who only does great wonders,
   who by his wisdom made the heavens,*
   who spread out the earth upon the waters,
   for his mercy endures for ever;

3 Who created great lights,
   the sun to rule the day,*
   the moon and the stars to govern the night,
   for his mercy endures for ever;

4 Who struck down the first-born of Egypt,
   and brought out Israel from among them,*
   with a mighty hand and a stretched out arm,
   for his mercy endures for ever;

5 Who divided the Red Sea in two,
   and made Israel to pass through the midst of it,*
   but swept Pharaoh and his army into the Red Sea,
   for his mercy endures for ever;

5 Who led his people through the wilderness,
   who struck down great kings,*
   and slew mighty kings,
   for his mercy endures for ever.

6 He gave away their lands for an inheritance,
   an inheritance for Israel his servant;*
   he remembered us in our low estate,
   for his mercy endures for ever.

7 He delivered us from our enemies,
   and gives food to all creatures.*
   Give thanks to the God of heaven,
   for his mercy endures for ever.

   Remember us, Lord, as you have in ages past.
   You made the world and our human race;
   you shaped its history,
   correcting your people with judgement yet with love.
   Your mercy endures for ever
   and we give you thanks, for you alone are good.
   Blessèd be God for ever! **Amen.**   16

1   Give thanks to the Lord, for he is good,*
    and his mercy endures for ever.

2   Let all those whom the Lord has redeemed proclaim*
    that he redeemed them from the hand of the foe.

3   He gathered them out of the lands;*
    from the east and from the west,
       from the north and from the south.

4   Some wandered in desert wastes;*
    they found no way to a city where they might dwell.

5   They were hungry and thirsty;*
    their spirits languished within them.

6   Then they cried to the Lord in their trouble,*
    and he delivered them from their distress.

7   He put their feet on a straight path*
    to go to a city where they might dwell.

8   Let them give thanks to the Lord for his mercy*
    and the wonders he does for his children.

9   For he satisfies the thirsty*
    and fills the hungry with good things.

10 Some sat in darkness and deep gloom,*
    bound fast in misery and iron;

11 Because they rebelled against the words of God*
    and despised the counsel of the Most High.

12 So he humbled their spirits with hard labour;*
    they stumbled and there was none to help.

13 Then they cried to the Lord in their trouble,*
    and he delivered them from their distress.

14 He led them out of darkness and deep gloom*
    and broke their bonds asunder.

15 Let them give thanks to the Lord for his mercy*
    and the wonders he does for his children.

16 For he shatters the doors of bronze*
    and breaks in two the iron bars.

17 Some went down to the sea in ships*
    and plied their trade in deep waters;

18 They beheld the works of the Lord*
and his wonders in the deep.

19 Then he spoke and a stormy wind arose,*
which tossed high the waves of the sea.

20 They mounted up to the heavens
and fell back to the depths;*
their hearts melted because of their peril.

21 They reeled and staggered like drunkards*
and were at their wits' end.

22 Then they cried to the Lord in their trouble,*
and he delivered them from their distress.

23 He stilled the storm to a whisper*
and quieted the waves of the sea.

24 Then were they glad because of the calm,*
and he brought them
to the harbour they were bound for.

25 Let them give thanks to the Lord for his mercy*
and the wonders he does for his children.

26 Let them exalt him in the congregation of the people*
and praise him in the council of the elders.

*Lord, here we have no abiding city,
but seek that which is to come:
guide and deliver us in all earthly changes
and direct our way towards the haven of salvation;
through Jesus Christ our Lord.* **Amen.**   14

Week 7 & Saturdays in Eastertide — from Psalm 116

1   I love the Lord,
      because he has heard the voice of my supplication,*
    because he has inclined his ear to me
      whenever I called upon him.

2   The cords of death entangled me;*
     the grip of the grave took hold of me.

3   Then I called upon the name of the Lord:*
    'O Lord, I pray you, save my life.'

4   Gracious is the Lord and righteous;*
    our God is full of compassion.

5   The Lord watches over the innocent;*
    I was brought very low and he helped me.

6   Turn again to your rest, O my soul,*
    for the Lord has treated you well.

7   For you have rescued my life from death,*
    my eyes from tears and my feet from stumbling.

8   I will walk in the presence of the Lord*
    in the land of the living.

9   How shall I repay the Lord*
    for all the good things he has done for me?

10 I will lift up the cup of salvation*
    and call upon the name of the Lord.

11 I will fulfil my vows to the Lord*
    in the presence of all his people.

12 Precious in the sight of the Lord*
    is the death of his servants.

13 O Lord, I am your servant;*
    you have freed me from my bonds.

14 I will offer you the sacrifice of thanksgiving*
    and call upon the name of the Lord.

15 In the presence of all his people,*
    in the courts of the Lord's house. Alleluia!

Faithful God,
rescue us from our faithlessness
that we may fulfil our vows to you
and ever call on your holy Name;
through Jesus Christ, our Saviour. **Amen.**   7

THE NEW TESTAMENT CANTICLE

Either: A SONG OF THE HEAVENLY CITY

1   I saw no temple in the city,*
    for its temple is the Lord God the Almighty
      and the Lamb.

2   And the city has no need of sun or moon
      to shine upon it,*
    for the glory of God is its light,
    and its lamp is the Lamb.

3   By its light the nations shall walk,*
    and the rulers of the earth
      shall bring their glory.

4   Its gates shall never be shut by day,
      nor shall there be any night;*
    they shall bring into it
      the glory and honour of the nations.

5   I saw the river of the water of life,
      bright as crystal,*
    flowing from the throne of God and of the Lamb.

6   And either side of the river stood the tree of life,
      yielding its fruit each month,*
    and the leaves of the tree
      were for the healing of the nations.

7   The throne of God and of the Lamb shall be there,
      and his servants shall worship him;*
    and they shall see God's face
      and his name shall be on their foreheads.

To the One who sits on the throne and to the Lamb*
be blessing and honour and glory and might,
    for ever and ever. Amen. *From Revelation 21 & 22*

Or: A SONG OF FAITH

1   Blessèd be the God and Father of our Lord Jesus Christ,*
    who in his great mercy
       gave us a new birth as his children.

2   He has raised Jesus Christ from the dead,*
    so that we have a sure hope in him.

3   We have the promise of an inheritance
       that can never be spoilt,*
    because it is kept for us in heaven.

4   The ransom that was paid to free us*
    was not paid in silver or gold,

5   But in the precious blood of Christ,*
    the Lamb without spot or stain.

6   God raised him from the dead and gave him glory*
    so that we might have faith and hope in God.

                                        From 1 Peter 1

    Glory to the Father, and to the Son,
       and to the Holy Spirit:*
    as it was in the beginning, is now,
       and shall be for ever. Amen.

THE SCRIPTURE READING

Week 1 & Sundays in Eastertide

Jesus took with him Peter, James and John and led them up a high mountain apart, by themselves. And he was transfigured before them and his clothes became dazzling white, such as no one on earth could bleach them. Then a cloud overshadowed them and from the cloud there came a voice, 'This is my Son, the Belovèd; listen to him!' *Mark 9. 2, 3, 7*

Week 2 & Mondays in Eastertide

Thus says the Lord God: 'I myself will be the shepherd of my sheep and I will make them lie down. I will seek the lost and I will bring back the strayed. I will bind up the injured and I will strengthen the weak, but the fat and the strong I will destroy. I will feed them with justice.' *Ezekiel 34. 15-16*

Week 3 & Tuesdays in Eastertide

Jesus said, 'Do not lay up for yourselves treasures on earth, where moth and rust consume and where thieves break in and steal; but lay up for yourselves treasures in heaven, where neither moth nor rust consumes and where thieves do not break in and steal. For where your treasure is, there will your heart be also.' *Matthew 6. 19-21*

Week 4 & Wednesdays in Eastertide

From now on, therefore, we regard no one from a human point of view; even though we once knew Christ from a human point of view, we know him no longer in that way. So if anyone is in Christ, there is a new creation: the old has passed away; behold, the new has come! *2 Corinthians 5. 16-17*

Week 5 & Thursdays in Eastertide

Two of the disciples were going to a village called Emmaus, and while they were talking, Jesus himself came near and went with them, but their eyes were kept from recognising him. As they came near to the village, Jesus walked ahead as if he were going on. But they urged him strongly, saying, 'Stay with us, because it is almost evening and the day is now nearly over.' So he went in to stay with them. When he was at the table with them, he took bread, blessed and broke it, and gave it to them. Then their eyes were opened and they recognised him; and he vanished from their sight. *Luke 24. 13, 15, 28-31*

Week 6 & Fridays in Eastertide

Thus says the Lord who created you, O Jacob, he who formed you, O Israel: Fear not, for I have redeemed you; I have called you by name, you are mine. When you pass through the waters, I will be with you; and through the rivers, they shall not overwhelm you; when you walk through fire, you shall not be burned and the flame shall not consume you. For I am the Lord your God, the Holy One of Israel, your Saviour. *Isaiah 43. 1-3a*

Week 7 & Saturdays in Eastertide

Jesus said to Martha, 'I am the resurrection and the life. Those who believe in me, even though they die, yet shall they live, and everyone who lives and believes in me will never die. Do you believe this?' She said to him, 'Yes, Lord, I believe that you are the Messiah, the Son of God, the one coming into the world.' *John 11. 25-26*

* * *

This RESPONSE to the reading may be used:
The Lord is my light and my salvation;
The Lord is the strength of my life.

THE GOSPEL CANTICLE: THE MAGNIFICAT

1   My soul proclaims the greatness of the Lord,*
     my spirit rejoices in God my Saviour,

2   For you, Lord, have looked with favour
        on your lowly servant.*
     From this day all generations will call me blessèd:

3   You, the Almighty, have done great things for me*
     and holy is your name.

4   You have mercy on those who fear you,*
     from generation to generation.

5   You have shown strength with your arm*
     and scattered the proud in their conceit,

6   Casting down the mighty from their thrones*
     and lifting up the lowly.

7   You have filled the hungry with good things*
     and sent the rich away empty.

8   You have come to the aid of your servant, Israel,*
     to remember the promise of mercy,

9   The promise made to our forebears,*
     to Abraham and his children for ever.   *Luke 1. 46-55*

   Glory to the Father, and to the Son,
     and to the Holy Spirit:*
  as it was in the beginning, is now,
     and shall be for ever. Amen.

THE PRAYERS

Intercession and thanksgiving are offered in free prayer or in silence, ending with the following:

To you, O Lord, we lift our eyes;
  to you, enthroned in the heavens.
Lord, have mercy.

Let our cry come before you, O Lord;
  grant us understanding, according to your word.
Christ, have mercy.

Let your merciful goodness come to us, O Lord;
   and your salvation, according to your promise.
Lord, have mercy.

Satisfy those who thirst,
   and fill the hungry with good things.
Christ, have mercy.

Your kingship has dominion over all,
   and with you is our redemption.
Lord, have mercy.

THE COLLECT for Sundays:

Grant to us, Lord, we pray,
the spirit to think and do always
such things as be rightful;
that we,
who cannot do anything that is good without you,
may by you be enabled to live
   according to your will;
through Jesus Christ our Lord . . .   1›

Or for Eastertide:

God,
through the mighty resurrection
   of your Son, Jesus Christ,
you have delivered us from the power of darkness
and brought us into the kingdom of your love:
grant that, as he was raised from the dead
so we may walk in newness of life
and seek those things which are above;
where with you, Father, and the Holy Spirit,
he is alive and reigns,
now and for ever. **Amen.**

THE LORD'S PRAYER may be said.

Let us bless the Lord.
Thanks be to God.

Morning Prayer - Form 2
Monday and daily in Pentecost

THE PREPARATION

O Lord, open our lips;
And our mouth shall proclaim your praise.

Blessèd are you, creator God;
to you be glory and praise for ever!
Your Spirit moved over the face of the waters
to bring light and life to your creation.
Pour out your Spirit on us this day,
that we may walk as children of light
and by your grace reveal your presence,
Father, Son and Holy Spirit;
Blessèd be God for ever!

THE WORD OF GOD
Week 1 & Sundays in Pentecost — Psalm 103

1   Bless the Lord, O my soul,*
    and all that is within me, bless his holy name.

2   Bless the Lord, O my soul,*
    and forget not all his benefits.

3   He forgives all your sins*
    and heals all your infirmities;

4   He redeems your life from the grave*
    and crowns you with mercy and loving-kindness;

5   He satisfies you with good things,*
    and your youth is renewed like an eagle's.

6   The Lord executes righteousness*
    and judgement for all who are oppressed.

7   He made his ways known to Moses*
    and his works to the children of Israel.

8   The Lord is full of compassion and mercy,*
    slow to anger and of great kindness.

9   He will not always accuse us,*
    nor will he keep his anger for ever.

10   He has not dealt with us according to our sins,*
      nor rewarded us according to our wickedness.

11   For as the heavens are high above the earth,*
      so is his mercy great upon those who fear him.

12   As far as the east is from the west,*
      so far has he removed our sins from us.

13   As a father cares for his children,*
      so does the Lord care for those who fear him.

14   For he himself knows whereof we are made;*
      he remembers that we are but dust.

15   Our days are like the grass;*
      we flourish like a flower of the field;

16   When the wind goes over it, it is gone,*
      and its place shall know it no more.

17   But the merciful goodness of the Lord
      endures for ever on those who fear him,*
      and his righteousness on children's children;

18   On those who keep his covenant*
      and remember his commandments and do them.

19   The Lord has set his throne in heaven,*
      and his kingship has dominion over all.

20   Bless the Lord, you angels of his,
      you mighty ones who do his bidding,*
      and hearken to the voice of his word.

21   Bless the Lord, all you his hosts,*
      you ministers of his who do his will.

22   Bless the Lord, all you works of his,
      in all places of his dominion;*
      bless the Lord, O my soul.

*As your merciful goodness endures for ever, O Lord,
remember the frailty of your children;
deal with us not according to our sins
but, in your compassion, redeem our life
and crown us with your mercy and loving-kindness;
through Jesus Christ our Lord.* **Amen.**   18

Week 2 & Mondays in Pentecost — Psalm 65

1 You are to be praised, O God, in Zion;*
   to you shall vows be performed in Jerusalem.

2 To you that hear prayer shall all flesh come,*
   because of their transgressions.

3 Our sins are stronger than we are,*
   but you will blot them out.

4 Happy are they whom you choose
      and draw to your courts to dwell there!*
   they will be satisfied by the beauty of your house,
      by the holiness of your temple.

5 Awesome things will you show us in your righteousness,
      O God of our salvation,*
   O Hope of all the ends of the earth
      and of the seas that are far away.

6 You make fast the mountains by your power;*
   they are girded about with might.

7 You still the roaring of the seas,*
   the roaring of their waves,
      and the clamour of the peoples.

8 Those who dwell at the ends of the earth
      will tremble at your marvellous signs;*
   you make the dawn and the dusk to sing for joy.

9 You visit the earth and water it abundantly;
      you make it very plenteous;*
   the river of God is full of water.

10 You prepare the grain,*
   for so you provide for the earth.

11 You drench the furrows and smooth out the ridges;*
   with heavy rain you soften the ground
      and bless its increase.

12 You crown the year with your goodness,*
   and your paths overflow with plenty.

13 May the fields of the wilderness be rich for grazing,*
   and the hills be clothed with joy.

14 May the meadows cover themselves with flocks
        and the valleys cloak themselves with grain;*
    let them shout for joy and sing.

May the richness of your creation, O God,
and the mystery of your sovereign rule,
lead us to that heavenly city
where all peoples will bring their wealth,
forsake their sins and find their true joy
in Jesus Christ our Lord. **Amen.**   19

Week 3 & Tuesdays in Pentecost — Psalm 121

1   I lift up my eyes to the hills;*
    from where is my help to come?

2   My help comes from the Lord,*
    the maker of heaven and earth.

3   He will not let your foot be moved*
    and he who watches over you will not fall asleep.

4   Behold, he who keeps watch over Israel*
    shall neither slumber nor sleep;

5   The Lord himself watches over you;*
    the Lord is your shade at your right hand,

6   So that the sun shall not strike you by day,*
    nor the moon by night.

7   The Lord shall preserve you from all evil;*
    it is he who shall keep you safe.

8   The Lord shall watch over your going out
        and your coming in,*
    from this time forth for evermore.

Lord, ever watchful and faithful,
we look to you to be our defence
and we lift up our hearts to know your help;
through Jesus Christ our Lord. **Amen.**   16

Week 4 & Wednesdays in Pentecost – Psalm 93

1 The Lord is king; he has put on splendid apparel;*
   the Lord has put on his apparel
      and girded himself with strength.

2 He has made the whole world so sure*
   that it cannot be moved;

3 Ever since the world began,
      your throne has been established;*
   you are from everlasting.

4 The waters have lifted up, O Lord,
      the waters have lifted up their voice;*
   the waters have lifted up their pounding waves.

5 Mightier than the sound of many waters,
      mightier than the breakers of the sea,*
   mightier is the Lord who dwells on high.

6 Your testimonies are very sure,*
   and holiness adorns your house, O Lord,
      for ever and for evermore.

*You have established your throne, O Lord,
above the chaos of this world:
may your truth, which is for everlasting,
be ours, now and for ever.* **Amen.**   18

Week 5 & Thursdays in Pentecost – Psalm 47

1 Clap your hands, all you peoples;*
   shout to God with a cry of joy.

2 For the Lord Most High is to be feared;*
   he is the great king over all the earth.

3 He subdues the peoples under us,*
   and the nations under our feet.

4 He chooses our inheritance for us,*
   the pride of Jacob whom he loves.

5 God has gone up with a shout,*
   the Lord with the sound of the ram's horn.

6 Sing praises to God, sing praises;*
   sing praises to our king, sing praises.

7   For God is king of all the earth;*
    sing praises with all your skill.

8   God reigns over the nations;*
    God sits upon his holy throne.

9   The nobles of the peoples have gathered together*
    with the people of the God of Abraham.

10 The rulers of the earth belong to God,*
    and he is highly exalted.

    As Christ was raised by your glory, O Father,
    so may we walk in newness of life
    and rejoice to be called the children of God;
    now and for ever. **Amen.**   18

Week 6 and Fridays in Pentecost – Psalm 111

1   Alleluia!
       I will give thanks to the Lord with my whole heart,*
    in the assembly of the upright, in the congregation.

2   Great are the deeds of the Lord!*
    they are studied by all who delight in them.

3   His work is full of majesty and splendour,*
    and his righteousness endures for ever.

4   He makes his marvellous works to be remembered;*
    the Lord is gracious and full of compassion.

5   He gives food to those who fear him;*
    he is ever mindful of his covenant.

6   He has shown his people the power of his works*
    in giving them the lands of the nations.

7   The works of his hands are faithfulness and justice;*
    all his commandments are sure.

8   They stand fast for ever and ever,*
    because they are done in truth and equity.

9   He sent redemption to his people;
       he commanded his covenant for ever;*
    holy and awesome is his name.

10 The fear of the Lord is the beginning of wisdom;*
     those who act accordingly have a good understanding;
        his praise endures for ever.

Holy Father,
you have revealed in your only begotten Son
the power of the new and everlasting covenant:
on this day, which we have made your own,
feed your people with the bread of heaven
as they recount your marvellous deeds;
through Jesus Christ our Lord. **Amen.**   14

Week 7 & Saturdays in Pentecost – Psalm 150

1 Alleluia!
     Praise God in his holy temple;*
   praise him in the firmament of his power.

2 Praise him for his mighty acts;*
   praise him for his excellent greatness.

3 Praise him with the blast of the ram's horn;*
   praise him with lyre and harp.

4 Praise him with timbrel and dance;*
   praise him with strings and pipe.

5 Praise him with resounding cymbals;*
   praise him with loud clanging cymbals.

6 Let everything that has breath*
   praise the Lord.
     Alleluia!

God of life and love,
whose Son was victorious over sin and death:
make us alive with his life,
that the whole world may resound with your praise;
through Jesus Christ our Lord. **Amen.**   13

THE OLD TESTAMENT CANTICLE
Either: A SONG OF DELIVERANCE

1   'Behold, God is my salvation;*
    I will trust and will not be afraid;

2   'For the Lord God is my strength and my song,*
    and has become my salvation.'

3   With joy you will draw water*
    from the wells of salvation.

4   On that day you will say,*
    'Give thanks to the Lord, call upon his name;

5   'Make known his deeds among the nations,*
    proclaim that his name is exalted.

6   'Sing God's praises, who has triumphed gloriously;*
    let this be known in all the world.

7   'Shout and sing for joy, you that dwell in Zion,*
    for great in your midst is the Holy One of Israel.'

                                            Isaiah 12. 2-6

    Glory to the Father, and to the Son,
        and to the Holy Spirit:*
    as it was in the beginning, is now,
        and shall be for ever. Amen.

Or: A SONG OF EZEKIEL

1   I will take you from the nations,*
    and gather you from all the countries.

2   I will sprinkle clean water upon you,*
    and purify you from all defilement.

3   A new heart I will give you,*
    and put a new spirit within you,

4   And I will remove from your body the heart of stone*
    and give you a heart of flesh.

5   You shall be my people,*
    and I will be your God. *Ezekiel 36. 24-28*

    Glory to the Father, and to the Son,
        and to the Holy Spirit:*
    as it was in the beginning, is now,
        and shall be for ever. Amen.

THE SCRIPTURE READING

Week 1 & Sundays in Pentecost

God said, 'Let us make man in our image, according to our
likeness, and let them have dominion over the fish of the sea, and
over the birds of the air, and over the cattle, and over all the
wild animals of the earth, and over every creeping thing that
creeps upon the earth.' So God created man in his image,
in the image of God he created him, male and female he created
them. God blessed them and said to them, 'Be fruitful and
multiply, and fill the earth and subdue it; and have dominion
over the fish of the sea and over the birds of the air and over
every living thing that moves upon the earth.' *Genesis 1. 26-28*

Week 2 & Mondays in Pentecost

Since we are justified by faith, we have peace with God through
our Lord Jesus Christ, through whom we have obtained access to
this grace in which we stand; and we boast in our hope of sharing
the glory of God. And not only that, but we also boast in our
sufferings, knowing that suffering produces endurance, and
endurance produces character, and character produces hope, and
hope does not disappoint us, because God's love has been poured
into our hearts through the Holy Spirit that has been given to us
Romans 5. 1-5

Week 3 & Tuesdays in Pentecost

Moses said to God, 'If I come to the Israelites and say to them,
"The God of your ancestors has sent me to you", and they ask me,
"What is his name?" what shall I say to them?' God said to Moses
'I AM WHO I AM.' He said further, 'Thus you shall say to the
Israelites, "I AM has sent me to you." ' *Exodus 3. 13-14*

Week 4 & Wednesdays in Pentecost

Moses said, 'Lay up these words of mine in your heart and
soul, and you shall bind them as a sign on your hand and fix them
as frontlets between your eyes. Teach them to your children,
talking about them when you are at home and when you are away,
when you lie down and when you rise.' *Deuteronomy 11. 18-21*

Week 5 & Thursdays in Pentecost

I bow my knees before the Father, from whom every family in heaven and on earth takes its name. I pray that, according to the riches of his glory, he may grant that you may be strengthened in your inner being with power through his Spirit, and that Christ may dwell in your hearts through faith, as you are being rooted and grounded in love. I pray that you may have the power to comprehend, with all the saints, what is the breadth and length and height and depth, and to know the love of Christ that surpasses knowledge, so that you may be filled with all the fullness of God.   *Ephesians 3. 14-19*

Week 6 & Fridays in Pentecost

There are varieties of gifts but the same Spirit; and there are varieties of service but the same Lord; and there are varieties of activities but it is the same God who inspires them all in everyone. To each is given the manifestation of the Spirit for the common good. For just as the body is one and has many members, and all the members of the body, though many, are one body, so it is with Christ. For in the one Spirit we were all baptised into one body – Jews or Greeks, slaves or free – and we were all made to drink of one spirit.
                              1 Corinthians 12. 4-7, 12-13

Week 7 & Saturdays in Pentecost

Job answered the Lord: 'I know that you can do all things and that no purpose of yours can be thwarted. "Who is this that hides counsel without knowledge?" Therefore, I have uttered what I did not understand; things too wonderful for me which I did not know. "Hear, and I will speak; I will question you, and you declare to me." I had heard of you by the hearing of the ear, but now my eye sees you; therefore I despise myself, and repent in dust and ashes.'   *Job 42. 1-6*

*   *   *

This RESPONSE to the reading may be used:
Come, Holy Spirit, fill the hearts of your people,
And kindle in us the fire of your love.

THE GOSPEL CANTICLE: THE BENEDICTUS

1   Blessèd are you, Lord, the God of Israel,*
    you have come to your people and set them free.

2   You have raised up for us a mighty Saviour,*
    born of the house of your servant, David.

3   Through your holy prophets, you promised of old*
    to save us from our enemies,
      from the hands of all who hate us,

4   To show mercy to our forebears,*
    and to remember your holy covenant.

5   This was the oath you swore to our father, Abraham,*
    to set us free from the hands of our enemies,

6   Free to worship you without fear,*
    holy and righteous before you,
      all the days of our life.

7   And you, child,
      shall be called the prophet of the Most High,*
    for you will go before the Lord to prepare the way,

8   To give God's people knowledge of salvation*
    by the forgiveness of their sins.

9   In the tender compassion of our God*
    the dawn from on high shall break upon us,

10 To shine on those who dwell in darkness
      and the shadow of death,*
    and to guide our feet into the way of peace. *Luke 1. 68-79*

    Glory to the Father, and to the Son,
      and to the Holy Spirit:*
    as it was in the beginning, is now,
      and shall be for ever. Amen.

THE PRAYERS

Intercession and thanksgiving are offered in free prayer or in silence, ending with the following:

In the morning, Lord, you hear our voice:
we make our appeal and watch for you.
Lord, have mercy.

Come, O Lord, and bless the righteous;
defend them with your favour as with a shield.
Christ, have mercy.

Let all the earth fear you, O Lord our God;
let all who dwell in the world stand in awe of you.
Lord, have mercy.

THE COLLECT for Mondays:

Eternal God and Father,
you create us by your power
and redeem us by your love:
guide and strengthen us by your Spirit,
that we may give ourselves in love and service
to one another and to you;
through Jesus Christ our Lord . . .   3

Or for the Pentecost Season:

Almighty God,
who sent your Holy Spirit
to be the life and light of your Church:
open our hearts to the riches of your grace,
that we may bring forth the fruit of the Spirit
in love and joy and peace;
through Jesus Christ our Lord . . .   3›

THE LORD'S PRAYER may be said.

Let us bless the Lord.
Thanks be to God.

Evening Prayer – Form 2

Monday and daily in Pentecost

THE BLESSING OF THE LIGHT

With you, O God, is the well of life
and in your light shall we see light.

The light and peace of Jesus Christ be with you all
And also with you.

Let us give thanks to the Lord our God
Who is worthy of all thanksgiving and praise.

Blessèd are you, Sovereign God, our light and our life;
to you be glory and praise for ever!
When we turned away to darkness and chaos,
like a mother you would not forsake us.
You cried out like a woman in labour
and rejoiced to bring forth a new people.
Your living Word brings light out of darkness
and daily your Spirit renews the face of the earth,
bending our wills to the gentle rule of your love,
Father, Son and Holy Spirit:
Blessèd be God for ever!

A SONG OF THE LIGHT

1   O gladsome light, of the holy glory of the immortal Father,*
    heavenly, holy, blessèd Jesus Christ.

2   Now that we have come to the setting of the sun
        and behold the light of evening,*
    we praise you, Father, Son and Holy Spirit.

3   For it is right at all times to worship you
        with voices of praise,*
    O Son of God and giver of life:
        therefore all the world glorifies you.

THE WORD OF GOD
Week 1 and Sundays in Pentecost – from Psalm 68

1 Let God arise and let his enemies be scattered;*
  let those who hate him flee before him.

2 Let them vanish like smoke
    when the wind drives it away;*
  as the wax melts at the fire,
    so let the wicked perish at the presence of God.

3 But let the righteous be glad and rejoice before God;*
  let them also be merry and joyful.

4 Sing to God, sing praises to his name;
    exalt him who rides upon the heavens;*
  Yahweh is his name, rejoice before him!

5 Father of orphans, defender of widows,*
  God in his holy habitation!

6 God gives the solitary a home
    and brings forth prisoners into freedom;*
  but the rebels shall live in dry places.

7 O God, when you went forth before your people,*
  when you marched through the wilderness,

8 The earth shook and the skies poured down rain,
    at the presence of God, the God of Sinai,*
  at the presence of God, the God of Israel.

9 You sent a gracious rain, O God, upon your inheritance;*
  you refreshed the land when it was weary.

10 Your people found their home in it;*
  in your goodness, O God,
    you have made provision for the poor.

11 The Lord gave the word;*
  great was the company of women who bore the tidings:

12 'Kings with their armies are fleeing away;*
  the women at home are dividing the spoils.'

13 Why do you look with envy, O rugged mountain,
    at the hill which God chose for his resting place?*
  truly, the Lord will dwell there for ever.

14 The chariots of God are twenty thousand,
   even thousands of thousands;*
   the Lord comes in holiness from Sinai.

15 You have gone up on high and led captivity captive;
   you have received gifts even from your enemies,*
   that the Lord God might dwell among them.

16 Blessèd be the Lord day by day,*
   the God of our salvation, who bears our burdens.

17 He is our God, the God of our salvation;*
   God is the Lord, by whom we escape death.

   We praise your holy Name, O God of hosts,
   and bless you day by day,
   for you bring healing and wholeness to your people:
   look with love on those in the shadow of death
   and let the light of Christ lead us all
   to your heavenly kingdom,
   to the fullness of life in the Spirit. **Amen.**

Week 2 & Mondays in Pentecost – from Psalm 68

24 Your procession is seen, O God,*
   your procession into the sanctuary, my God and my King.

25 The singers go before, musicians follow after,*
   in the midst of maidens playing upon the hand drums.

26 Bless God in the congregation;*
   bless the Lord, you that are of the fountain of Israel.

27 There is Benjamin, least of the tribes, at the head;
   the princes of Judah in a company;*
   and the princes of Zebulon and Naphtali.

28 Send forth your strength, O God;*
   establish, O God, what you have wrought for us.

29 Kings shall bring gifts to you,*
   for your temple's sake at Jerusalem.

30 Rebuke the wild beast of the reeds,*
   and the peoples, a herd of wild bulls with its calves.

31 Trample down those who lust after silver;*
   scatter the peoples that delight in war.

32 Let tribute be brought out of Egypt;*
   let Ethiopia stretch out her hands to God.

33 Sing to God, O kingdoms of the earth;*
   sing praises to the Lord.

34 He rides in the heavens, the ancient heavens;*
   he sends forth his voice, his mighty voice.

35 Ascribe power to God;*
   his majesty is over Israel;
     his strength is in the skies.

36 How wonderful is God in his holy places!*
   the God of Israel giving strength and power to his people!
     Blessèd be God!

Blessèd be God
whose victory creates a new people,
who makes his home among the weak,
who delivers us from death,
and who brings joy and blessings beyond our imagining.
Blessèd be God for ever. **Amen.**   19

Week 3 & Tuesdays in Pentecost – Psalm 127

1 Unless the Lord builds the house,*
   their labour is in vain who build it.

2 Unless the Lord watches over the city,*
   in vain the guard keeps vigil.

3 It is in vain that you rise so early
   and go to bed so late;*
   vain, too, to eat the bread of toil,
     for he gives to his belovèd sleep.

4 Children are a heritage from the Lord,*
   and the fruit of the womb is a gift.

5 Like arrows in the hand of a warrior*
   are the children of one's youth.

6 Happy are they who have their quiver full of them!*
   they shall not be put to shame
     when they contend with their enemies in the gate.

Lord, you are ever watchful,
you bless us with your gifts,
you provide for all our needs:
help us to build only what pleases you;
through Jesus Christ our Lord. **Amen.**   16

1 I love you, O Lord my strength,*
    O Lord my stronghold, my crag and my haven.

2 My God, my rock in whom I put my trust,*
    my shield, the horn of my salvation and my refuge;
        you are worthy of praise.

3 I will call upon the Lord,*
    and so shall I be saved from my enemies.

4 The breakers of death rolled over me,*
    and the torrents of oblivion made me afraid.

5 The cords of hell entangled me,*
    and the snares of death were set for me.

6 I called upon the Lord in my distress*
    and cried out to my God for help.

7 He heard my voice from his heavenly dwelling;*
    my cry of anguish came to his ears.

8 The earth reeled and rocked;*
    the roots of the mountains shook;
        they reeled because of his anger.

9 Smoke rose from his nostrils
        and a consuming fire out of his mouth;*
    hot burning coals blazed forth from him.

10 He parted the heavens and came down*
    with a storm cloud under his feet.

11 He mounted on cherubim and flew;*
    he swooped on the wings of the wind.

12 He wrapped darkness about him;*
    he made dark waters and thick clouds his pavilion.

13 From the brightness of his presence, through the clouds,*
    burst hailstones and coals of fire.

14 The Lord thundered out of heaven;*
    the Most High uttered his voice.

15 He loosed his arrows and scattered them;*
    he hurled thunderbolts and routed them.

16 The beds of the seas were uncovered,
and the foundations of the world laid bare,*
at your battle cry, O Lord,
at the blast of the breath of your nostrils.

17 He reached down from on high and grasped me;*
he drew me out of great waters.

18 He delivered me from my strong enemies
and from those who hated me;*
for they were too mighty for me.

19 They confronted me in the day of my disaster;*
but the Lord was my support.

20 He brought me out into an open place;*
he rescued me because he delighted in me.

Spirit of God,
bring us into all truth,
deliver us from all evil,
reach down and touch us,
guide us to the Father,
through Jesus, our risen Lord. **Amen.** 7

Week 5 & Thursdays in Pentecost — Psalm 18, Part II

21 The Lord rewarded me because of my righteous dealing;*
because my hands were clean he rewarded me;

22 For I have kept the ways of the Lord*
and have not offended against my God;

23 For all his judgements are before my eyes,*
and his decrees I have not put away from me;

24 For I have been blameless with him*
and have kept myself from iniquity;

25 Therefore the Lord rewarded me
according to my righteous dealing,*
because of the cleanness of my hands in his sight.

26 With the faithful you show yourself faithful, O God;*
with the forthright you show yourself forthright.

27 With the pure you show yourself pure,*
but with the crooked you are wily.

28 You will save a lowly people;*
   but you will humble the haughty eyes.

29 You, O Lord, are my lamp;*
   my God, you make my darkness bright.

30 With you I will break down an enclosure;*
   with the help of my God I will scale any wall.

31 As for God, his ways are perfect;
      the words of the Lord are tried in the fire;*
   he is a shield to all who trust in him.

32 For who is God, but the Lord?*
   who is the rock, except our God?

33 It is God who girds me about with strength*
   and makes my way secure.

34 He makes me sure-footed like a deer*
   and lets me stand firm on the heights.

35 He trains my hands for battle*
   and my arms for bending even a bow of bronze.

36 You have given me your shield of victory;*
   your right hand also sustains me;
      your loving care makes me great.

37 You lengthen my stride beneath me,*
   and my ankles do not give way.

38 I pursue my enemies and overtake them;*
   I will not turn back till I have destroyed them.

39 I strike them down and they cannot rise;*
   they fall defeated at my feet.

40 You have girded me with strength for the battle;*
   you have cast down my adversaries beneath me;
      you have put my enemies to flight.

41 I destroy those who hate me;
      they cry out, but there is none to help them;*
   they cry to the Lord, but he does not answer.

42 I beat them small like dust before the wind;*
   I trample them like mud in the streets.

43 You deliver me from the strife of the peoples;*
   you put me at the head of the nations.

44 A people I have not known shall serve me;
    no sooner shall they hear than they shall obey me;*
strangers will cringe before me.

45 The foreign peoples will lose heart;*
they shall come trembling out of their strongholds.

46 The Lord lives! Blessèd is my rock!*
Exalted is the God of my salvation!

47 He is the God who gave me victory*
and cast down the peoples beneath me.

48 You rescued me from the fury of my enemies;
    you exalted me above those who rose against me;*
you saved me from my deadly foe;

49 Therefore will I extol you among the nations, O Lord,*
and sing praises to your name.

50 He multiplies the victories of his king;*
he shows loving-kindness to his anointed,
    to David and his descendants for ever.

Guard us, O Lord, with the shield of faith
and fight for us with the sword of the Spirit,
that in all our spiritual warfare
    against the powers of darkness
we may gain the victory
through Jesus Christ our Lord. **Amen.** 14

1   I will give thanks to you, O Lord, with my whole heart;*
    before the gods I will sing your praise.

2   I will bow down towards your holy temple
        and praise your name,*
    because of your love and faithfulness;

3   For you have glorified your name*
    and your word above all things.

4   When I called, you answered me;*
    you increased my strength within me.

5   All the kings of the earth will praise you, O Lord,*
    when they have heard the words of your mouth.

6   They will sing of the ways of the Lord,*
    that great is the glory of the Lord.

7   Though the Lord be high, he cares for the lowly;*
    he perceives the haughty from afar.

8   Though I walk in the midst of trouble,
        you keep me safe;*
    you stretch forth your hand
        against the fury of my enemies;
        your right hand shall save me.

9   The Lord will make good his purpose for me;*
    O Lord, your love endures for ever;
        do not abandon the works of your hands.

Lord our God, supreme over all things,
we ask you to look upon the humble and lowly,
to put new strength into our souls
and to complete your purpose for us,
in Christ Jesus our Lord. **Amen.**   16

1   O how good and pleasant it is,*
    when a family lives together in unity!

2   It is like fine oil upon the head*
    that runs down upon the beard,

3   Upon the beard of Aaron,*
    and runs down upon the collar of his robe.

4   It is like the dew of Hermon*
    that falls upon the hills of Zion.

5   For there the Lord has ordained the blessing:*
    life for evermore.

Holy Trinity, God in perfect Unity,
send your life-giving blessing
upon the brothers and sisters of Christ,
that they may live for evermore with joy
the life of unity that springs from you,
God, to all eternity.   **Amen.**   16

Psalm 134

1   Behold now, bless the Lord,
       all you servants of the Lord,*
    you that stand by night in the house of the Lord.

2   Lift up your hands in the holy place
       and bless the Lord;*
    the Lord who made heaven and earth
       bless you out of Zion.

Blessèd are you, Lord our God,
our creator and sustainer:
in the darkness we look to your light
and we place ourselves and all your household
under your protection through the night.
Blessèd be God for ever! **Amen.**   16

THE NEW TESTAMENT CANTICLE

Either: A SONG OF GOD'S GRACE

1   Blessèd are you,
        the God and Father of our Lord Jesus Christ,*
    for you have blest us in Christ Jesus
        with every spiritual blessing in the heavenly places.

2   You chose us to be yours in Christ
        before the foundation of the world,*
    that we should be holy and blameless before you.

3   In love you destined us to be your children,
        through Jesus Christ,*
    according to the purpose of your will,

4   To the praise of your glorious grace,*
    which you freely bestowed on us in the Belovèd.

5   In you, we have redemption
        through the blood of Christ,*
    the forgiveness of our sins,

6   According to the riches of your grace,*
    which you have lavished upon us.

7   You have made known to us, in all wisdom and insight,*
    the mystery of your will,

8   According to your purpose
        which you set forth in Christ,*
    as a plan for the fullness of time,

9   To unite all things in Christ,*
    things in heaven and things on earth.   *Ephesians 1. 3-10*

    **Glory to the Father, and to the Son,
        and to the Holy Spirit:***
    **as it was in the beginning, is now,
        and shall be for ever. Amen.**

Or: A SONG OF GOD'S CHILDREN

1 In Christ Jesus, the life-giving law of the Spirit*
   has set us free from the law of sin and death.

2 All who are led by the Spirit of God are children of God;*
   it is the Spirit that enables us to cry, 'Abba!' Father.

3 The Spirit itself bears witness
      that we are God's children;*
   and if God's children, then heirs of God.

4 We are heirs of God and fellow-heirs with Christ;*
   if we share his sufferings now
      we shall be glorified with him hereafter.

5 These sufferings that we now endure*
   are not worth comparing
      with the glory that shall be revealed.

6 For the creation waits with eager longing*
   for the revealing of the children of God.   *From Romans 8*

   Glory to the Father, and to the Son,
      and to the Holy Spirit:*
   as it was in the beginning, is now,
      and shall be for ever.   Amen.

THE SCRIPTURE READING

Week 1 & Sundays in Pentecost

Jesus came from Nazareth of Galilee and was baptised by John in the Jordan. And just as he was coming up out of the water, he saw the heavens torn apart and the Spirit descending like a dove on him. And a voice came from heaven, 'You are my Son, the Belovèd; with you I am well pleased.'   *Mark 1. 9-11*

Week 2 & Mondays in Pentecost

The Lord said: I will pour out my spirit on all flesh; your sons and your daughters shall prophesy, your old men shall dream dreams and your young men shall see visions. Even upon the menservants and maidservants in those days, I will pour out my spirit.   *Joel 2. 28-29*

Week 3 & Tuesdays in Pentecost

Jesus put before them another parable: 'The kingdom of heaven is like a mustard seed that someone took and sowed in his field; it is the smallest of all the seeds but, when it has grown, it is the greatest of shrubs and becomes a tree, so that the birds of the air come and make nests in its branches.' *Matthew 13. 31-32*

Week 4 & Wednesdays in Pentecost

Since, then, we have such a hope, we act with great boldness, not like Moses, who put a veil over his face to keep the people of Israel from gazing at the end of the glory that was being set aside. But their minds were hardened. Indeed, to this very day when they hear the reading of the old covenant, that same veil is still there, since only in Christ is it set aside. Indeed, to this very day, whenever Moses is read, a veil lies over their minds; but when one turns to the Lord, the veil is removed. Now the Lord is the Spirit and where the Spirit of the Lord is, there is freedom. And all of us, with unveiled faces, seeing the glory of the Lord as though reflected in a mirror, are being transformed into the same image from one degree of glory to another; for this comes from the Lord, the Spirit.
2 Corinthians 3. 12-18

Week 5 & Thursdays in Pentecost

Jesus entered Capernaum and a centurion there had a servant whom he valued highly, who was ill and close to death and he sent to ask Jesus to come and heal his servant. Jesus went and, when he was not far from the house, the centurion sent friends to say to him, 'Lord, do not trouble yourself, for I am not worthy to have you come under my roof. But only speak the word, and let my servant be healed.' When Jesus heard this, he was amazed at him and, turning to the crowd that followed him, he said, 'I tell you, not even in Israel have I found such faith.' When those who had been sent returned to the house, they found the servant in good health.   *From Luke 7. 1-10*

Week 6 & Fridays in Pentecost

'Now hear, O Jacob my servant, Israel whom I have chosen! Thus says the Lord who made you, who formed you in the womb and will help you: Do not fear, for I will pour water on the thirsty land and streams on the dry ground; I will pour my spirit upon your descendants and my blessing on your offspring. They shall spring up like a green tamarisk, like willows by flowing streams.'
                          Isaiah 44. 1-4

Week 7 & Saturdays in Pentecost

Jesus said, 'I am the vine, you are the branches. Anyone who abides in me and I in him bears much fruit, because apart from me you can do nothing. If you abide in me and my words abide in you, ask for whatever you wish and it will be done for you. My Father is glorified by this, that you bear much fruit and become my disciples.'   *John 15. 5, 7-8*

*   *   *

This RESPONSE to the reading may be used:
When you send forth your Spirit, we are created:
You renew the face of the earth.

THE GOSPEL CANTICLE: THE MAGNIFICAT

1 My soul proclaims the greatness of the Lord,*
  my spirit rejoices in God my Saviour,

2 For you, Lord, have looked with favour
      on your lowly servant.*
  From this day all generations will call me blessèd:

3 You, the Almighty, have done great things for me*
  and holy is your name.

4 You have mercy on those who fear you,*
  from generation to generation.

5 You have shown strength with your arm*
  and scattered the proud in their conceit,

6 Casting down the mighty from their thrones*
  and lifting up the lowly.

7 You have filled the hungry with good things*
  and sent the rich away empty.

8 You have come to the aid of your servant, Israel,*
  to remember the promise of mercy,

9 The promise made to our forebears,*
  to Abraham and his children for ever.   *Luke 1. 46-55*

  **Glory to the Father, and to the Son,
    and to the Holy Spirit:***
  **as it was in the beginning, is now,
    and shall be for ever. Amen.**

THE PRAYERS

Intercession and thanksgiving are offered in free prayer or in silence, ending with the following:

Lord, make your face to shine upon your servants
and in your loving kindness save us.
Lord, have mercy.

Hear the cry of the needy
and never forget the lives of the poor.
Christ, have mercy.

Ride on and conquer in the cause of truth;
may your Kingdom of justice and righteousness break upon us.
Lord, have mercy.

THE COLLECT for Mondays:

Guide us, Lord, in all our doings,
with your most gracious favour
and further us with your continual help;
that in all our works begun, continued
  and ended in you,
we may glorify your holy name,
and by your mercy attain everlasting life;
through Jesus Christ our Lord . . .   1›

Or for the Pentecost Season:

Lord, you have taught us
that all our doings without love are nothing worth:
send your Holy Spirit
and pour into our hearts
that most excellent gift of love,
the true bond of peace and of all virtues,
without which whoever lives
is counted dead before you.
Grant this for the sake of your only Son,
Jesus Christ our Lord . . .   3

THE LORD'S PRAYER may be said.

Let us bless the Lord.
Thanks be to God.

Morning Prayer – Form 3

Tuesday and daily in Advent

THE PREPARATION

O Lord, open our lips
And our mouth shall proclaim your praise.

Blessèd are you, Sovereign God of all,
to you be glory and praise for ever!
In your tender compassion,
the dawn from on high is breaking upon us
to dispel the lingering shadows of night.
As we look for your coming among us this day,
open our eyes to behold your presence
and strengthen our hands to do your will,
that the world may rejoice and give you praise,
Father, Son and Holy Spirit:
Blessèd be God for ever!

THE WORD OF GOD

Week 1 and Sundays in Advent – Psalm 24

1 The earth is the Lord's and all that is in it,*
   the world and all who dwell therein.

2 For it is he who founded it upon the seas*
   and made it firm upon the rivers of the deep.

3 'Who can ascend the hill of the Lord?*
   and who can stand in his holy place?'

4 'Those who have clean hands and a pure heart,*
   who have not pledged themselves to falsehood,
   nor sworn by what is a fraud.

5 'They shall receive a blessing from the Lord*
   and a just reward from the God of their salvation.'

6 Such is the generation of those who seek him,*
   of those who seek your face, O God of Jacob.

7 Lift up your heads, O gates;
      lift them high, O everlasting doors;*
   and the King of glory shall come in.

8   'Who is this King of glory?'*
    'The Lord, strong and mighty,
        the Lord, mighty in battle.'

9   Lift up your heads, O gates;
        lift them high, O everlasting doors;*
    and the King of glory shall come in.

10 'Who is he, this King of glory?'*
    'The Lord of hosts,
        he is the King of glory.'

O Lord of Hosts,
purify our hearts
that the King of glory may come in,
even your Son, Jesus our Redeemer. **Amen.**   7

Week 2 & Mondays in Advent – Psalm 75

1   We give you thanks, O God, we give you thanks,*
    calling upon your name
        and declaring all your wonderful deeds.

2   'I will appoint a time', says God;*
    'I will judge with equity.

3   'Though the earth and all its inhabitants are quaking,*
    I will make its pillars fast.

4   'I will say to the boasters, "Boast no more",*
    and to the wicked, "Do not toss your horns;

5   ' "Do not toss your horns so high,*
    nor speak with a proud neck." '

6   For judgement is neither from the east
        nor from the west,*
    nor yet from the wilderness or the mountains.

7   It is God who judges;*
    he puts down one and lifts up another.

8   For in the Lord's hand there is a cup,
        full of spiced and foaming wine, which he pours out,*
    and all the wicked of the earth
        shall drink and drain the dregs.

9   But I will rejoice for ever;*
     I will sing praises to the God of Jacob.

10   He shall break off all the horns of the wicked;*
     but the horns of the righteous shall be exalted.

     Judge of all the earth,
     restrain the ambitions of the proud
     and the turmoil of the nations;
     establish among us the reign of the Messiah,
     who drained for us the cup of judgement
     and is alive with you and the Holy Spirit,
     one God, for ever and ever. **Amen.**   19

Week 3 & Tuesdays in Advent – Psalm 25

1   To you, O Lord, I lift up my soul;
        my God, I put my trust in you;*
     let me not be humiliated,
        nor let my enemies triumph over me.

2   Let none who look to you be put to shame;*
     let the treacherous be disappointed in their schemes.

3   Show me your ways, O Lord,*
     and teach me your paths.

4   Lead me in your truth and teach me,*
     for you are the God of my salvation;
        in you have I trusted all the day long.

5   Remember, O Lord, your compassion and love,*
     for they are from everlasting.

6   Remember not the sins of my youth
        and my transgressions;*
     remember me according to your love
        and for the sake of your goodness, O Lord.

7   Gracious and upright is the Lord;*
     therefore he teaches sinners in his way.

8   He guides the humble in doing right*
     and teaches his way to the lowly.

9 All the paths of the Lord are love and faithfulness*
   to those who keep his covenant and his testimonies.

10 For your name's sake, O Lord,*
   forgive my sin, for it is great.

11 Who are they who fear the Lord?*
   he will teach them the way that they should choose.

12 They shall dwell in prosperity,*
   and their offspring shall inherit the land.

13 The Lord is a friend to those who fear him*
   and will show them his covenant.

14 My eyes are ever looking to the Lord,*
   for he shall pluck my feet out of the net.

15 Turn to me and have pity on me,*
   for I am left alone and in misery.

16 The sorrows of my heart have increased;*
   bring me out of my troubles.

17 Look upon my adversity and misery*
   and forgive me all my sin.

18 Look upon my enemies, for they are many,*
   and they bear a violent hatred against me.

19 Protect my life and deliver me;*
   let me not be put to shame, for I have trusted in you.

20 Let integrity and uprightness preserve me,*
   for my hope has been in you.

21 Deliver Israel, O God,*
   out of all his troubles.

Free us, God of mercy,
from all that keeps us from you,
relieve the misery of the poor and destitute
and fulfil us all with the hope of peace;
through Jesus Christ our Lord. **Amen.**   7

1   O Lord, I call to you;
    my rock, do not be deaf to my cry;*
  lest, if you do not hear me,
    I become like those who go down to the Pit.

2   Hear the voice of my prayer when I cry out to you,*
  when I lift up my hands to your holy of holies.

3   Do not snatch me away with the wicked
    or with the evildoers,*
  who speak peaceably with their neighbours,
    while strife is in their hearts.

4   Repay them according to their deeds,*
  and according to the wickedness of their actions.

5   According to the work of their hands repay them,*
  and give them their just deserts.

6   They have no understanding of the Lord's doings,
    nor of the works of his hands;*
  therefore he will break them down
    and not build them up.

7   Blessèd is the Lord!*
  for he has heard the voice of my prayer.

8   The Lord is my strength and my shield;*
  my heart trusts in him and I have been helped;

9   Therefore my heart dances for joy,*
  and in my song will I praise him.

10 The Lord is the strength of his people,*
  a safe refuge for his anointed.

11 Save your people and bless your inheritance;*
  shepherd them and carry them for ever.

Hear us, Shepherd of your people,
you who commanded us to love our neighbours
with our whole hearts:
forgive us our sins
and make us whole in body and soul;
through Jesus Christ our Lord. **Amen.**

                                7

Week 5 & Thursdays in Advent — from Psalm 62

1   For God alone my soul in silence waits;*
    from him comes my salvation.

2   He alone is my rock and my salvation,*
    my stronghold, so that I shall not be greatly shaken.

3   For God alone my soul in silence waits;*
    truly, my hope is in him.

4   He alone is my rock and my salvation,*
    my stronghold, so that I shall not be shaken.

5   In God is my safety and my honour;*
    God is my strong rock and my refuge.

6   Put your trust in him always, O people,*
    pour out your hearts before him, for God is our refuge.

7   Those of high degree are but a fleeting breath,*
    even those of low estate cannot be trusted.

8   On the scales they are lighter than a breath,*
    all of them together.

9   Put no trust in extortion;
        in robbery take no empty pride;*
    though wealth increase, set not your heart upon it.

10 God has spoken once, twice have I heard it,*
    that power belongs to God.

11 Steadfast love is yours, O Lord,*
    for you repay everyone according to his deeds.

O God, we seek security and deliverance
not in money or theft,
not in human ambition or malice,
not in our own ability or power,
but in you, the only God,
our rock and our salvation. **Amen.**

Week 6 & Fridays in Advent – Psalm 40

1   I waited patiently upon the Lord;*
   he stooped to me and heard my cry.

2   He lifted me out of the desolate pit,
     out of the mire and clay;*
   he set my feet upon a high cliff and made my footing sure.

3   He put a new song in my mouth,
     a song of praise to our God;*
   many shall see and stand in awe
     and put their trust in the Lord.

4   Happy are they who trust in the Lord!*
   they do not resort to evil spirits or turn to false gods.

5   Great things are they that you have done, O Lord my God!
     how great your wonders and your plans for us!*
   there is none who can be compared with you.

6   O that I could make them known and tell them!*
   but they are more than I can count.

7   In sacrifice and offering you take no pleasure*
   (you have given me ears to hear you);

8   Burnt-offering and sin-offering you have not required,*
   and so I said, 'Behold, I come.

9   'In the roll of the book it is written concerning me:*
   "I love to do your will, O my God;
   your law is deep in my heart." '

10 I proclaimed righteousness in the great congregation;*
   behold, I did not restrain my lips;
   and that, O Lord, you know.

11 Your righteousness have I not hidden in my heart;
     I have spoken of your faithfulness and your deliverance;*
   I have not concealed your love and faithfulness
     from the great congregation.

12 You are the Lord;
     do not withhold your compassion from me;*
   let your love and your faithfulness keep me safe for ever,

13 For innumerable troubles have crowded upon me;
    my sins have overtaken me and I cannot see;*
they are more in number than the hairs of my head,
    and my heart fails me.

14 Be pleased, O Lord, to deliver me;*
O Lord, make haste to help me.

15 Let them be ashamed and altogether dismayed
    who seek after my life to destroy it;*
let them draw back and be disgraced
    who take pleasure in my misfortune.

16 Let those who say 'Aha!' and gloat over me be confounded,*
because they are ashamed.

17 Let all who seek you rejoice in you and be glad;*
let those who love your salvation continually say,
    'Great is the Lord!'

18 Though I am poor and afflicted,*
the Lord will have regard for me.

19 You are my helper and my deliverer;*
do not tarry, O my God.

*Free us from our sins, O God,
and may we never be ashamed
to confess you to all the nations,
through your Son, our Redeemer,
Jesus Christ, the Lord of all.* **Amen.**   7

Week 7 & Saturdays in Advent – Psalm 146

1   Alleluia!
       Praise the Lord, O my soul!*
    I will praise the Lord as long as I live;
       I will sing praises to my God while I have my being.

2   Put not your trust in rulers,
       nor in any child of earth,*
    for there is no help in them.

3   When they breathe their last, they return to earth,*
    and in that day their thoughts perish.

4   Happy are they who have the God of Jacob
       for their help!*
    whose hope is in the Lord their God;

5   Who made heaven and earth, the seas,
       and all that is in them;*
    who keeps his promise for ever;

6   Who gives justice to those who are oppressed,*
    and food to those who hunger.

7   The Lord sets the prisoners free;
       the Lord opens the eyes of the blind;*
    the Lord lifts up those who are bowed down;

8   The Lord loves the righteous;
       the Lord cares for the stranger;*
    he sustains the orphan and widow,
       but frustrates the way of the wicked.

9   The Lord shall reign for ever,*
    your God, O Zion, throughout all generations.
       Alleluia!

Lord God, creator of all things,
who in your loving-kindness and care
meet our human needs:
with the dawn of each day
help us to set our hearts and hope upon you,
that we may show you in the world
as the universal and eternal king;
through Jesus Christ our Lord. **Amen.**   13

THE OLD TESTAMENT CANTICLE
Either: A SONG OF THE WILDERNESS

1 The wilderness and the dry land shall rejoice,*
   the desert shall blossom and burst into song.

2 They shall see the glory of the Lord,*
   the majesty of our God.

3 Strengthen the weary hands,*
   and make firm the feeble knees.

4 Say to the anxious, 'Be strong, fear not,
      your God is coming with judgement,*
   coming with judgement to save you.'

5 Then shall the eyes of the blind be opened,*
   and the ears of the deaf unstopped;

6 Then shall the lame leap like a hart,*
   and the tongue of the dumb sing for joy.

7 For waters shall break forth in the wilderness,*
   and streams in the desert;

8 The ransomed of the Lord shall return with singing,*
   with everlasting joy upon their heads.

9 Joy and gladness shall be theirs,*
   and sorrow and sighing shall flee away. *From Isaiah 35*

   Glory to the Father, and to the Son,
      and to the Holy Spirit:*
   as it was in the beginning, is now,
      and shall be for ever. Amen.

Or: A SONG OF GOD'S HERALD

1   Go up to a high mountain,
        herald of good tidings to Zion;*
     lift up your voice with strength,
        herald of good tidings to Jerusalem.

2   Lift up your voice, fear not;*
     say to the cities of Judah, 'Behold your God!'

3   See the Lord God, coming with power,*
     coming to rule with his mighty arm.

4   He brings his reward for the people of God,*
     the recompense for those who are saved.

5   God will feed his flock like a shepherd,*
     and gather the lambs in his arms;

6   He will hold them to his breast,*
     and gently lead those that are with young.   *Isaiah 40. 9-11*

     Glory to the Father, and to the Son,
        and to the Holy Spirit:*
     as it was in the beginning, is now,
        and shall be for ever. Amen.

*A SONG OF PEACE (page 237) is a particularly appropriate
alternative Canticle on Tuesdays and in Advent.*

THE SCRIPTURE READING

Week 1 & Sundays in Advent

The Lord said to Cain, 'Where is your brother Abel?' He said, 'I do not know; am I my brother's keeper?' And the Lord said, 'What have you done? Listen; your brother's blood is crying out to me from the ground! And now you are cursed from the ground, which has opened its mouth to receive your brother's blood from your hand.' *Genesis 4. 9-11*

Week 2 & Mondays in Advent

Now it is full time for you to awake from sleep, for salvation is nearer to us now than when we first believed; the night is far gone, the day is at hand. Let us then cast aside the works of darkness and put on the armour of light. Put on the Lord Jesus Christ and make no provision for the flesh, to gratify its desires. *Romans 13. 11-12, 14*

Week 3 & Tuesdays in Advent

Moses and Aaron went to Pharaoh and said, 'Thus says the Lord, the God of Israel, "Let my people go, so that they may celebrate a festival to me in the wilderness." ' But Pharaoh said, 'Who is the Lord, that I should heed him and let Israel go? I do not know the Lord and I will not let Israel go.' *Exodus 5. 1-2*

Week 4 & Wednesdays in Advent

Moses said, 'Remember the long way that the Lord your God has led you these forty years in the wilderness, in order to humble you, testing you to know what was in your heart, whether or not you would keep his commandments. He humbled you by letting you hunger, then by feeding you with manna, with which neither you nor your ancestors were acquainted, in order to make you understand that man does not live by bread alone, but by every word that comes from the mouth of the Lord.' *Deuteronomy 8. 2-3*

Week 5 & Thursdays in Advent

Take up the whole armour of God, so that you may be able to withstand on that evil day, and having done everything, to stand firm.

Stand, therefore, having girded your loins with truth, and having put on the breastplate of righteousness, and having shod your feet with the equipment of the gospel of peace; above all, taking the shield of faith, with which you will be able to quench all the flaming arrows of the evil one. Take the helmet of salvation and the sword of the Spirit, which is the word of God. Pray in the Spirit at all times in every prayer and supplication.

Ephesians 6. 13-18a

Week 6 & Fridays in Advent

All of you must clothe yourselves with humility in your dealings with one another, for 'God opposes the proud but gives grace to the humble.' Humble yourselves, therefore, under the mighty hand of God, so that he may exalt you in due time. Cast all your anxiety on him, because he cares for you.   *1 Peter 5. 5b-7*

Week 7 & Saturdays in Advent

Elijah came to a cave and spent the night there. Then the word of the Lord came to him, saying, 'What are you doing here, Elijah?' He answered, 'I have been very zealous for the Lord, the God of hosts; for the Israelites have forsaken your covenant, thrown down your altars and killed your prophets with the sword. I alone am left, and they are seeking my life, to take it away.' He said, 'Go out and stand on the mountain before the Lord, for the Lord is passing by.' Now there was a great wind, so strong that it was splitting mountains and breaking rocks in pieces before the Lord; but the Lord was not in the wind. And after the wind, an earthquake; but the Lord was not in the earthquake. And after the earthquake, a fire; but the Lord was not in the fire. And after the fire, a still small voice. When Elijah heard it, he wrapped his face in his mantle and went out and stood at the entrance to the cave.   *1 Kings 19. 9-13a*

*   *   *

This RESPONSE to the reading may be used:
Now it is time to awake out of sleep,
For the night is far spent and the day is at hand.

THE GOSPEL CANTICLE: THE BENEDICTUS

1 Blessèd are you, Lord, the God of Israel,*
   you have come to your people and set them free.

2 You have raised up for us a mighty Saviour,*
   born of the house of your servant, David.

3 Through your holy prophets, you promised of old*
   to save us from our enemies,
      from the hands of all who hate us,

4 To show mercy to our forebears,*
   and to remember your holy covenant.

5 This was the oath you swore to our father, Abraham,*
   to set us free from the hands of our enemies,

6 Free to worship you without fear,*
   holy and righteous before you,
      all the days of our life.

7 And you, child,
      shall be called the prophet of the Most High,*
   for you will go before the Lord to prepare the way,

8 To give God's people knowledge of salvation*
   by the forgiveness of their sins.

9 In the tender compassion of our God*
   the dawn from on high shall break upon us,

10 To shine on those who dwell in darkness
      and the shadow of death,*
   and to guide our feet into the way of peace. *Luke 1. 68-79*

   **Glory to the Father, and to the Son,
      and to the Holy Spirit:***
   **as it was in the beginning, is now,
      and shall be for ever. Amen.**

THE PRAYERS

Intercession and thanksgiving are offered in free prayer or in silence, ending with the following:

O God, be merciful to us and bless us;
show us the light of your countenance and come to us.
Lord, have mercy.

Let your ways be known upon earth,
your saving help among the nations.
Christ, have mercy.

Let the peoples praise you, O God,
let all the peoples praise you.
Lord, have mercy.

THE COLLECT for Tuesdays:

O God,
who set before us the great hope
that your Kingdom shall come on earth
and taught us to pray for its coming:
give us grace to discern the signs of its dawning
and to work for the perfect day
when the whole world shall reflect your glory;
through Jesus Christ our Lord . . .   *Percy Dearmer/17*

Or for Advent:

Almighty God,
give us grace to cast away the works of darkness
and to put on the armour of light,
now in the time of this mortal life,
in which your Son Jesus Christ came to us in great humility:
so that on the last day,
when he shall come again in his glorious majesty
   to judge the living and the dead,
we may rise to the life immortal;
through him who is alive and reigns
   with you and the Holy Spirit,
one God, now and for ever. **Amen.**   3

THE LORD'S PRAYER may be said.

Let us bless the Lord.
Thanks be to God.

Evening Prayer – Form 3

Tuesday and daily in Advent

THE BLESSING OF THE LIGHT

Your word, O God, is a lantern to our feet
  and a light upon our path.

The light and peace of Jesus Christ be with you all
And also with you.

Let us give thanks to the Lord our God
Who is worthy of all thanksgiving and praise.

Blessèd are you, Sovereign God, creator of light and darkness!
As evening falls, you renew your promise
to reveal among us the light of your presence.
May your word be a lantern to our feet
and a light upon our path,
that we may behold your glory coming among us.
Strengthen us in our stumbling weakness
and free our tongues to sing your praise,
Father, Son and Holy Spirit:
Blessèd be God for ever!

A SONG OF THE LIGHT

Light of the world, in grace and beauty,
Mirror of God's eternal face,
Transparent flame of love's free duty,
You bring salvation to our race.
Now, as we see the lights of evening,
We raise our voice in hymns of praise;
Worthy are you of endless blessing,
Sun of our night, lamp of our days.   12

THE WORD OF GOD

Week 1 & Sundays in Advent – Psalm 80

1   Hear, O Shepherd of Israel, leading Joseph like a flock;*
     shine forth, you that are enthroned upon the cherubim.

2   In the presence of Ephraim, Benjamin and Manasseh,*
     stir up your strength and come to help us.

3   Restore us, O God of hosts;*
     show the light of your countenance
       and we shall be saved.

4   O Lord God of hosts,*
     how long will you be angered
       despite the prayers of your people?

5   You have fed them with the bread of tears;*
     you have given them bowls of tears to drink.

6   You have made us the derision of our neighbours,*
     and our enemies laugh us to scorn.

7   Restore us, O God of hosts;*
     show the light of your countenance
       and we shall be saved.

8   You have brought a vine out of Egypt;*
     you cast out the nations and planted it.

9   You prepared the ground for it;*
     it took root and filled the land.

10   The mountains were covered by its shadow*
     and the towering cedar trees by its boughs.

11   You stretched out its tendrils to the Sea*
     and its branches to the River.

12   Why have you broken down its wall,*
     so that all who pass by pluck off its grapes?

13   The wild boar of the forest has ravaged it,*
     and the beasts of the field have grazed upon it.

14   Turn now, O God of hosts, look down from heaven;
       behold and tend this vine;*
     preserve what your right hand has planted.

15 They burn it with fire like rubbish;*
   at the rebuke of your countenance let them perish.

16 Let your hand be upon the man of your right hand,*
   the son of man you have made so strong for yourself.

17 And so will we never turn away from you;*
   give us life, that we may call upon your name.

18 Restore us, O Lord God of hosts;*
   show the light of your countenance
      and we shall be saved.

Faithful Shepherd of your people,
as we look for the light of your countenance
restore in us the image of your glory
and graft us into the risen life
of your Son, Jesus Christ our Lord. **Amen.**   18

Week 2 & Mondays in Advent – Psalm 123

1 To you I lift up my eyes,*
   to you enthroned in the heavens.

2 As the eyes of servants look to the hand of their masters,*
   and the eyes of a maid to the hand of her mistress,

3 So our eyes look to the Lord our God,*
   until he show us his mercy.

4 Have mercy upon us, O Lord, have mercy,*
   for we have had more than enough of contempt,

5 Too much of the scorn of the indolent rich,*
   and of the derision of the proud.

Sovereign God, enthroned in the heavens,
look upon us with your eyes of mercy
as we look upon you with humility and love
and fill our souls with your peace;
through Jesus Christ our Lord. **Amen.**   16

Week 3 & Tuesdays in Advent – Psalm 144

1   Blessèd be the Lord my rock!*
    who trains my hands to fight and my fingers to battle;

2   My help and my fortress,
        my stronghold and my deliverer,*
    my shield in whom I trust,
        who subdues the peoples under me.

3   O Lord, what are we that you should care for us?*
    mere mortals that you should think of us?

4   We are like a puff of wind;*
    our days are like a passing shadow.

5   Bow your heavens, O Lord, and come down;*
    touch the mountains and they shall smoke.

6   Hurl the lightning and scatter them;*
    shoot out your arrows and rout them.

7   Stretch out your hand from on high;*
    rescue me and deliver me from the great waters,
        from the hand of foreign peoples,

8   Whose mouths speak deceitfully*
    and whose right hand is raised in falsehood.

9   O God, I will sing to you a new song;*
    I will play to you on a ten-stringed lyre.

10 You give victory to kings*
    and have rescued David your servant.

11 Rescue me from the hurtful sword*
    and deliver me from the hand of foreign peoples,

12 Whose mouths speak deceitfully*
    and whose right hand is raised in falsehood.

13 May our sons be like plants
        well nurtured from their youth,*
    and our daughters like sculptured corners of a palace.

14 May our barns be filled to overflowing*
    with all manner of crops;

15 May the flocks in our pastures
        increase by thousands and tens of thousands;*
    may our cattle be fat and sleek.

16 May there be no breaching of the walls,
     no going into exile,*
   no wailing in the public squares.

17 Happy are the people of whom this is so!*
   happy are the people whose God is the Lord!

   Eternal God,
   whose Son struggled against the forces
   which enfeeble and enslave your people:
   shield us from evil and all deception,
   that we may enter your truth
   and enjoy the abundance of his risen life;
   who with you and the Holy Spirit
   is alive and reigns for ever and ever. **Amen.**   13

Week 4 & Wednesdays in Advent — Psalm 11

1 In the Lord have I taken refuge;*
  how then can you say to me,
    'Fly away like a bird to the hilltop;

2 'For see how the wicked bend the bow
    and fit their arrows to the string,*
  to shoot from ambush at the true of heart.

3 'When the foundations are being destroyed,*
  what can the righteous do?'

4 The Lord is in his holy temple;*
  the Lord's throne is in heaven.

5 His eyes behold the inhabited world;*
  his piercing eye weighs our worth.

6 The Lord weighs the righteous as well as the wicked,*
  but those who delight in violence he abhors.

7 Upon the wicked he shall rain coals of fire
    and burning sulphur;*
  a scorching wind shall be their lot.

8 For the Lord is righteous;
    he delights in righteous deeds;*
  and the just shall see his face.

O God, who from the midst of your holy temple
behold all the dwellers upon earth:
guard your faithful in the time of trial
and save us from the dangers and temptations of this life;
through Jesus Christ our Lord. **Amen.**   14

Week 5 & Thursdays in Advent – Psalm 12

1   Help me, Lord, for there is no godly one left;*
    the faithful have vanished from among us.

2   Everyone speaks falsely with their neighbour;*
    with a smooth tongue they speak from a double heart.

3   O that the Lord would cut off all smooth tongues,*
    and close the lips that utter proud boasts!

4   Those who say, 'With our tongue will we prevail;*
    our lips are our own; who is lord over us?'

5   'Because the needy are oppressed,
        and the poor cry out in misery,*
    I will rise up', says the Lord,
        'and give them the help they long for.'

6   The words of the Lord are pure words,*
    like silver refined from ore
        and purified seven times in the fire.

7   O Lord, watch over us*
    and save us from this generation for ever.

8   The wicked prowl on every side,*
    and that which is worthless is highly prized by everyone.

O Father, whose Son, for lies, was falsely accused
and by falsehood, wrongly condemned:
watch over your people and guard them in the way of truth,
that by your grace they may overcome the world;
through Jesus Christ our Lord. **Amen.**   14

Week 6 & Fridays in Advent – Psalm 42

1   As the deer longs for the water-brooks,*
    so longs my soul for you, O God.

2   My soul is athirst for God, athirst for the living God;*
    when shall I come to appear before the presence of God?

3   My tears have been my food day and night,*
    while all day long they say to me,
      'Where now is your God?'

4   I pour out my soul when I think on these things:*
    how I went with the multitude
      and led them into the house of God,

5   With the voice of praise and thanksgiving,*
    among those who keep holy day.

6   Why are you so full of heaviness, O my soul?*
    and why are you so disquieted within me?

7   Put your trust in God;*
    for I will yet give thanks to him,
      who is the help of my countenance, and my God.

8   My soul is heavy within me;*
    therefore I will remember you from the land of Jordan,
      and from the peak of Mizar among the heights of Hermon.

9   One deep calls to another in the noise of your cataracts;*
    all your rapids and floods have gone over me.

10 The Lord grants his loving-kindness in the daytime;*
    in the night season his song is with me,
      a prayer to the God of my life.

11 I will say to the God of my strength,
      'Why have you forgotten me?*
    and why do I go so heavily
      while the enemy oppresses me?'

12 While my bones are being broken,*
    my enemies mock me to my face;

13 All day long they mock me*
    say to me, 'Where now is your God?'

14 Why are you so full of heaviness, O my soul?*
    and why are you so disquieted within me?

15 Put your trust in God;*
      for I will yet give thanks to him,
        who is the help of my countenance, and my God.

      O God,
      as we come before your presence
      satisfy the hearts of all who wait in hope for your coming;
      fill our soul with streams of living water
      as we place all our hope in you;
      through Jesus Christ our Lord. **Amen.**   14

Week 7 & Saturdays in Advent – Psalm 130

1   Out of the depths have I called to you, O Lord;
      Lord, hear my voice;*
      let your ears consider well the voice of my supplication.

2   If you, Lord, were to note what is done amiss,*
      O Lord, who could stand?

3   For there is forgiveness with you;*
      therefore you shall be feared.

4   I wait for the Lord; my soul waits for him;*
      in his word is my hope.

5   My soul waits for the Lord,
        more than the night-watch for the morning,*
      more than the night-watch for the morning.

6   O Israel, wait for the Lord,*
      for with the Lord there is mercy;

7   With him there is plenteous redemption,*
      and he shall redeem Israel from all their sins.

      Lord of mercy and redemption,
      rescue us, we pray, from the depths of sin and death;
      forgive us what we do wrong,
      and give us grace to stand in your presence,
      to serve you in Jesus Christ our Lord. **Amen.**   16

THE SECOND CANTICLE

Either: A SONG OF THE LAMB

1   Salvation and glory and power belong to our God,*
    whose judgements are true and just.

2   Praise our God, all you servants of God,*
    you who fear him, both small and great.

3   The Lord our God, the Almighty, reigns:*
    let us rejoice and exult and give glory and homage.

4   The marriage of the Lamb has come*
    and his bride has made herself ready.

5   Happy are those who are invited*
    to the wedding banquet of the Lamb.   *From Revelation 19*

To the One who sits on the throne and to the Lamb*
be blessing and honour and glory and might,
    for ever and ever. Amen.

Or: A SONG OF THE SPIRIT

1   'Behold, I am coming soon', says the Lord,
    'and bringing my reward with me,*
   to give to everyone according to their deeds.

2   'I am the Alpha and the Omega, the first and the last,*
    the beginning and the end.'

3   Blessèd are those who do God's commandments,
    that they may have the right to the tree of life,*
   and may enter into the city through the gates.

4   'I, Jesus, have sent my angel to you,*
    with this testimony for all the churches.

5   'I am the root and the offspring of David,*
    I am the bright morning star.'

6   'Come!' say the Spirit and the Bride;*
    'Come!' let each hearer reply!

7   Come forward, you who are thirsty,*
    let those who desire
      take the water of life as a gift.

Surely I am coming soon!*
Amen! Come, Lord Jesus!   *From Revelation 22*

THE SCRIPTURE READING

Week 1 & Sundays in Advent

They brought to Jesus a deaf man who had an impediment in his speech, and they begged him to lay his hand on him. He took him aside in private, away from the crowd, and put his fingers into his ears and he spat and touched his tongue. Then, looking up to heaven, he sighed and said to him, 'Ephphatha', that is, 'Be opened.' And immediately his ears were opened, his tongue released and he spoke plainly.

Mark 7. 32-35

Week 2 & Mondays in Advent

See, I am sending my messenger to prepare the way before me, and the Lord whom you seek will suddenly come to my temple. The messenger of the covenant in whom you delight – indeed, he is coming, says the Lord of hosts. But who can endure the day of his coming, and who can stand when he appears? Then the offering of Judah and Jerusalem will be pleasing to the Lord as in the days of old and as in former years.

Malachi 3. 1-2a, 4

Week 3 & Tuesdays in Advent

Jesus said, 'You have heard it said, "You shall love your neighbour and hate your enemy." But I say to you, Love your enemies and pray for those who persecute you, so that you may be children of your Father in heaven; for he makes his sun rise on the evil and on the good and sends rain on the righteous and on the unrighteous.'

Matthew 5. 43-45

Week 4 & Wednesdays in Advent

In Christ, God was reconciling the world to himself, not counting their trespasses against them, and entrusting the message of reconciliation to us. So we are ambassadors for Christ, since God is making his appeal through us; we entreat you on behalf of Christ: be reconciled to God.

2 Corinthians 5. 19-20

Week 5 & Thursdays in Advent

John summoned two of his disciples and sent them to the Lord to ask, 'Are you the one who is to come or are we to wait for another?' And Jesus answered them, 'Go and tell John what you have seen and heard: the blind receive their sight, the lame walk, the lepers are cleansed, the deaf hear, the dead are raised, the poor have good news brought to them. And blessèd is anyone who takes no offence at me.'   *Luke 7. 19, 22-23*

Week 6 & Fridays in Advent

How beautiful on the mountains are the feet of the messenger who announces peace, who brings good news, who announces salvation, who says to Zion, 'Your God reigns.' Listen! Your sentinels lift up their voices, together they sing for joy; for in plain sight they see the return of the Lord to Zion. Break forth into singing, you ruins of Jerusalem, for the Lord has comforted his people, he has redeemed Jerusalem.   *Isaiah 52. 7-9*

Week 7 & Saturdays in Advent

Jesus said, 'I am the door. Whoever enters by me will be saved and will come in and go out and find pasture. The thief comes only to steal and kill and destroy. I came that they may have life, and have it abundantly.'   *John 10. 9-10*

*   *   *

This RESPONSE to the reading may be used:
My soul is waiting for you, O Lord:
In your word is my hope.

THE GOSPEL CANTICLE: THE MAGNIFICAT

1   My soul proclaims the greatness of the Lord,*
    my spirit rejoices in God my Saviour,

2   For you, Lord, have looked with favour
        on your lowly servant.*
    From this day all generations will call me blessèd:

3   You, the Almighty, have done great things for me*
    and holy is your name.

4   You have mercy on those who fear you,*
    from generation to generation.

5   You have shown strength with your arm*
    and scattered the proud in their conceit,

6   Casting down the mighty from their thrones*
    and lifting up the lowly.

7   You have filled the hungry with good things*
    and sent the rich away empty.

8   You have come to the aid of your servant, Israel,*
    to remember the promise of mercy,

9   The promise made to our forebears,*
    to Abraham and his children for ever. *Luke 1. 46-55*

**Glory to the Father, and to the Son,
    and to the Holy Spirit:***
**as it was in the beginning, is now,
    and shall be for ever. Amen.**

THE PRAYERS

Intercession and thanksgiving are offered in free prayer or in silence, ending with the following:

For you alone, O God, our soul in silence waits,
for truly our hope is found in you.
Lord, have mercy.

Awake, O God, and decree justice;
let the peoples gather around you.
Christ, have mercy.

Send forth your strength, O Lord;
establish, O God, what you have wrought in us.
Lord, have mercy.

THE COLLECT for Tuesdays:

O Lord our God,
make us watchful and keep us faithful
as we await the coming of your Son our Lord;
that, when he shall appear,
he may not find us sleeping in sin
but active in his service
and joyful in his praise;
through Jesus Christ our Lord . . .   17

Or for Advent:

O God, by whose command
   the order of time runs its course:
forgive our restlessness, perfect our faith
and, while we await the fulfilment of your promise,
grant us to have a good hope
through the Word made flesh,
even Jesus Christ our Lord . . .   17›

THE LORD'S PRAYER may be said.

Let us bless the Lord.
Thanks be to God.

Morning Prayer – Form 4

Wednesday and daily in Christmastide

THE PREPARATION

O Lord, open our lips
And our mouth shall proclaim your praise.

Blessèd are you, Sovereign God, creator of all;
To you be glory and praise for ever!
You founded the earth in the beginning
and the heavens are the work of your hands.
As we rejoice in the gift of your presence among us,
let the light of your love always shine in our hearts
and your praises ever be on our lips,
Father, Son and Holy Spirit:
Blessèd be God for ever!

THE WORD OF GOD

Week 1 & Sundays in Christmastide – Psalm 8

1   O Lord our governor,*
    how exalted is your name in all the world!

2   Out of the mouths of infants and children*
    your majesty is praised above the heavens.

3   You have set up a stronghold against your adversaries,*
    to quell the enemy and the avenger.

4   When I consider your heavens, the work of your fingers,*
    the moon and the stars you have set in their courses,

5   What are mortals, that you should be mindful of them?*
    mere human beings, that you should seek them out?

6   You have made them little lower than the angels;*
    you adorn them with glory and honour.

7   You give them mastery over the works of your hands;*
    and put all things under their feet,

8   All sheep and oxen,*
    even the wild beasts of the field,

9   The birds of the air, the fish of the sea,*
    and whatsoever walks in the paths of the sea.

10 O Lord our governor,*
   how exalted is your name in all the world!

O God the Word and Son of God,
exalted is your name in all creation,
yet you have stooped to become one with us:
as you have ordained humanity the steward of your creation,
so minister through us the mystery of your salvation;
to the glory of your holy Name. **Amen.**   14

Week 2 and Mondays in Christmastide – Psalm 85

1 You have been gracious to your land, O Lord,*
   you have restored the good fortune of Jacob.

2 You have forgiven the iniquity of your people*
   and blotted out all their sins.

3 You have withdrawn all your fury*
   and turned yourself from your wrathful indignation.

4 Restore us then, O God our Saviour;*
   let your anger depart from us.

5 Will you be displeased with us for ever?*
   will you prolong your anger from age to age?

6 Will you not give us life again,*
   that your people may rejoice in you?

7 Show us your mercy, O Lord,*
   and grant us your salvation.

8 I will listen to what the Lord God is saying,*
   for he is speaking peace to his faithful people
      and to those who turn their hearts to him.

9 Truly, his salvation is very near to those who fear him,*
   that his glory may dwell in our land.

10 Mercy and truth have met together;*
   righteousness and peace have kissed each other.

11 Truth shall spring up from the earth,*
   and righteousness shall look down from heaven.

12 The Lord will indeed grant prosperity,*
   and our land will yield its increase.

13 Righteousness shall go before him,*
    and peace shall be a pathway for his feet.

*Be gracious to us, Lord our God,
and restore us to fullness of life with you;
that mercy and truth may be our guide
and peace be a pathway for our feet;
through our Saviour, Jesus Christ our Lord.* **Amen.** 18

Week 3 & Tuesdays in Christmastide — Psalm 112

1   Alleluia!
      Happy are they who fear the Lord*
    and have great delight in his commandments!

2   Their descendants will be mighty in the land;*
    the generation of the upright will be blessed.

3   Wealth and riches will be in their house,*
    and their righteousness will last for ever.

4   Light shines in the darkness for the upright;*
    the righteous are merciful and full of compassion.

5   It is good for them to be generous in lending*
    and to manage their affairs with justice.

6   For they will never be shaken;*
    the righteous will be kept in everlasting remembrance.

7   They will not be afraid of any evil rumours;*
    their heart is right;
      they put their trust in the Lord.

8   Their heart is established and will not shrink,*
    until they see their desire upon their enemies.

9   They have given freely to the poor,*
    and their righteousness stands fast for ever;
      they will hold up their head with honour.

10 The wicked will see it and be angry;
      they will gnash their teeth and pine away;*
    the desires of the wicked will perish.

*Lord our God,
you have given us the light of Christ to banish darkness
and to lead us in the way of your commandments:
make it ever our delight to fulfil your will,
and truly to love one another;
through Jesus Christ our Lord.* **Amen.**   14

1 The heavens declare the glory of God,*
  and the firmament shows his handiwork.

2 One day tells its tale to another,*
  and one night imparts knowledge to another.

3 Although they have no words or language,*
  and their voices are not heard,

4 Their sound has gone out into all lands,*
  and their message to the ends of the world.

5 In the deep has he set a pavilion for the sun;*
  it comes forth like a bridegroom out of his chamber;
    it rejoices like a champion to run its course.

6 It goes forth from the uttermost edge of the heavens
    and runs about to the end of it again;*
  nothing is hidden from its burning heat.

7 The law of the Lord is perfect
    and revives the soul;*
  the testimony of the Lord is sure
    and gives wisdom to the innocent.

8 The statutes of the Lord are just
    and rejoice the heart;*
  the commandment of the Lord is clear
    and gives light to the eyes.

9 The fear of the Lord is clean
    and endures for ever;*
  the judgements of the Lord are true
    and righteous altogether.

10 More to be desired are they than gold,
     more than much fine gold,*
   sweeter far than honey,
     than honey in the comb.

11 By them also is your servant enlightened,*
   and in keeping them there is great reward.

12 Who can tell how often he offends?*
   Cleanse me from my secret faults.

13 Above all, keep your servant from presumptuous sins;
        let them not get dominion over me;*
    then shall I be whole and sound,
        and innocent of a great offence.

14 Let the words of my mouth and the meditation of my heart
        be acceptable in your sight,*
    O Lord, my strength and my redeemer.

Let the Sun of Righteousness arise, O God,
with healing in his wings;
may he come forth as the bridegroom to rejoice with the bride
and make your people acceptable in his sight;
through Jesus Christ our Lord. **Amen.**   14

Week 5 & Thursdays in Christmastide — Psalm 113

1   Alleluia!
        Give praise, you servants of the Lord;*
    praise the name of the Lord.

2   Let the name of the Lord be blessed,*
    from this time forth for evermore.

3   From the rising of the sun to its going down*
    let the name of the Lord be praised.

4   The Lord is high above all nations,*
    and his glory above the heavens.

5   Who is like the Lord our God,
        who sits enthroned on high,*
    but stoops to behold the heavens and the earth?

6   He takes up the weak out of the dust*
    and lifts up the poor from the ashes.

7   He sets them with the princes,*
    with the princes of his people.

8   He makes the woman of a childless house*
    to be a joyful mother of children.

From the rising of the sun to its going down,
your Name is praised, O Lord,
for you have raised us from the dust and set before us
the vision of your glory.
As you bestowed upon us the dignity of a royal priesthood,
lift up our hearts as we celebrate your praise;
through Jesus Christ our Lord. **Amen.**   14

Week 6 & Fridays in Christmastide — Psalm 20

1 May the Lord answer you in the day of trouble,*
  the name of the God of Jacob defend you;

2 Send you help from his holy place*
  and strengthen you out of Zion;

3 Remember all your offerings*
  and accept your burnt sacrifice;

4 Grant you your heart's desire*
  and prosper all your plans.

5 We will shout for joy at your victory
    and triumph in the name of our God;*
  may the Lord grant all your requests.

6 Now I know that the Lord gives victory
    to his anointed;*
  he will answer him out of his holy heaven,
    with the victorious strength of his right hand.

7 Some put their trust in chariots and some in horses,*
  but we will call upon the name of the Lord our God.

8 They collapse and fall down,*
  but we will arise and stand upright.

9 O Lord, give victory to the king*
  and answer us when we call.

*O God, whose Son was born in our flesh
    to be our Redeemer:
hear and defend us, who call upon his holy Name,
and grant us to share in his victory;
through Jesus Christ our Lord.* **Amen.**   14

13 Alleluia! Worship the Lord, O Jerusalem;*
    praise your God, O Zion;

14 For he has strengthened the bars of your gates;*
    he has blessed your children within you.

15 He has established peace on your borders;*
    he satisfies you with the finest wheat.

16 He sends out his command to the earth,*
    and his word runs very swiftly.

17 He gives snow like wool;*
    he scatters hoarfrost like ashes.

18 He scatters his hail like bread crumbs;*
    who can stand against his cold?

19 He sends forth his word and melts them;*
    he blows with his wind and the waters flow.

20 He declares his word to Jacob,*
    his statutes and his judgements to Israel.

21 He has not done so to any other nation;*
    to them he has not revealed his judgements.
      Alleluia!

King of the Universe,
whose wisdom gives order and fruitfulness to the earth:
help us to respond trustfully to your call,
that being drawn into the unity of your kingdom
we may continually praise you
for your providential care;
through Jesus Christ our Lord. **Amen.**   13

THE OLD TESTAMENT CANTICLE

Either: A SONG OF THE MESSIAH

1   The people who walked in darkness
        have seen a great light;*
    those who dwelt in a land of deep darkness,
        upon them the light has dawned.

2   You have increased their joy
        and given them great gladness;*
    they rejoiced before you as with joy at the harvest.

3   For you have shattered the yoke that burdened them;*
    the collar that lay heavy on their shoulders.

4   For to us a child is born and to us a son is given,*
    and the government will be upon his shoulder.

5   And his name will be called: Wonderful Counsellor;
        the Mighty God;*
    the Everlasting Father; the Prince of Peace.

6   Of the increase of his government and of peace*
    there will be no end,

7   Upon the throne of David and over his kingdom,*
    to establish and uphold it
        with justice and righteousness.

8   From this time forth and for evermore;*
    the zeal of the Lord of hosts will do this.   *Isaiah 9. 2-7*

    **Glory to the Father, and to the Son,
        and to the Holy Spirit:***
    **as it was in the beginning, is now,
        and shall be for ever. Amen.**

*A SONG OF JERUSALEM OUR MOTHER (page 238) is a
particularly appropriate alternative Canticle on Wednesdays.*

Or: A SONG OF GOD'S CHOSEN ONE

1   There shall come forth a shoot from the stock of Jesse,*
     and a branch shall grow out of his roots.

2   And the Spirit of the Lord shall rest upon him,*
     the spirit of wisdom and understanding,

3   The spirit of counsel and might,*
     the spirit of knowledge and the fear of the Lord.

4   He shall not judge by what his eyes see,*
     or decide by what his ears hear,

5   But with righteousness he shall judge the poor,*
     and decide with equity for the meek of the earth.

6   The wolf shall dwell with the lamb,*
     and the leopard shall lie down with the kid.

7   The calf and the lion cub together,*
     with a little child to lead them.

8   They shall not hurt or destroy in all my holy mountain,*
     for the earth shall be full of the knowledge of the Lord
       as the waters cover the sea. *From Isaiah 11*

     Glory to the Father, and to the Son,
       and to the Holy Spirit:*
   as it was in the beginning, is now,
       and shall be for ever. Amen.

THE SCRIPTURE READING

Week 1 & Sundays in Christmastide

God said to Noah, 'I establish my covenant with you, that never again shall all flesh be cut off by the waters of a flood, and never again shall there be a flood to destroy the earth. This is the sign of the covenant that I make between me and you and every living creature that is with you, for all future generations: I have set my bow in the clouds, and it shall be a sign of the covenant between me and the earth.'   *Genesis 9. 11-13*

Week 2 & Mondays in Christmastide

We know that all things work together for good for those who love God, who are called according to his purpose. For those whom he foreknew he also predestined to be conformed to the image of his Son, in order that he might be the first-born within a large family. And those whom he predestined he also called; and those whom he called he also justified; and those whom he justified he also glorified.   *Romans 8. 28-30*

Week 3 & Tuesdays in Christmastide

Moses said, 'You shall make this response before the Lord: "A wandering Aramean was my father; he went down into Egypt and lived there as an alien, few in number, and there he became a great nation, mighty and populous. When the Egyptians treated us harshly and afflicted us, by imposing hard labour on us, we cried to the Lord, the God of our ancestors; the Lord heard our voice and saw our affliction, our toil and our oppression. The Lord brought us out of Egypt with a mighty hand and an outstretched arm, with great terror, and with signs and wonders; and he brought us into this place and gave us this land, a land flowing with milk and honey." '   *Deuteronomy 26. 5-9*

Week 4 & Wednesdays in Christmastide

Moses said, 'For this commandment which I command you this day is not too hard for you, nor is it too far off. It is not in heaven, that you should say, "Who will go up to heaven for us, and get it for us so that we may fear it and observe it?"

Neither is it beyond the sea, that you should say, "Who will go over the sea for us and bring it to us. that we may hear it and do it?" No, the word is very near to you; it is in your mouth and in your heart so that you can do it.' *Deuteronomy 30. 11-14*

Week 5 & Thursdays in Christmastide

Let the word of Christ dwell in you richly; teach and admonish one another in all wisdom; and with thankfulness in your hearts sing psalms, hymns and spiritual songs to God. And whatever you do, in word or deed, do everything in the name of the Lord Jesus giving thanks to God the Father through him. *Colossians 3. 16-17*

Week 6 & Fridays in Christmastide

Come to him, that living stone, rejected by mortals yet in God's sight chosen and precious; and like living stones be yourselves built into a spiritual house, to be a holy priesthood, to offer spiritual sacrifices acceptable to God through Jesus Christ. For it stands in scripture: 'Behold, I am laying in Zion a stone, a corner-stone chosen and precious, and whoever believes in him will not be put to shame.' *1 Peter 2. 4-6*

Week 7 & Saturdays in Christmastide

God, who at sundry times and in diverse manners spoke in time past to our ancestors by the prophets, has, in these latter days spoken to us by his Son, whom he has appointed heir of all things, through whom also he created the worlds. He reflects the glory of God and bears the very stamp of his nature, upholding the universe by his word of power. When he had made purification for sins, he sat down at the right hand of the Majesty on high, having become as much superior to angels as the name he has obtained is more excellent than theirs. *Hebrews 1. 1-4*

* * *

This RESPONSE to the reading may be used:
The Word of Life which was from the beginning,
We proclaim to you.

THE GOSPEL CANTICLE: THE BENEDICTUS

1   Blessèd are you, Lord, the God of Israel,*
    you have come to your people and set them free.

2   You have raised up for us a mighty Saviour,*
    born of the house of your servant, David.

3   Through your holy prophets, you promised of old*
    to save us from our enemies,
      from the hands of all who hate us,

4   To show mercy to our forebears,*
    and to remember your holy covenant.

5   This was the oath you swore to our father, Abraham,*
    to set us free from the hands of our enemies,

6   Free to worship you without fear,*
    holy and righteous before you,
      all the days of our life.

7   And you, child,
      shall be called the prophet of the Most High,*
    for you will go before the Lord to prepare the way,

8   To give God's people knowledge of salvation*
    by the forgiveness of their sins.

9   In the tender compassion of our God*
    the dawn from on high shall break upon us,

10 To shine on those who dwell in darkness
      and the shadow of death,*
    and to guide our feet into the way of peace. *Luke 1. 68-79*

Glory to the Father, and to the Son,
    and to the Holy Spirit:*
as it was in the beginning, is now,
    and shall be for ever. Amen.

THE PRAYERS

Intercession and thanksgiving are offered in free prayer or in silence, ending with the following:

O Lord, you are the king of glory:
help us at the break of day.
Lord, have mercy.

You love righteousness and justice:
may your loving kindness fill the earth.
Christ, have mercy.

Hear our cry, O God,
and listen to our prayer.
Lord, have mercy.

THE COLLECT for Wednesdays:

Lord of all power and might,
the author and giver of all good things:
graft in our hearts the love of your name,
increase in us true religion,
nourish us with all goodness
and of your great mercy keep us in the same;
through Jesus Christ our Lord . . .   3›

Or for Christmastide:

Almighty God,
who wonderfully created us in your own image
and yet more wonderfully restored us
  in your Son Jesus Christ:
grant that, as he came to share our human nature,
so we may be partakers in his divine glory;
who is alive and reigns with you and the Holy Spirit,
one God, now and for ever. **Amen.**   2›/6

THE LORD'S PRAYER may be said.

Let us bless the Lord.
Thanks be to God.

Evening Prayer - Form 4

Wednesday and daily in Christmastide

THE BLESSING OF THE LIGHT

In the beginning was the Word,
and the Word was with God and the Word was God.
In him was life, and the life was the light of all.

The light and peace of Jesus Christ be with you all
And also with you.

Let us give thanks to the Lord our God
Who is worthy of all thanksgiving and praise.

Blessèd are you, Sovereign God, our light and our salvation,
to you be glory and praise for ever!
In the beginning you laid the foundation of the earth,
and the heavens are the work of your hands.
To dispel the darkness of our night,
you sent forth your Son, the first-born of all creation.
He is our Christ, the light of the world,
and him we acclaim, as all creation sings to you,
Father, Son and Holy Spirit:
Blessèd be God for ever!

A SONG OF THE LIGHT

1   O joyful light,
       from the pure glory of the eternal heavenly Father,*
     O holy, blessèd Jesus Christ.

2   As we come to the setting of the sun*
     and see the evening light,

3   We give thanks and praise to the Father and to the Son*
     and to the Holy Spirit of God.

4   Worthy are you at all times
       to be sung with holy voices,
       O Son of God, O Giver of life,*
     and to be glorified through all creation.

THE WORD OF GOD

Week 1 & Sundays in Christmastide – Psalm 110

1   The Lord said to my lord, 'Sit at my right hand,*
    until I make your enemies your footstool.'

2   The Lord will send the sceptre of your power
        out of Zion,*
    saying, 'Rule over your enemies round about you.

3   'Princely state has been yours
        from the day of your birth,*
    in the beauty of holiness have I begotten you,
        like dew from the womb of the morning.'

4   The Lord has sworn and he will not recant:*
    'You are a priest for ever after the order of Melchizedek.'

5   The Lord who is at your right hand
        will smite kings in the day of his wrath;*
    he will rule over the nations.

6   He will heap high the corpses;*
    he will smash heads over the wide earth.

7   He will drink from the brook beside the road;*
    therefore he will lift high his head.

O Christ, our king and our great high priest,
as in humility you were born among us
so now in power may you ever plead for us;
for you are alive and reign in the glory of the Father,
now and for ever. **Amen.**   14

Week 2 & Mondays in Christmastide – from Psalm 89

1   Your love, O Lord, for ever will I sing;*
    from age to age my mouth will proclaim your faithfulness.

2   For I am persuaded that your love is established for ever;*
    you have set your faithfulness firmly in the heavens.

3   'I have made a covenant with my chosen one;*
    I have sworn an oath to David my servant:

4 ' "I will establish your line for ever,*
and preserve your throne for all generations." '

5 You spoke once in a vision
    and said to your faithful people:*
'I have set the crown upon a warrior
    and have exalted one chosen out of the people.

6 'I have found David my servant;*
with my holy oil have I anointed him.

7 'My hand will hold him fast*
and my arm will make him strong.

8 'No enemy shall deceive him,*
nor the wicked bring him down.

9 'I will crush his foes before him*
and strike down those who hate him.

10 'My faithfulness and love shall be with him,*
and he shall be victorious through my name.

11 'I shall make his dominion extend*
from the Great Sea to the River.

12 'He will say to me, "You are my Father,*
my God and the rock of my salvation."

13 'I will make him my first-born*
and higher than the kings of the earth.

14 'I will keep my love for him for ever,*
and my covenant will stand firm for him.

15 'I will establish his line for ever*
and his throne as the days of heaven.'

*Faithful God,
you have established with us
your covenant of love:
remember your promise,
fulfilled in your anointed Son Jesus Christ,
and count us worthy to stand in his strength alone;
who, with you and the Holy Spirit, lives and reigns,
one God for ever and ever.* **Amen.** 18

Week 3 & Tuesdays in Christmastide – Psalm 96

1 Sing to the Lord a new song;*
 sing to the Lord, all the whole earth.

2 Sing to the Lord and bless his name;*
 proclaim the good news of his salvation from day to day.

3 Declare his glory among the nations*
 and his wonders among all peoples.

4 For great is the Lord and greatly to be praised;*
 he is more to be feared than all gods.

5 As for all the gods of the nations, they are but idols;*
 but it is the Lord who made the heavens.

6 O the majesty and magnificence of his presence!*
 O the power and the splendour of his sanctuary!

7 Ascribe to the Lord, you families of the peoples;*
 ascribe to the Lord honour and power.

8 Ascribe to the Lord the honour due to his name;*
 bring offerings and come into his courts.

9 Worship the Lord in the beauty of holiness;*
 let the whole earth tremble before him.

10 Tell it out among the nations: 'The Lord is king!*
 he has made the world so firm that it cannot be moved;
  he will judge the peoples with equity.'

11 Let the heavens rejoice and let the earth be glad;
  let the sea thunder and all that is in it;*
 let the field be joyful and all that is therein.

12 Then shall all the trees of the wood shout for joy
  before the Lord when he comes,*
 when he comes to judge the earth.

13 He will judge the world with righteousness*
 and the peoples with his truth.

*Heaven and earth, O Lord, are full of your glory
and all creation resounds with your praise.
As your Son has appeared in the likeness of our flesh
so may all creation share in the beauty of holiness;
through Jesus Christ our Lord.* **Amen.**   14

1   My heart is stirring with a noble song;
    let me recite what I have fashioned for the king;*
  my tongue shall be the pen of a skilled writer.

2   You are the fairest of men;*
  grace flows from your lips,
    because God has blessed you for ever.

3   Strap your sword upon your thigh, O mighty warrior,*
  in your pride and in your majesty.

4   Ride out and conquer in the cause of truth*
  and for the sake of justice.

5   Your right hand will show you marvellous things;*
  your arrows are very sharp, O mighty warrior.

6   The peoples are falling at your feet,*
  and the king's enemies are losing heart.

7   Your throne, O God, endures for ever and ever,*
  a sceptre of righteousness is the sceptre of your kingdom;
    you love righteousness and hate iniquity;

8   Therefore God, your God, has anointed you*
  with the oil of gladness above your fellows.

9   All your garments are fragrant with myrrh, aloes and cassia,*
  and the music of strings from ivory palaces makes you glad.

10 Kings' daughters stand among the ladies of the court;*
  on your right hand is the queen,
    adorned with the gold of Ophir.

11 'Hear, O daughter; consider and listen closely;*
  forget your people and your family's house.

12 'The king will have pleasure in your beauty;*
  he is your master; therefore do him honour.

13 'The people of Tyre are here with a gift;*
  the rich among the people seek your favour.'

14 All glorious is the princess as she enters;*
  her gown is cloth-of-gold.

15 In embroidered apparel she is brought to the king;*
  after her the bridesmaids follow in procession.

16 With joy and gladness they are brought,*
    and enter into the palace of the king.

17 'In place of fathers, O king, you shall have sons;*
    you shall make them princes over all the earth.

18 'I will make your name to be remembered
        from one generation to another;*
    therefore nations will praise you for ever and ever.'

    You have anointed us, O Lamb of God,
    with the oil of gladness
    and clothed us in the garments of salvation:
    come and unite us in the joy of heaven wedded to earth;
    through Jesus Christ our Lord. **Amen.**   14

Week 5 & Thursdays in Christmastide – Psalm 128

1 Happy are they all who fear the Lord,*
   and who follow in his ways!

2 You shall eat the fruit of your labour;*
   happiness and prosperity shall be yours.

3 Your wife shall be like a fruitful vine
       within your house,*
   your children like olive shoots round about your table.

4 Whoever fears the Lord*
   shall thus indeed be blessed.

5 The Lord bless you from Zion,*
   and may you see the prosperity of Jerusalem
       all the days of your life.

6 May you live to see your children's children;*
   may peace be upon Israel.

   Creator God,
   whose Son is the true vine and we the branches:
   make us fruitful in your service,
   sharing your love and joy and peace
   with all your children,
   in the power of the Spirit
   of Jesus Christ our Lord. **Amen.**   16

1 Lord, remember David*
   and all the hardships he endured;

2 How he swore an oath to the Lord*
   and vowed a vow to the Mighty One of Jacob:

3 'I will not come under the roof of my house,*
   nor climb up into my bed;

4 'I will not allow my eyes to sleep,*
   nor let my eyelids slumber;

5 'Until I find a place for the Lord,*
   a dwelling for the Mighty One of Jacob.'

6 'The Ark! We heard it was in Ephratha;*
   we found it in the fields of Jearim.

7 'Let us go to God's dwelling place;*
   let us fall upon our knees before his footstool.'

8 Arise, O Lord, into your resting-place,*
   you and the ark of your strength.

9 Let your priests be clothed with righteousness;*
   let your faithful people sing with joy.

10 For your servant David's sake,*
   do not turn away the face of your anointed.

11 The Lord has sworn an oath to David;*
   in truth, he will not break it:

12 'A son, the fruit of your body*
   will I set upon your throne.

13 'If your children keep my covenant
      and my testimonies that I shall teach them,*
   their children will sit upon your throne for evermore.'

14 For the Lord has chosen Zion,*
   he has desired her for his habitation:

15 'This shall be my resting-place for ever;*
   here will I dwell, for I delight in her.

16 'I will surely bless her provisions,*
   and satisfy her poor with bread.

17 'I will clothe her priests with salvation,*
  and her faithful people will rejoice and sing.

18 'There will I make the horn of David flourish;*
  I have prepared a lamp for my anointed.

19 'As for his enemies, I will clothe them with shame;*
  but as for him, his crown will shine.'

  Jesus, Son of David, Mighty One of God,
  you have called us to be priests of the new covenant:
  clothe us with righteousness,
  make us faithful
  and give us hearts to shout for joy
    in your salvation.
  To you be glory for ever! **Amen.**   16

Week 7 & Saturdays in Christmastide – Psalm 84

1 How dear to me is your dwelling, O Lord of hosts!*
  My soul has a desire and longing
    for the courts of the Lord;
    my heart and my flesh rejoice in the living God.

2 The sparrow has found her a house
    and the swallow a nest
    where she may lay her young;*
  by the side of your altars, O Lord of hosts,
    my King and my God.

3 Happy are they who dwell in your house!*
  they will always be praising you.

4 Happy are the people whose strength is in you!*
  whose hearts are set on the pilgrims' way.

5 Those who go through the desolate valley
    will find it a place of springs,*
  for the early rains have covered it with pools of water.

6 They will climb from height to height,*
  and the God of gods will reveal himself in Zion.

7 Lord God of hosts, hear my prayer;*
  hearken, O God of Jacob.

8   Behold our defender, O God;*
    and look upon the face of your anointed.

9   For one day in your courts
    is better than a thousand in my own room,*
    and to stand at the threshold of the house of my God
      than to dwell in the tents of the wicked.

10 For the Lord God is both sun and shield;*
    he will give grace and glory;

11 No good thing will the Lord withhold*
    from those who walk with integrity.

12 O Lord of hosts,*
    happy are they who put their trust in you!

Lord God,
sustain us in this vale of tears
with the vision of your grace and glory;
that as we journey towards your presence
we may go from strength to strength
in the power of Jesus Christ our Lord. **Amen.**   18

THE SECOND CANTICLE
Either: A SONG OF REDEMPTION

1   The Father has delivered us
    from the dominion of darkness,*
    and transferred us to the kingdom of his belovèd Son;

2   In whom we have redemption,*
    the forgiveness of our sins.

3   He is the image of the invisible God,*
    the first-born of all creation.

4   For in him all things were created,*
    in heaven and on earth, visible and invisible.

5   All things were created through him and for him,*
    he is before all things
      and in him all things hold together.

6   He is the head of the body, the Church,*
    he is the beginning, the first-born from the dead.

7 For it pleased God that in him
     all fullness should dwell,*
  and through him all things be reconciled to himself.
                                        Colossians 1. 13-20

  Glory to the Father, and to the Son,
     and to the Holy Spirit:*
  as it was in the beginning, is now,
     and shall be for ever. Amen.

Or: A SONG OF GOD'S LOVE

1 Belovèd, let us love one another,
     for love is of God;*
  everyone who loves is born of God and knows God.

2 Whoever does not love does not know God,*
     for God is love.

3 In this the love of God was revealed among us,*
     that God sent his only Son into the world,
        so that we might live through him.

4 In this is love,
     not that we loved God but that he loved us,*
  and sent his Son to be the expiation for our sins.

5 Belovèd, since God loved us so much,*
     we ought also to love one another.

6 For if we love one another, God abides in us,*
  and God's love will be perfected in us. *1 John 4. 7-11*

  Glory to the Father, and to the Son,
     and to the Holy Spirit:*
  as it was in the beginning, is now,
     and shall be for ever. Amen.

THE SCRIPTURE READING

Week 1 & Sundays in Christmastide

Jesus said to his disciples, 'You know that among the Gentiles those whom they recognise as their rulers lord it over them and their great ones exercise authority over them. But it shall not be so among you; but whoever wishes to become great among you must be your servant, and whoever wishes to be first among you must be servant of all. For the Son of Man came not to be served but to serve, and to give his life as a ransom for many.'

Mark 10. 43-45

Week 2 & Mondays in Christmastide

Now the word of the Lord came to me, saying, 'Before I formed you in the womb, I knew you. And before you were born I consecrated you. I appointed you a prophet to the nations.' Then I said, 'Ah, Lord God! Truly I do not know how to speak, for I am only a youth.' But the Lord said to me, 'Do not say "I am only a youth", for you shall go to all to whom I send you, and you shall speak whatever I command you. Do not be afraid of them for I am with you to deliver,' says the Lord. *Jeremiah 1. 4-6*

Week 3 & Tuesdays in Christmastide

Jesus said, 'You are the light of the world. A city set on a hill cannot be hid. No one after lighting a lamp puts it under a bushel but on the lampstand and it gives light to all in the house. In the same way, let your light so shine before others that they may see your good works and glorify your Father who is in heaven.' *Matthew 5. 14-16*

Week 4 & Wednesdays in Christmastide

You know the grace of our Lord Jesus Christ, that though he was rich, yet for your sakes he became poor, so that, by his poverty, you might become rich. *2 Corinthians 8. 9*

Week 5 & Thursdays in Christmastide

Jesus said, 'When you are invited to a wedding feast, do not sit down at the place of honour, in case someone more distinguished than you has been invited by your host. But when you are invited, sit down at the lowest place so that, when your host comes, he may say to you, "Friend, go up higher"; then you will be honoured in the presence of all who sit at the table with you. For all who exalt themselves will be humbled, and those who humble themselves will be exalted.' *Luke 14. 8, 10-11*

Week 6 & Fridays in Christmastide

Is not this the fast that I choose: to loose the bonds of injustice, to undo the thongs of the yoke, to let the oppressed go free, and to break every yoke? Is it not to share your bread with the hungry and bring the homeless poor into your house; when you see the naked, to cover them, and not to hide yourself from your own kin? Then shall your light break forth like the dawn and your healing shall spring up speedily; your vindicator shall go before you, the glory of the Lord shall be your rear guard.
Isaiah 58. 6-8

Week 7 & Saturdays in Christmastide

Jesus spoke to the Pharisees, saying, 'I am the light of the world. Whoever follows me will never walk in darkness but will have the light of life.' *John 8. 12*

*　　　　*　　　　*

This RESPONSE to the reading may be used:
Your salvation is near to those who fear you,
That glory may dwell in our land.

THE GOSPEL CANTICLE: THE MAGNIFICAT

1   My soul proclaims the greatness of the Lord,*
     my spirit rejoices in God my Saviour,

2   For you, Lord, have looked with favour
       on your lowly servant.*
     From this day all generations will call me blessèd:

3   You, the Almighty, have done great things for me*
     and holy is your name.

4   You have mercy on those who fear you,*
     from generation to generation.

5   You have shown strength with your arm*
     and scattered the proud in their conceit,

6   Casting down the mighty from their thrones*
     and lifting up the lowly.

7   You have filled the hungry with good things*
     and sent the rich away empty.

8   You have come to the aid of your servant, Israel,*
     to remember the promise of mercy,

9   The promise made to our forebears,*
     to Abraham and his children for ever. *Luke 1. 46-55*

Glory to the Father, and to the Son,
   and to the Holy Spirit:*
as it was in the beginning, is now,
   and shall be for ever. Amen.

THE PRAYERS

Intercession and thanksgiving are offered in free prayer or in silence, ending with the following:

Have mercy, O Lord, upon us,
as we have hoped in you.
Lord, have mercy.

Give justice to the orphan and the oppressed
and break the power of wickedness and evil.
Christ, have mercy.

Lord, hear our prayer
and answer us in your righteousness.
Lord, have mercy.

THE COLLECT for Wednesdays:

Almighty God,
in Christ you make all things new:
transform the poverty of our nature
   by the riches of your grace,
and in the renewal of our lives
make known your heavenly glory;
through Jesus Christ our Lord . . .   3

Or for Christmastide:

Almighty God,
who called your Church to witness
that you were in Christ reconciling the world to yourself:
help us so to proclaim the good news of your love
that all who hear it may be reconciled to you;
through him who died for us and rose again
and reigns with you and the Holy Spirit,
one God, now and for ever. **Amen.**   3/5

THE LORD'S PRAYER may be said.

Let us bless the Lord.
Thanks be to God.

Morning Prayer – Form 5

Thursday and daily in Epiphanytide

THE PREPARATION

O Lord, open our lips
And our mouth shall proclaim your praise.

Blessèd are you, Sovereign God, King of the nations,
to you be praise and glory for ever!
From the rising of the sun to its setting
your name is proclaimed in all the world.
As the Sun of Righteousness dawns in our hearts,
anoint our lips with the seal of your Spirit
that we may witness to your gospel
and sing your praise in all the world,
Father, Son and Holy Spirit:
Blessèd be God for ever!

THE WORD OF GOD

Week 1 & Sundays in Epiphany – Psalm 67

1   May God be merciful to us and bless us,*
    show us the light of his countenance and come to us.

2   Let your ways be known upon earth,*
    your saving health among all nations.

3   Let the peoples praise you, O God;*
    let all the peoples praise you.

4   Let the nations be glad and sing for joy,*
    for you judge the peoples with equity
       and guide all the nations upon earth.

5   Let the peoples praise you, O God;*
    let all the peoples praise you.

6   The earth has brought forth her increase;*
    may God, our own God, give us his blessing.

7   May God give us his blessing,*
    and may all the ends of the earth stand in awe of him.

In the face of Jesus Christ,
your light and glory have blazed forth
to all the nations, O God;
with all your people may we make known your grace
and live out your ways of peace. **Amen.**   19

1   The Lord is king; let the people tremble;*
    he is enthroned upon the cherubim; let the earth shake.

2   The Lord is great in Zion;*
    he is high above all peoples.

3   Let them confess his name, which is great and awesome;*
    he is the Holy One.

4   'O mighty King, lover of justice,
        you have established equity;*
    you have executed justice and righteousness in Jacob.'

5   Proclaim the greatness of the Lord our God
        and fall down before his footstool;*
    he is the Holy One.

6   Moses and Aaron among his priests,
        and Samuel among those who call upon his name,*
    they called upon the Lord and he answered them.

7   He spoke to them out of the pillar of cloud;*
    they kept his testimonies
        and the decree that he gave them.

8   'O Lord our God, you answered them indeed;*
    you were a God who forgave them,
        yet punished them for their evil deeds.'

9   Proclaim the greatness of the Lord our God
        and worship him upon his holy hill;*
    for the Lord our God is the Holy One.

O Lord our king, exalted on high,
yet stooping to the measure of our lowliness,
you have called us to be holy for you are holy:
as in our worship we confess your glory,
so may our lives be directed in righteousness;
through Jesus Christ our Lord. **Amen.**   14

1 The Lord is king; let the earth rejoice;*
    let the multitude of the isles be glad.

2 Clouds and darkness are round about him,*
    righteousness and justice
      are the foundations of his throne.

3 A fire goes before him*
    and burns up his enemies on every side.

4 His lightnings light up the world;*
    the earth sees it and is afraid.

5 The mountains melt like wax
      at the presence of the Lord,*
    at the presence of the Lord of the whole earth.

6 The heavens declare his righteousness,*
    and all the peoples see his glory.

7 Confounded be all who worship carved images
      and delight in false gods!*
    Bow down before him, all you gods.

8 Zion hears and is glad and the cities of Judah rejoice,*
    because of your judgements, O Lord.

9 For you are the Lord: most high over all the earth;*
    you are exalted far above all gods.

10 The Lord loves those who hate evil;*
    he preserves the lives of his saints
      and delivers them from the hand of the wicked.

11 Light has sprung up for the righteous,*
    and joyful gladness for those who are true-hearted.

12 Rejoice in the Lord, you righteous,*
    and give thanks to his holy name.

   *All creation was astonished at your appearing, O Christ,
   for in your presence no one living can be justified,
   yet you have redeemed us and we rejoice in your salvation:
   grant that your righteousness may illuminate our hearts
   to the glory of your Name.* **Amen.**   14

Week 4 & Wednesdays in Epiphany – Psalm 21

1   The king rejoices in your strength, O Lord;*
     how greatly he exults in your victory!

2   You have given him his heart's desire;*
     you have not denied him the request of his lips.

3   For you meet him with blessings of prosperity,*
     and set a crown of fine gold upon his head.

4   He asked you for life and you gave it to him;*
     length of days, for ever and ever.

5   His honour is great, because of your victory;*
     splendour and majesty have you bestowed upon him.

6   For you will give him everlasting felicity*
     and will make him glad with the joy of your presence.

7   For the king puts his trust in the Lord;*
     because of the loving-kindness of the Most High,
       he will not fall.

8   Your hand will lay hold upon all your enemies;*
     your right hand will seize all those who hate you.

9   You will make them like a fiery furnace*
     at the time of your appearing, O Lord;

10   You will swallow them up in your wrath,*
     and fire shall consume them.

11   Though they intend evil against you
      and devise wicked schemes,*
     yet they shall not prevail.

12   Be exalted, O Lord, in your might;*
     we will sing and praise your power.

*Go before us, Lord Christ,
with the blessings of your goodness
and guide all those you call to authority
in the way of your justice,
the knowledge of your liberty
and the wisdom of your gentleness;
for your Name's sake.* **Amen.**

7

1   Ascribe to the Lord, you gods,*
      ascribe to the Lord glory and strength.

2   Ascribe to the Lord the glory due to his name;*
      worship the Lord in the beauty of holiness.

3   The voice of the Lord is upon the waters;
       the God of glory thunders;*
      the Lord is upon the mighty waters.

4   The voice of the Lord is a powerful voice;*
      the voice of the Lord is a voice of splendour.

5   The voice of the Lord breaks the cedar trees;*
      the Lord breaks the cedars of Lebanon;

6   He makes Lebanon skip like a calf,*
      and Mount Hermon like a young wild ox.

7   The voice of the Lord splits the flames of fire;
       the voice of the Lord shakes the wilderness;*
      the Lord shakes the wilderness of Kadesh.

8   The voice of the Lord makes the oak trees writhe*
      and strips the forests bare.

9   And in the temple of the Lord*
      all are crying, 'Glory!'

10   The Lord sits enthroned above the flood;*
      the Lord sits enthroned as king for evermore.

11   The Lord shall give strength to his people;*
      the Lord shall give his people the blessing of peace.

Open our ears to hear you, O God,
and our mouths to proclaim your glory
and the beauty of your holiness
as revealed to us in your Son,
Jesus Christ our Lord. **Amen.**   7

1   Be merciful to me, O God, be merciful,
        for I have taken refuge in you;*
    in the shadow of your wings will I take refuge
        until this time of trouble has gone by.

2   I will call upon the Most High God,*
    the God who maintains my cause.

3   He will send from heaven and save me;
        he will confound those who trample upon me;*
    God will send forth his love and his faithfulness.

4   I lie in the midst of lions that devour the people;*
    their teeth are spears and arrows,
        their tongue a sharp sword.

5   They have laid a net for my feet and I am bowed low;*
    they have dug a pit before me
        but have fallen into it themselves.

6   Exalt yourself above the heavens, O God,*
    and your glory over all the earth.

7   My heart is firmly fixed, O God, my heart is fixed;*
    I will sing and make melody.

8   Wake up, my spirit; awake, lute and harp;*
    I myself will waken the dawn.

9   I will confess you among the peoples, O Lord;*
    I will sing praise to you among the nations.

10 For your loving-kindness is greater than the heavens,*
    and your faithfulness reaches to the clouds.

11 Exalt yourself above the heavens, O God,*
    and your glory over all the earth.

Tender God,
gentle protector in time of trouble:
pierce the gloom of despair
and give us, with all your people,
the song of freedom and the shout of praise,
in Jesus Christ our Lord. **Amen.**   19

Week 7 & Saturdays in Epiphany – Psalm 148

1   Alleluia! Praise the Lord from the heavens;*
    praise him in the heights.

2   Praise him, all you angels of his;*
    praise him, all his host.

3   Praise him, sun and moon;*
    praise him, all you shining stars.

4   Praise him, heaven of heavens,*
    and you waters above the heavens.

5   Let them praise the name of the Lord;*
    for he commanded and they were created.

6   He made them stand fast for ever and ever;*
    he gave them a law which shall not pass away.

7   Praise the Lord from the earth,*
    you sea monsters and all deeps;

8   Fire and hail, snow and fog,*
    tempestuous wind, doing his will;

9   Mountains and all hills, fruit trees and all cedars;*
    wild beasts and all cattle, creeping things and winged birds;

10 Kings of the earth and all peoples,*
    princes and all rulers of the world;

12 Young men and maidens, old and young together:*
    let them praise the name of the Lord,

13 For his name only is exalted,*
    his splendour is over earth and heaven.

14 He has raised up strength for his people
        and praise for all his loyal servants,*
    the children of Israel, a people who are near him.
        Alleluia!

O glorious God,
the whole of creation proclaims your marvellous work:
increase in us a capacity to wonder and delight in it,
that heaven's praise may echo in our hearts
and our lives be spent as good stewards of the earth;
through Jesus Christ our Lord. **Amen.**   13

THE OLD TESTAMENT CANTICLE
Either: A SONG OF THE COVENANT

1   Thus says God, who created the heavens,*
     who fashioned the earth and all that dwells in it;

2   Who gives breath to the people upon it*
     and spirit to those who walk in it,

3   'I am the Lord and I have called you in righteousness,*
     I have taken you by the hand and kept you;

4   'I have given you as a covenant to the people,*
     a light to the nations, to open the eyes that are blind,

5   'To bring out the captives from the dungeon,*
     from the prison, those who sit in darkness.

6   'I am the Lord, that is my name;*
     my glory I give to no other.' *Isaiah 42. 5-8a*

     **Glory to the Father, and to the Son,
        and to the Holy Spirit:***
     **as it was in the beginning, is now,
        and shall be for ever. Amen.**

Or: A SONG OF THE NEW JERUSALEM

1   Arise, shine out, for your light has come,*
     the glory of the Lord is rising upon you.

2   Though night still covers the earth,*
     and darkness the peoples;

3   Above you the Holy One arises,*
     and above you God's glory appears.

4   The nations will come to your light,*
     and kings to your dawning brightness.

5   Your gates will lie open continually;*
     shut neither by day nor by night.

6   The sound of violence
        shall be heard no longer in your land,*
     or ruin and devastation within your borders.

7   You will call your walls, Salvation,*
     and your gates, Praise.

8   No more will the sun give you daylight,*
     nor moonlight shine upon you;

9   But the Lord will be your everlasting light,*
      your God will be your splendour.

10   For you shall be called the city of God,*
      the dwelling of the Holy One of Israel.   *From Isaiah 60*

Glory to the Father, and to the Son,
    and to the Holy Spirit:*
as it was in the beginning, is now,
    and shall be for ever.   Amen.

THE SCRIPTURE READING

Week 1 & Sundays in Epiphanytide

The Lord said to Abraham, 'I will surely return to you in due
season and your wife Sarah shall have a son.' Now Abraham and
Sarah were old and it had ceased to be with Sarah after the
manner of women. So Sarah laughed to herself, saying, 'After I
have grown old, and my husband is old, shall I have pleasure?'
The Lord said to Abraham, 'Why did Sarah laugh and say, "Shall I
indeed bear a child, now that I am old?" Is anything too hard
for the Lord? At the appointed time I will return to you, in the
spring, and Sarah shall have a son.'   *Genesis 18. 10-14*

Week 2 & Mondays in Epiphanytide

How are they to call on one in whom they have not believed? And
how are they to believe in one of whom they have never heard?
And how are they to hear without a preacher? And how are they to
preach him unless they are sent? As it is written, 'How
beautiful are the feet of those who bring good news!'
                                        Romans 10. 14-15

Week 3 & Tuesdays in Epiphanytide

Moses said, 'You shall offer the passover sacrifice to the Lord
your God, from the flock and the herd, at the place that the Lord
will choose as a dwelling for his name. You shall eat no
leavened bread with it; seven days you shall eat it with
unleavened bread, the bread of affliction – because you came out
of the land of Egypt in great haste – so that all the days of
your life you may remember the day when you came out of the land
of Egypt.'   *Deuteronomy 16. 2-3*

Week 4 & Wednesdays in Epiphanytide

Moses said, 'I call heaven and earth to witness against you today
that I have set before you life and death, blessing and curse.
Therefore, choose life, that you and your descendants may live,
loving the Lord your God, obeying his voice and holding fast to
him; for that means life to you and length of days, that you may
live in the land that the Lord swore to your ancestors, to
Abraham, to Isaac and to Jacob, to give them.'

Deuteronomy 30. 19-20

Week 5 & Thursdays in Epiphanytide

As many of you as were baptised into Christ have put on Christ.
There is no longer Jew or Greek, there is no longer slave or
free, there is no longer male and female; for you are all one in
Christ Jesus. And if you are Christ's, then you are Abraham's
offspring, heirs according to the promise. *Galatians 3. 27-29*

Week 6 & Fridays in Epiphanytide

You are a chosen race, a royal priesthood, a holy nation, God's
own people, in order that you may proclaim the wonderful deeds o
him who called you out of darkness into his marvellous light.
Once you were no people, but now you are God's people; once you
had not received mercy, but now you have received mercy.

1 Peter 2. 9-10

Week 7 & Saturdays in Epiphanytide

Elijah said to Elisha, 'Tell me what I may do for you, before I
am taken from you.' Elisha said, 'I pray you let me inherit a
double share of your spirit.' He responded, 'You have asked a
hard thing; yet, if you see me as I am being taken from you, it
will be granted you; if not, it will not.' As they continued
walking and talking, a chariot of fire and horses of fire
separated the two of them and Elijah ascended in a whirlwind into
heaven. Elisha saw it and cried out, 'My father, my father! The
chariots of Israel and its horsemen.' *2 Kings 2. 9-12a*

*   *   *

This RESPONSE to the reading may be used:
O worship the Lord in the beauty of holiness,
Let the whole earth stand in awe of him.

THE GOSPEL CANTICLE: THE BENEDICTUS

1 Blessèd are you, Lord, the God of Israel,*
   you have come to your people and set them free.

2 You have raised up for us a mighty Saviour,*
   born of the house of your servant, David.

3 Through your holy prophets, you promised of old*
   to save us from our enemies,
      from the hands of all who hate us,

4 To show mercy to our forebears,*
   and to remember your holy covenant.

5 This was the oath you swore to our father, Abraham,*
   to set us free from the hands of our enemies,

6 Free to worship you without fear,*
   holy and righteous before you,
      all the days of our life.

7 And you, child,
      shall be called the prophet of the Most High,*
   for you will go before the Lord to prepare the way,

8 To give God's people knowledge of salvation*
   by the forgiveness of their sins.

9 In the tender compassion of our God*
   the dawn from on high shall break upon us,

10 To shine on those who dwell in darkness
      and the shadow of death,*
   and to guide our feet into the way of peace. *Luke 1. 68-79*

   Glory to the Father, and to the Son,
      and to the Holy Spirit:*
   as it was in the beginning, is now,
      and shall be for ever. Amen.

THE PRAYERS

Intercession and thanksgiving are offered in free prayer or in silence, ending with the following:

Lord, send us your loving-kindness in the morning
and so shall we rejoice and be glad.
Lord, have mercy.

Let not the oppressed turn away ashamed;
let the poor and needy praise your name.
Christ, have mercy.

Teach us your ways, O Lord,
and we will walk in your truth.
Lord, have mercy.

THE COLLECT for Thursdays:

O God, the author of peace
and lover of concord,
whom to know is eternal life,
whose service is perfect freedom:
defend us your servants
from all assaults of our enemies,
that we, surely trusting in your defence,
may not fear the power of any adversaries;
through Jesus Christ our Lord . . .   1›

Or for Epiphanytide:

Lord our God,
who anointed your only Son
with the Spirit at the river Jordan,
and so hallowed the waters of new birth
to bring us forth to salvation:
keep us strong in the life of grace,
direct the ways of your people,
and open the door of your Kingdom
to all who stand on the threshold of faith;
through Jesus our Messiah and Saviour . . .   17

THE LORD'S PRAYER may be said.

Let us bless the Lord.
Thanks be to God.

Evening Prayer – Form 5

Thursday and daily in Epiphanytide

THE BLESSING OF THE LIGHT

Jesus Christ is the light of the world,
a light no darkness can quench.

The light and peace of Jesus Christ be with you all
And also with you.

Let us give thanks to the Lord our God
Who is worthy of all thanksgiving and praise.

Blessèd are you, Sovereign God of all,
to you be glory and praise for ever!
From the rising of the sun to its setting
your glory is proclaimed in all the world.
You gave the Christ as a light to the nations,
and through the anointing of his Spirit
you established us as a royal priesthood.
As you call us into his marvellous light,
may our lives bear witness to your truth
and our lips never cease to proclaim your praise,
Father, Son and Holy Spirit:
Blessèd be God for ever!

A SONG OF THE LIGHT

1   O gladsome light,
        of the holy glory of the immortal Father,*
    heavenly, holy, blessèd Jesus Christ.

2   Now that we have come to the setting of the sun
        and behold the light of evening,*
    we praise you, Father, Son and Holy Spirit.

3   For it is right at all times to worship you
        with voices of praise,*
    O Son of God and giver of life:
        therefore all the world glorifies you.

THE WORD OF GOD

Week 1 & Sundays in Epiphany – Psalm 72

1   Give the king your justice, O God,*
    and your righteousness to the king's son;

2   That he may rule your people righteously*
    and the poor with justice;

3   That the mountains may bring prosperity to the people,*
    and the little hills bring righteousness.

4   He shall defend the needy among the people;*
    he shall rescue the poor and crush the oppressor.

5   He shall live as long as the sun and moon endure,*
    from one generation to another.

6   He shall come down like rain upon the mown field,*
    like showers that water the earth.

7   In his time shall the righteous flourish;*
    there shall be abundance of peace
      till the moon shall be no more.

8   He shall rule from sea to sea,*
    and from the River to the ends of the earth.

9   His foes shall bow down before him,*
    and his enemies lick the dust.

10 The kings of Tarshish and of the isles shall pay tribute,*
    and the kings of Arabia and Saba offer gifts.

11 All kings shall bow down before him,*
    and all the nations do him service.

12 For he shall deliver the poor who cries out in distress,*
    and the oppressed who has no helper.

13 He shall have pity on the lowly and poor;*
    he shall preserve the lives of the needy.

14 He shall redeem their lives from oppression and violence,*
    and dear shall their blood be in his sight.

15 Long may he live,
    and may there be given to him gold from Arabia;*
    may prayer be made for him always,
      and may they bless him all the day long.

16 May there be abundance of grain on the earth,
    growing thick even on the hilltops;*
may its fruit flourish like Lebanon,
    and its grain like grass upon the earth.

17 May his name remain for ever
    and be established as long as the sun endures;*
may all the nations bless themselves in him
    and call him blessèd.

18 Blessèd be the Lord God, the God of Israel,*
who alone does wondrous deeds!

19 And blessèd be his glorious name for ever!*
and may all the earth be filled with his glory.
    Amen. Amen.

*Your kingdom come, O Lord,
with deliverance for the needy,
with peace for the righteous,
with overflowing blessing for all nations,
with glory, honour and praise
    for the only Saviour,*
Jesus Christ our Lord. **Amen.**
                              19

Week 2 & Mondays in Epiphany – Psalm 48

1 Great is the Lord and highly to be praised;*
in the city of our God is his holy hill.

2 Beautiful and lofty, the joy of all the earth,
    is the hill of Zion,*
the very centre of the world
    and the city of the great king.

3 God is in her citadels;*
he is known to be her sure refuge.

4 Behold, the kings of the earth assembled*
and marched forward together.

5 They looked and were astounded;*
they retreated and fled in terror.

6   Trembling seized them there;*
     they writhed like a woman in childbirth,
       like ships of the sea when the east wind shatters them.

7   As we have heard, so have we seen,
     in the city of the Lord of hosts, in the city of our God;*
   God has established her for ever.

8   We have waited in silence
     on your loving-kindness, O God,*
   in the midst of your temple.

9   Your praise, like your name, O God,
     reaches to the world's end;*
   your right hand is full of justice.

10   Let Mount Zion be glad
     and the cities of Judah rejoice,*
   because of your judgements.

11   Make the circuit of Zion; walk round about her;*
   count the number of her towers.

12   Consider well her bulwarks; examine her strongholds;*
   that you may tell those who come after.

13   This God is our God for ever and ever;*
   he shall be our guide for evermore.

*We wait on your loving-kindness, O God,
in the midst of your temple;
as your praise reaches to the ends of the earth,
so gather in the nations to the beauty of your house;
through Jesus Christ our Lord.* **Amen.**   14

1   I was glad when they said to me,*
    'Let us go to the house of the Lord.'

2   Now our feet are standing*
    within your gates, O Jerusalem.

3   Jerusalem is built as a city*
    that is at unity with itself.

4   To which the tribes go up, the tribes of the Lord,*
    the assembly of Israel, to praise the name of the Lord.

5   For there are the thrones of judgement,*
    the thrones of the house of David.

6   Pray for the peace of Jerusalem:*
    'May they prosper who love you.

7   'Peace be within your walls*
    and quietness within your towers.

8   'For my family and companions' sake,*
    I pray for your prosperity.

9   'Because of the house of the Lord our God,*
    I will seek to do you good.'

10 Praise the Lord, all you nations;*
    laud him, all you peoples.

11 For his loving-kindness towards us is great,*
    and the faithfulness of the Lord endures for ever.
       Alleluia!

God of our joy and gladness,
hear our prayer for the peace of this world
and bring us at last,
with all our companions in faith,
to the peace of that city where you live and reign,
Father, Son and Holy Spirit,
now and to all eternity. **Amen.**   16

1   Sing with joy to God our strength*
    and raise a loud shout to the God of Jacob.

2   Raise a song and sound the timbrel,*
    the merry harp and the lyre.

3   Blow the ram's horn at the new moon,*
    and at the full moon, the day of our feast.

4   For this is a statute for Israel,*
    a law of the God of Jacob.

5   He laid it as a solemn charge upon Joseph,*
    when he came out of the land of Egypt.

6   I heard an unfamiliar voice saying,*
    'I eased his shoulder from the burden;
        his hands were set free from bearing the load.'

7   You called on me in trouble and I saved you;*
    I answered you from the secret place of thunder
        and tested you at the waters of Meribah.

8   Hear, O my people, and I will admonish you:*
    O Israel, if you would but listen to me!

9   There shall be no strange god among you;*
    you shall not worship a foreign god.

10 I am the Lord your God,
        who brought you out of the land of Egypt and said,*
    'Open your mouth wide and I will fill it.'

11 And yet my people did not hear my voice,*
    and Israel would not obey me.

12 So I gave them over to the stubbornness
        of their hearts,*
    to follow their own devices.

13 O that my people would listen to me!*
    that Israel would walk in my ways!

14 I should soon subdue their enemies*
    and turn my hand against their foes.

15 Those who hate the Lord would cringe before him,*
    and their punishment would last for ever.

16 But Israel would I feed with the finest wheat*
    and satisfy him with honey from the rock.

Father of mercy,
keep us joyful in your salvation
and faithful to your covenant;
and, as we journey to your kingdom,
ever feed us with the bread of life,
your Son, our Saviour Jesus Christ. **Amen.**　　　18

Week 5 & Thursdays in Epiphany – Psalm 98

1　Sing to the Lord a new song,*
　　for he has done marvellous things.

2　With his right hand and his holy arm*
　　has he won for himself the victory.

3　The Lord has made known his victory;*
　　his righteousness has he openly shown
　　　in the sight of the nations.

4　He remembers his mercy and faithfulness
　　　to the house of Israel,*
　　and all the ends of the earth have seen
　　　the victory of our God.

5　Shout with joy to the Lord, all you lands;*
　　lift up your voice, rejoice and sing.

6　Sing to the Lord with the harp,*
　　with the harp and the voice of song.

7　With trumpets and the sound of the horn*
　　shout with joy before the King, the Lord.

8　Let the sea make a noise and all that is in it,*
　　the lands and those who dwell therein.

9　Let the rivers clap their hands,*
　　and let the hills ring out with joy before the Lord,
　　　when he comes to judge the earth.

10　In righteousness shall he judge the world,*
　　and the peoples with equity.

　　O God, mindful of your promises,
　　you have visited and redeemed your people:
　　as we rejoice in the power of your victory,
　　so hasten the day of your appearing;
　　through Jesus Christ our Lord. **Amen.**　　　14

1 There is a voice of rebellion deep in the heart of the wicked
   there is no fear of God before their eyes.

2 They flatter themselves in their own eyes*
   that their hateful sin will not be found out.

3 The words of their mouths are wicked and deceitful;*
   they have left off acting wisely and doing good.

4 They think up wickedness upon their beds
      and have set themselves in no good way;*
   they do not abhor that which is evil.

5 Your love, O Lord, reaches to the heavens,*
   and your faithfulness to the clouds.

6 Your righteousness is like the strong mountains,
      your justice like the great deep;*
   you save both human and beast, O Lord.

7 How priceless is your love, O God!*
   your people take refuge under the shadow of your wings.

8 They feast upon the abundance of your house;*
   you give them drink from the river of your delights.

9 For with you is the well of life,*
   and in your light we see light.

10 Continue your loving-kindness to those who know you,*
    and your favour to those who are true of heart.

11 Let not the foot of the proud come near me,*
    nor the hand of the wicked push me aside.

12 See how they are fallen, those who work wickedness!*
    they are cast down and shall not be able to rise.

   O God,
   the fountain and source of everlasting life,
   in your light we see light:
   increase in us the the brightness of knowledge
   that we may be lightened with the radiance of your wisdom;
   through Jesus Christ our Lord. **Amen.**   7

1 God is our refuge and strength,*
   a very present help in trouble;

2 Therefore we will not fear, though the earth be moved,*
   and though the mountains be toppled
     into the depths of the sea;

3 Though its waters rage and foam,*
   and though the mountains tremble at its tumult.

4 The Lord of hosts is with us;*
   the God of Jacob is our stronghold.

5 There is a river whose streams
    make glad the city of God,*
   the holy habitation of the Most High.

6 God is in the midst of her;
    she shall not be overthrown;*
   God shall help her at the break of day.

7 The nations make much ado
    and the kingdoms are shaken;*
   God has spoken and the earth shall melt away.

8 The Lord of hosts is with us;*
   the God of Jacob is our stronghold.

9 Come now and look upon the works of the Lord,*
   what awesome things he has done on earth.

10 It is he who makes war to cease in all the world;*
   he breaks the bow and shatters the spear
    and burns the shields with fire.

11 'Be still, then, and know that I am God;*
   I will be exalted among the nations;
    I will be exalted in the earth.'

12 The Lord of hosts is with us;*
   the God of Jacob is our stronghold.

Assuage our fear, O God,
and quieten our hearts to know you,
that being our refuge and strength
you may dwell in our midst
and make glad the place of your habitation;
through Jesus Christ our Lord. **Amen.**   14

THE NEW TESTAMENT CANTICLE
Either: A SONG OF PRAISE

1 You are worthy, our Lord and God,*
   to receive glory and honour and power.

2 For you have created all things,*
   and by your will they have their being.

3 You are worthy, O Lamb, for you were slain,*
   and by your blood you ransomed for God
      saints from every tribe and language and nation.

4 You have made them to be a kingdom and priests
      serving our God,*
   and they will reign with you on earth.

From Revelation 4 & 5

To the One who sits on the throne and to the Lamb*
be blessing and honour and glory and might,
   for ever and ever. Amen.

Or: A SONG OF CHRIST'S APPEARING

1 Christ Jesus was revealed in the flesh*
   and vindicated in the spirit.

2 He was seen by angels*
   and proclaimed among the nations.

3 Believed in throughout the world,*
   he was taken up in glory.

4 This will be made manifest at the proper time*
   by the blessèd and only Sovereign,

5 Who alone has immortality,*
   and dwells in unapproachable light.

To the King of kings and Lord of lords*
be honour and eternal dominion. Amen.

From 1 Timothy 3 & 6

THE SCRIPTURE READING

Week 1 & Sundays in Epiphanytide

While they were eating, Jesus took bread, and after blessing it he broke it, gave it to his disciples and said, 'Take, this is my body.' Then he took a cup and, after giving thanks, he gave it to them, and all of them drank from it. He said to them, 'This is my blood of the covenant, which is poured out for many. Truly I tell you, I shall not drink again of the fruit of the vine until that day when I drink it new in the kingdom of God.'

Mark 14. 22-25

Week 2 & Mondays in Epiphanytide

Come, let us go up to the mountain of the Lord, to the house of the God of Jacob, that he may teach us his ways and that we may walk in his paths. For out of Zion shall go forth instruction and the word of the Lord from Jerusalem. He shall judge between many peoples and shall decide for strong nations far off. They shall beat their swords into ploughshares and their spears into pruning hooks. Nation shall not lift up sword against nation, neither shall they learn war any more. But they shall each sit under their own vines and under their own fig trees and no one shall make them afraid, for the mouth of the Lord of hosts has spoken. For all the peoples walk, each in the name of its god, but we will walk in the name of the Lord our God for ever and ever.

Micah 4. 2b-5

Week 3 & Tuesdays in Epiphanytide

Jesus said, 'Every one who hears these words of mine and acts on them will be like a wise man who built his house on rock. The rain fell, the floods came, and the winds blew and beat on that house, but it did not fall, because it had been founded on rock. And everyone who hears these words of mine and does not act on them will be like a foolish man who built his house on sand. The rain fell, and the floods came, and the winds blew and beat against that house, and it fell – and great was its fall!'

Matthew 7. 24-27

Week 4 & Wednesdays in Epiphanytide

We proclaim not ourselves but Christ Jesus as Lord and ourselves as your servants for Jesus' sake. For it is the God who said,

'Let light shine out of darkness' who has shone in our hearts to give the light of the knowledge of the glory of God in the face of Jesus Christ.   *2 Corinthians 4. 5-7*

Week 5 & Thursdays in Epiphanytide

Jesus said to Simon, 'Do you see this woman? I entered your house: you gave me no water for my feet, but she has bathed my feet with her tears and dried them with her hair. You gave me no kiss, but from the time I came in she has not ceased to kiss my feet. You did not anoint my head with oil, but she has anointed my feet with ointment. Therefore, I tell you, her sins, which are many, are forgiven, for she loved much, but the one who is forgiven little, loves little.'   *Luke 7. 44-47*

Week 6 & Fridays in Epiphanytide

The spirit of the Lord God is upon me, because the Lord has anointed me; he has sent me to bring good news to the oppressed, to bind up the brokenhearted, to proclaim liberty to the captives and release to the prisoners; to proclaim the year of the Lord's favour and the day of vengeance of our God; to comfort all who mourn, to give them a garland instead of ashes, the oil of gladness instead of mourning, the mantle of praise instead of a faint spirit. They shall be called oaks of righteousness, the planting of the Lord, that he may be glorified.   *Isaiah 61. 1-3*

Week 7 & Saturdays in Epiphanytide

Jesus said, 'I am the living bread that came down from heaven. Whoever eats of this bread will live for ever; and the bread that I will give for the life of the world is my flesh.'   *John 6. 51*

*   *   *

This RESPONSE to the reading may be used:
Arise, shine, for your light has come;
The glory of the Lord is rising upon you.

THE GOSPEL CANTICLE: THE MAGNIFICAT

1   My soul proclaims the greatness of the Lord,*
    my spirit rejoices in God my Saviour,

2   For you, Lord, have looked with favour
         on your lowly servant.*
    From this day all generations will call me blessèd:

3   You, the Almighty, have done great things for me*
    and holy is your name.

4   You have mercy on those who fear you,*
    from generation to generation.

5   You have shown strength with your arm*
    and scattered the proud in their conceit,

6   Casting down the mighty from their thrones*
    and lifting up the lowly.

7   You have filled the hungry with good things*
    and sent the rich away empty.

8   You have come to the aid of your servant, Israel,*
    to remember the promise of mercy,

9   The promise made to our forebears,*
    to Abraham and his children for ever. *Luke 1. 46-55*

    Glory to the Father, and to the Son,
       and to the Holy Spirit:*
    as it was in the beginning, is now,
       and shall be for ever. Amen.

THE PRAYERS

Intercession and thanksgiving are offered in free prayer or in silence, ending with the following:

You, Lord, are the light of the world;
come and make our darkness bright.
Lord, have mercy.

O God, give the solitary a home
and bring forth prisoners into freedom.
Christ, have mercy.

Restore us again, O God of hosts;
show the light of your countenance and we shall be saved.
Lord, have mercy.

THE COLLECT for Thursdays:

O God, the source of all good desires,
all right judgements and all just works:
give to your servants that peace
  which the world cannot give;
that our hearts may be set to obey
  your commandments
and that, freed from the fear of our enemies,
we may pass our time in rest and quietness;
through Jesus Christ our Lord . . .   3›

Or for Epiphanytide:

Almighty God,
from whom all thoughts of truth and peace proceed:
kindle, we pray, in every heart, the true love of peace
and guide with your pure and peaceable wisdom
those who take counsel for the nations of the earth;
that in tranquillity your Kingdom may go forward
till the earth is filled with the knowledge of your love;
through Jesus Christ our Lord . . .   3/5

THE LORD'S PRAYER may be said.

Let us bless the Lord.
Thanks be to God.

Morning Prayer - Form 6

Friday and daily in Lent

THE PREPARATION

O Lord, open our lips
And our mouth shall proclaim your praise.

Blessèd are you, God of compassion and mercy,
to you be praise and glory for ever!
In the darkness of our sin,
your light breaks forth like the dawn
and your healing springs up for deliverance.
As we rejoice in the gift of your saving help,
sustain us with your bountiful Spirit
and open our lips to sing your praise,
Father, Son and Holy Spirit:
Blessèd be God for ever!

THE WORD OF GOD

Week 1 & Sundays in Lent - Psalm 95

1   Come, let us sing to the Lord;*
    let us shout for joy to the rock of our salvation.

2   Let us come before his presence with thanksgiving*
    and raise a loud shout to him with psalms.

3   For the Lord is a great God,*
    and a great king above all gods.

4   In his hand are the depths of the earth,*
    and the heights of the hills are his also.

5   The sea is his, for he made it,*
    and his hands have moulded the dry land.

6   Come, let us bow down and bend the knee,*
    and kneel before the Lord our Maker.

7   For he is our God,
        and we are the people of his pasture
        and the sheep of his hand.*
    O that today you would hearken to his voice!

8 'Harden not your hearts,
    as your forebears did in the wilderness,*
at Meribah, and on that day at Massah,
    when they tempted me.

9 'They put me to the test,*
though they had seen my works.

10 'Forty years long I detested that generation and said,*
"This people are wayward in their hearts;
they do not know my ways."

11 'So I swore in my wrath,*
"They shall not enter into my rest." '

Lord God, the creator of all,
before whom we bow down in worship:
make us joyful in your presence
and do not test us beyond our enduring;
through Jesus Christ our Lord. **Amen.**   18

Week 2 & Mondays in Lent – Psalm 51

1 Have mercy on me, O God,
    according to your loving-kindness;*
in your great compassion blot out my offences.

2 Wash me through and through from my wickedness*
and cleanse me from my sin.

3 For I know my transgressions,*
and my sin is ever before me.

4 Against you only have I sinned*
and done what is evil in your sight.

5 And so you are justified when you speak*
and upright in your judgement.

6 Indeed, I have been wicked from my birth,*
a sinner from my mother's womb.

7 For behold, you look for truth deep within me,*
and will make me understand wisdom secretly.

8   Purge me from my sin and I shall be pure;*
    wash me and I shall be clean indeed.

9   Make me hear of joy and gladness,*
    that the body you have broken may rejoice.

10 Hide your face from my sins*
    and blot out all my iniquities.

11 Create in me a clean heart, O God,*
    and renew a right spirit within me.

12 Cast me not away from your presence*
    and take not your holy Spirit from me.

13 Give me the joy of your saving help again*
    and sustain me with your bountiful Spirit.

14 I shall teach your ways to the wicked,*
    and sinners shall return to you.

15 Deliver me from death, O God,*
    and my tongue shall sing of your righteousness,
        O God of my salvation.

16 Open my lips, O Lord,*
    and my mouth shall proclaim your praise.

17 Had you desired it, I would have offered sacrifice,*
    but you take no delight in burnt offerings.

18 The sacrifice of God is a troubled spirit;*
    a broken and contrite heart, O God, you will not despise.

19 Be favourable and gracious to Zion,*
    and rebuild the walls of Jerusalem.

20 Then you will be pleased with the appointed sacrifices,
        with burnt offerings and oblations;*
    then shall they offer young bullocks upon your altar.

Take away, O Lord, the sin that corrupts us;
restore by grace your own image within us;
give us the sorrow that heals
and the joy that praises,
that we may take our place among your people,
in Jesus Christ our Lord. **Amen.**   19

1 Have mercy on me, O God,
    for my enemies are hounding me;*
  all day long they assault and oppress me.

2 They hound me all the day long;*
  truly there are many who fight against me, O Most High.

3 Whenever I am afraid,*
  I will put my trust in you.

4 In God, whose word I praise,
    in God I trust and will not be afraid,*
  for what can flesh do to me?

5 All day long they damage my cause;*
  their only thought is to do me evil.

6 They band together; they lie in wait;*
  they spy upon my footsteps; because they seek my life.

7 Shall they escape despite their wickedness?*
  O God, in your anger, cast down the peoples.

8 You have noted my lamentation;
    put my tears into your bottle;*
  are they not recorded in your book?

9 Whenever I call upon you,
    my enemies will be put to flight;*
  this I know, for God is on my side.

10 In God the Lord, whose word I praise,
    in God I trust and will not be afraid,*
  for what can mortals do to me?

11 I am bound by the vow I made to you, O God;*
  I will present to you thank-offerings;

12 For you have rescued my soul from death
    and my feet from stumbling,*
  that I may walk before God in the light of the living.

Faithful God,
your deliverance is near at hand:
keep us from fear
and help us to find courage and joy in your word;
through Jesus Christ our Lord. **Amen.**   19

Week 4 & Wednesdays in Lent – Psalm 6

1   Lord, do not rebuke me in your anger;*
    do not punish me in your wrath.

2   Have pity on me, Lord, for I am weak;*
    heal me, Lord, for my bones are racked.

3   My spirit shakes with terror;*
    how long, O Lord, how long?

4   Turn, O Lord, and deliver me;*
    save me for your mercy's sake.

5   For in death no one remembers you;*
    and who will give you thanks in the grave?

6   I grow weary because of my groaning;*
    every night I drench my bed
        and flood my couch with tears.

7   My eyes are wasted with grief*
    and worn away because of all my enemies.

8   Depart from me, all evildoers,*
    for the Lord has heard the sound of my weeping.

9   The Lord has heard my supplication;*
    the Lord accepts my prayer.

10 All my enemies shall be confounded and quake with fear;*
    they shall turn back and suddenly be put to shame.

*From the death of sin, raise us up, O Lord,
that with a troubled spirit and penitential tears
our prayer may find favour in your sight;
through Jesus Christ our Lord.* **Amen.**   14

Week 5 & Thursdays in Lent – Psalm 13

1   How long, O Lord;
        will you forget me for ever?*
    how long will you hide your face from me?

2   How long shall I have perplexity in my mind,
        and grief in my heart, day after day?*
    how long shall my enemy triumph over me?

3   Look upon me and answer me, O Lord my God;*
    give light to my eyes, lest I sleep in death;

4   Lest my enemy say, 'I have prevailed over him',*
    and my foes rejoice that I have fallen.

5   But I put my trust in your mercy;*
    my heart is joyful because of your saving help.

6   I will sing to the Lord,
        for he has dealt with me richly;*
    I will praise the name of the Lord Most High.

O God, we carry in our own bodies
the death of the Lord Jesus,
that likewise we might manifest his life:
let not our spiritual foe prevail against us,
but with the morning light
raise us up from the sleep of sin and death;
through Jesus Christ our Lord. **Amen.**   14

Week 6 & Fridays in Lent – from Psalm 22

1   My God, my God, why have you forsaken me?*
    and are so far from my cry
        and from the words of my distress?

2   O my God, I cry in the daytime,
        but you do not answer;*
    by night as well, but I find no rest.

3   Yet you are the Holy One,*
    enthroned upon the praises of Israel.

4   Our forebears put their trust in you;*
    they trusted and you delivered them.

5   They cried out to you and were delivered;*
    they trusted in you and were not put to shame.

6   But as for me, I am a worm and no man,*
    scorned by all and despised by the people.

7   All who see me laugh me to scorn;*
    they curl their lips and wag their heads, saying,

8   'He trusted in the Lord; let him deliver him;*
    let him rescue him, if he delights in him.'

9   Yet you are he who took me out of the womb,*
    and kept me safe upon my mother's breast.

10 I have been entrusted to you ever since I was born;*
    you were my God
        when I was still in my mother's womb.

11 Be not far from me, for trouble is near,*
    and there is none to help.

12 I am poured out like water;
        all my bones are out of joint;*
    my heart within my breast is melting wax.

13 My mouth is dried out like a pot-sherd;
        my tongue sticks to the roof of my mouth;*
    and you have laid me in the dust of the grave.

14 Packs of dogs close me in,
        and gangs of evildoers circle around me;*
    they pierce my hands and my feet;
        I can count all my bones.

15 They stare and gloat over me;*
  they divide my garments among them;
    they cast lots for my clothing.

16 Be not far away, O Lord;*
  you are my strength; hasten to help me.

17 Save me from the sword,*
  my life from the power of the dog.

18 Save me from the lion's mouth,*
  my wretched body from the horns of wild bulls.

19 I will declare your name to my people;*
  in the midst of the congregation I will praise you.

20 Praise the Lord, you that fear him;*
  stand in awe of him, O offspring of Israel;
    all you of Jacob's line, give glory.

21 For he does not despise nor abhor
    the poor in their poverty;
      neither does he hide his face from them;*
  but when they cry to him he hears them.

22 My praise is of him in the great assembly;*
  I will perform my vows
    in the presence of those who worship him.

23 The poor shall eat and be satisfied,
    and those who seek the Lord shall praise him:*
  'May your heart live for ever!'

24 All the ends of the earth
    shall remember and turn to the Lord,*
  and all the families of the nations shall bow before him.

25 To him alone all who sleep in the earth
    bow down in worship;*
  all who go down to the dust fall before him.

26 They shall come and make known to a people yet unborn*
  the saving deeds that he has done.

*Merciful God, your Son came to free us from sin,
overcoming death and rising in triumph:
may we, who are redeemed by his blood
be made ready to meet you face to face;
this we ask for Jesus' sake.* **Amen.**   7

1   How good it is to sing praises to our God!*
     how pleasant it is to honour him with praise!

2   The Lord rebuilds Jerusalem;*
     he gathers the exiles of Israel.

3   He heals the brokenhearted*
     and binds up their wounds.

4   He counts the number of the stars*
     and calls them all by their names.

5   Great is our Lord and mighty in power;*
     there is no limit to his wisdom.

6   The Lord lifts up the lowly,*
     but casts the wicked to the ground.

7   Sing to the Lord with thanksgiving;*
     make music to our God upon the harp.

8   He covers the heavens with clouds*
     and prepares rain for the earth;

9   He makes grass to grow upon the mountains*
     and green plants to serve us all.

10   He provides food for flocks and herds*
     and for the young ravens when they cry.

11   He is not impressed by the might of a horse,*
     he has no pleasure in human strength;

12   But the Lord has pleasure in those who fear him,*
     in those who await his gracious favour.

Be praised, O Lord, for sister death,
who greets each of us in life:
blessèd are those who do your will
and serve you with humility,
for from you, Most High, they receive the crown
of everlasting life in your Son, Jesus Christ. **Amen.**   7

THE OLD TESTAMENT CANTICLE
Either: A SONG OF HUMILITY

1   Come, let us return to the Lord*
    who has torn us and will heal us.

2   God has stricken us*
    and will bind up our wounds.

3   After two days, he will revive us,*
    and on the third day will raise us up,
        that we may live in his presence.

4   Let us humble ourselves;*
    let us strive to know our God,

5   Whose justice dawns like the morning star;*
    its dawning is as sure as the sunrise.

6   God's justice will come to us like the showers,*
    like the spring rains that water the earth.

7   'O Ephraim, how shall I deal with you?*
    How shall I deal with you, O Jacob?

8   'Your love for me is like the morning mist,*
    like the dew that goes early away.

9   'Therefore, I have hewn them by the prophets,*
    and my judgement goes forth as the light.

10 'For loyalty is my desire and not sacrifice,*
    and the knowledge of God
        rather than burnt offerings.' *Hosea 6. 1-6*

    Glory to the Father, and to the Son,
        and to the Holy Spirit:*
    as it was in the beginning, is now,
        and shall be for ever. Amen.

Or: A SONG OF THE WORD OF THE LORD

1   Seek the Lord while he may be found,*
     call upon him while he is near;

2   Let the wicked abandon their ways,*
     and the unrighteous their thoughts;

3   Return to the Lord,
         who will have mercy;*
     to our God, who will richly pardon.

4   'For my thoughts are not your thoughts,*
     neither are your ways my ways', says the Lord.

5   'For as the heavens are higher than the earth,*
     so are my ways higher than your ways
         and my thoughts than your thoughts.

6   'As the rain and the snow come down from above,*
     and return not again but water the earth,

7   'Bringing forth life and giving growth,*
     seed for sowing and bread to eat,

8   'So is my word that goes forth from my mouth;*
     it will not return to me fruitless,

9   'But it will accomplish that which I purpose,*
     and succeed in the task I·gave it.'   *Isaiah 55. 6-11*

     Glory to the Father, and to the Son,
         and to the Holy Spirit:*
     as it was in the beginning, is now,
         and shall be for ever. Amen.

*A SONG OF NEW LIFE (page 239) is a particularly appropriate
alternative Canticle in Lent and Passiontide.*

*A SONG OF SOLOMON (page 237) and
A SONG OF LAMENTATION (page 238) are particularly
appropriate alternative Canticles in Passiontide.*

THE SCRIPTURE READING

Week 1 & Sundays in Lent

Abraham bound his son Isaac, and laid him on the altar, on top of the wood. Then he reached out his hand and took the knife to slay his son. But the angel of the Lord called to him from heaven and said, 'Abraham, Abraham! Do not lay your hand on the boy or do anything to him, for now I know that you fear God, since you have not withheld your son, your only son, from me.'

Genesis 22. 9b-12

Week 2 & Mondays in Lent

While we were yet helpless, at the right time Christ died for the ungodly. Indeed, rarely will anyone die for a righteous person – though perhaps for a good person someone might actually dare to die. But God proves his love for us in that while we were still sinners Christ died for us.

Romans 5. 6-8

Week 3 & Tuesdays in Lent

The Lord said, 'Tell the whole congregation of Israel that on the tenth day of the first month of the year, they are to take a lamb for each household and in this manner you shall eat it: your loins girded, your sandals on your feet and your staff in your hand; and you shall eat it hurriedly. It is the passover of the Lord. For I will pass through the land of Egypt that night and I will strike down every first-born in the land of Egypt, both man and beast; on all the gods of Egypt I will execute judgements: I am the Lord. The blood shall be a sign for you on the houses where you live: when I see the blood, I shall pass over you and no plague shall destroy you when I strike the land of Egypt.'

Exodus 12. 3, 11-13

Week 4 & Wednesdays in Lent

Moses said, 'When all these things come upon you, the blessing and the curse, which I have set before you, and you call them to mind among all the nations where the Lord your God has driven you, and return to the Lord your God, and you and your children obey him with all your heart and with all your soul, in all that I command you this day, then the Lord your God will restore your fortunes and have compassion on you, and he will gather you again from all the peoples where the Lord your God has scattered you.

Even if you are exiled to the ends of the world, from there the Lord your God will gather you, and from there he will bring you back.'   *Deuteronomy 30. 1-4*

Week 5 & Thursdays in Lent

I have been crucified with Christ, and it is no longer I who live but it is Christ who lives in me.   And the life I now live in the flesh I live by faith in the Son of God, who loved me and gave himself for me.   *Galatians 2. 20*

Week 6 & Fridays in Lent

Whatever gain I had, these I have come to regard as loss because of Christ.   Indeed I count everything as loss because of the surpassing value of knowing Christ Jesus my Lord.   For his sake I have suffered the loss of all things and I regard them as refuse, in order that I may gain Christ and be found in him, not having a righteousness of my own that comes from the law, but one that comes through faith in Christ, the righteousness from God based on faith; that I may know him and the power of his resurrection, and may share his sufferings, becoming like him in his death, that if possible I may attain the resurrection from the dead.   *Philippians 3. 7-11*

Week 7 & Saturdays in Lent

I, Daniel, prayed to the Lord: 'O God, listen to the prayer of your servant and to his supplication and, for your own sake, Lord, let your face shine upon your desolated sanctuary.   Incline your ear, O my God, and hear.   Open your eyes and look at our desolation and the city that bears your name.   We do not present our supplication before you on the ground of our own righteousness but on the ground of your great mercies.   O Lord, hear; O Lord, forgive; O Lord, listen and act and do not delay! For your own sake, O my God, because your city and your people bear your name!'   *Daniel 9. 17-19*

*   *   *

This RESPONSE to the reading may be used:
To you, O Lord, I lift up my soul;
O my God, in you I trust.

THE GOSPEL CANTICLE: THE BENEDICTUS

1 Blessèd are you, Lord, the God of Israel,*
   you have come to your people and set them free.

2 You have raised up for us a mighty Saviour,*
   born of the house of your servant, David.

3 Through your holy prophets, you promised of old*
   to save us from our enemies,
      from the hands of all who hate us,

4 To show mercy to our forebears,*
   and to remember your holy covenant.

5 This was the oath you swore to our father, Abraham,*
   to set us free from the hands of our enemies,

6 Free to worship you without fear,*
   holy and righteous before you,
      all the days of our life.

7 And you, child,
      shall be called the prophet of the Most High,*
   for you will go before the Lord to prepare the way,

8 To give God's people knowledge of salvation*
   by the forgiveness of their sins.

9 In the tender compassion of our God*
   the dawn from on high shall break upon us,

10 To shine on those who dwell in darkness
      and the shadow of death,*
   and to guide our feet into the way of peace. *Luke 1. 68-79*

   Glory to the Father, and to the Son,
      and to the Holy Spirit:*
   as it was in the beginning, is now,
      and shall be for ever. Amen.

THE PRAYERS

Intercession and thanksgiving are offered in free prayer or in silence, ending with the following:

O Lord, you are our God:
we call upon you all day long.
Lord, have mercy.

Rescue the weak and poor,
deliver them from the power of the wicked.
Christ, have mercy.

Lord, our souls wait for you,
for our hope is in your word.
Lord, have mercy.

THE COLLECT for Fridays & Lent:

Almighty and everlasting God,
you hate nothing that you have made
and forgive the sins of all those who are penitent:
create and make in us new and contrite hearts
that we, worthily lamenting our sins
  and acknowledging our wretchedness,
may receive from you, the God of all mercy,
perfect remission and forgiveness;
through Jesus Christ our Lord . . .   1›

Or for Fridays and Passiontide:

Most merciful God,
who by the death and resurrection of your Son Jesus Christ
delivered and saved the world:
grant that by faith in him who suffered on the cross,
we may triumph in the power of his victory;
through Jesus Christ our Lord . . .   3›

THE LORD'S PRAYER may be said.

Let us bless the Lord.
Thanks be to God.

Evening Prayer – Form 6

Friday and daily in Lent

THE BLESSING OF THE LIGHT

Christ your light shall rise in the darkness
and your healing shall spring up like the dawn.

The light and peace of Jesus Christ be with you all
And also with you.

Let us give thanks to the Lord our God
Who is worthy of all thanksgiving and praise.

Blessèd are you, Sovereign God,
Shepherd of your pilgrim people:
their pillar of cloud by day, their pillar of fire by night.
Stir up in us the fire of your love
which shone forth from your Son enthroned on the cross,
that we may be cleansed of all our sins
and be made ready to come into your presence,
Father, Son and Holy Spirit:
Blessèd be God for ever!

Verses from Psalm 141 may be said:

**Let my prayer rise before you as incense,
the lifting up of my hands as the evening sacrifice.**

O Lord, I call to you; come to me quickly;
hear my voice when I cry to you.
Set a watch before my mouth, O Lord,
and guard the door of my lips.

**Let my prayer rise before you as incense,
the lifting up of my hands as the evening sacrifice.**

Let not my heart incline to any evil thing;
let me not be occupied in wickedness.
But my eyes are turned to you, Lord God,
in you I take refuge;
do not leave me defenceless.

**Let my prayer rise before you as incense,
the lifting up of my hands as the evening sacrifice.**

THE WORD OF GOD

Week 1 & Sundays in Lent — from Psalm 86

1   Bow down your ear, O Lord, and answer me,*
    for I am poor and in misery.

2   Keep watch over my life, for I am faithful;*
    save your servant who trusts in you.

3   Be merciful to me, O Lord, for you are my God;*
    I call upon you all the day long.

4   Gladden the soul of your servant,*
    for to you, O Lord, I lift up my soul.

5   For you, O Lord, are good and forgiving,*
    and great is your love towards all who call upon you.

6   Give ear, O Lord, to my prayer,*
    and attend to the voice of my supplications.

7   In the time of my trouble I will call upon you,*
    for you will answer me.

8   Among the gods there is none like you, O Lord,*
    nor anything like your works.

9   Teach me your way, O Lord,
        and I will walk in your truth;*
    knit my heart to you that I may fear your name.

10 I will thank you, O Lord my God, with all my heart,*
    and glorify your name for evermore.

11 For great is your love towards me;*
    you have delivered me from the nethermost Pit.

12 Turn to me and have mercy upon me;*
    give your strength to your servant;
        and save the child of your handmaid.

13 Show me a sign of your favour,
        so that those who hate me may see it and be ashamed;*
    because you, O Lord, have helped me and comforted me.

*God of mercy, who in your great love
drew your Son from the depths of the Pit:
bring your people from death to life,
that we may rejoice in your compassion
and praise you now and for ever.* **Amen.**   18

Week 2 & Mondays in Lent – Psalm 32

1 Happy are they whose transgressions are forgiven,*
   and whose sin is put away!

2 Happy are they to whom the Lord imputes no guilt,*
   and in whose spirit there is no guile!

3 While I held my tongue, my bones withered away,*
   because of my groaning all day long.

4 For your hand was heavy upon me day and night;*
   my moisture was dried up as in the heat of summer.

5 Then I acknowledged my sin to you,*
   and did not conceal my guilt.

6 I said, 'I will confess my transgressions to the Lord';*
   then you forgave me the guilt of my sin.

7 Therefore all the faithful will make their prayers to you
     in time of trouble;*
   when the great waters overflow, they shall not reach them.

8 You are my hiding-place;
     you preserve me from trouble;*
   you surround me with shouts of deliverance.

9 'I will instruct you and teach you
     in the way that you should go;*
   I will guide you with my eye.

10 'Do not be like horse or mule,
     which have no understanding;*
   who must be fitted with bit and bridle,
     or else they will not stay near you.'

11 Great are the tribulations of the wicked;*
   but mercy embraces those who trust in the Lord.

12 Be glad, you righteous, and rejoice in the Lord;*
   shout for joy, all who are true of heart.

*Have mercy on your prodigal children, O God,
and teach us to acknowledge our sinfulness,
so that, in repentance,
we may come to know your forgiveness
which is the fulfilment of our life in your Son,
Jesus Christ our Lord.* **Amen.**   7

Week 3 & Tuesdays in Lent — from Psalm 31

1 In you, O Lord, have I taken refuge;
    let me never be put to shame;*
  deliver me in your righteousness.

2 Incline your ear to me;*
  make haste to deliver me.

3 Be my strong rock, a castle to keep me safe,
    for you are my crag and my stronghold;*
  for the sake of your name, lead me and guide me.

4 Take me out of the net
    that they have secretly set for me,*
  for you are my tower of strength.

5 Into your hands I commend my spirit,*
  for you have redeemed me,
    O Lord, O God of truth.

6 I hate those who cling to worthless idols,*
  and I put my trust in the Lord.

7 I will rejoice and be glad because of your mercy;*
  for you have seen my affliction;
    you know my distress.

8 You have not shut me up in the power of the enemy;*
  you have set my feet in an open place.

9 Have mercy on me, O Lord, for I am in trouble;*
  my eye is consumed with sorrow,
    and also my throat and my belly.

10 For my life is wasted with grief,
    and my years with sighing;*
  my strength fails me because of affliction,
    and my bones are consumed.

11 I have become a reproach to all my enemies
    and even to my neighbours,
    a dismay to those of my acquaintance;*
  when they see me in the street they avoid me.

12 I am forgotten like the dead, out of mind;*
  I am as useless as a broken pot.

13 For I have heard the whispering of the crowd;
        fear is all around;*
    they put their heads together against me;
        they plot to take my life.

14 But as for me, I have trusted in you, O Lord.*
    I have said, 'You are my God.

15 'My times are in your hand;*
    rescue me from the hand of my enemies,
        and from those who persecute me.'

    *God of truth,
    have mercy on us, redeem us from sin,
    and bring us to new life in Christ.* **Amen.**   7

Week 4 and Wednesdays in Lent − from Psalm 31

16 'Make your face to shine upon your servant,*
    and in your loving-kindness save me.'

17 Lord, let me not be ashamed
        for having called upon you;*
    rather, let the wicked be put to shame;
        let them be silent in the grave.

18 Let the lying lips be silenced
        which speak against the righteous,*
    haughtily, disdainfully and with contempt.

19 How great is your goodness, O Lord,
        which you have laid up for those who fear you;*
    which you have done in the sight of all
        for those who put their trust in you.

20 You hide them in the covert of your presence
        from those who slander them;*
    you keep them in your shelter from the strife of tongues.

21 Blessèd be the Lord!*
    for he has shown me the wonders of his love
        in a besieged city.

22 Yet I said in my alarm,
        'I have been cut off from the sight of your eyes.'*
    Nevertheless, you heard the sound of my entreaty
        when I cried out to you.

23 Love the Lord, all you who worship him;*
   the Lord protects the faithful,
      but repays to the full those who act haughtily.

24 Be strong and let your heart take courage,*
   all you who wait for the Lord.

   Lord Jesus Christ,
   in our pilgrimage through this life,
   rescue us from evil,
   and make your face to shine on us,
   for you are our Lord and our God. **Amen.**   7

Week 5 & Thursdays in Lent – Psalm 27

1 The Lord is my light and my salvation;
      whom then shall I fear?*
   the Lord is the strength of my life;
      of whom then shall I be afraid?

2 When evildoers came upon me to eat up my flesh,*
   it was they, my foes and my adversaries,
      who stumbled and fell.

3 Though an army should encamp against me,*
   yet my heart shall not be afraid;

4 And though war should rise up against me,*
   yet will I put my trust in him.

5 One thing have I asked of the Lord;
      one thing I seek;*
   that I may dwell in the house of the Lord
      all the days of my life;

6 To behold the fair beauty of the Lord*
   and to seek him in his temple.

7 For in the day of trouble
      he shall keep me safe in his shelter;*
   he shall hide me in the secrecy of his dwelling
      and set me high upon a rock.

8 Even now he lifts up my head*
   above my enemies round about me;

9 Therefore I will offer in his dwelling an oblation
      with sounds of great gladness;*
   I will sing and make music to the Lord.

10 Hearken to my voice, O Lord, when I call;*
   have mercy on me and answer me.

11 You speak in my heart and say, 'Seek my face.'*
   Your face, Lord, will I seek.

12 Hide not your face from me,*
   nor turn away your servant in displeasure.

13 You have been my helper;
      cast me not away;*
   do not forsake me, O God of my salvation.

14 Though my father and my mother forsake me,*
   the Lord will sustain me.

15 Show me your way, O Lord;*
   lead me on a level path, because of my enemies.

16 Deliver me not into the hand of my adversaries,*
   for false witnesses have risen up against me,
      and also those who speak malice.

17 What if I had not believed
      that I should see the goodness of the Lord*
   in the land of the living!

18 O tarry and await the Lord's pleasure;
      be strong and he shall comfort your heart;*
   wait patiently for the Lord.

   O God our defender,
   give us the light of truth and wisdom
   that all our hope may be fixed on you,
   and on your Son, Jesus the Christ. **Amen.**   7

Week 6 & Fridays in Lent – from Psalm 69

1 Save me, O God,*
   for the waters have risen up to my neck.

2 I am sinking in deep mire,*
   and there is no firm ground for my feet.

3 I have come into deep waters,*
   and the torrent washes over me.

4 I have grown weary with my crying;
      my throat is inflamed;*
   my eyes have failed from looking for my God.

5   Those who hate me without a cause
        are more than the hairs of my head;
        my lying foes who would destroy me are mighty.*
    Must I then give back what I never stole?

6   O God, you know my foolishness,*
    and my faults are not hidden from you.

7   Let not those who hope in you
        be put to shame through me, Lord God of hosts;*
    let not those who seek you be disgraced because of me,
        O God of Israel.

8   Surely, for your sake have I suffered reproach,*
    and shame has covered my face.

9   I have become a stranger to my own kindred,*
    an alien to my mother's children.

10 Zeal for your house has eaten me up;*
    the scorn of those who scorn you has fallen upon me.

11 I humbled myself with fasting,*
    but that was turned to my reproach.

12 I put on sackcloth also,*
    and became a byword among them.

13 Those who sit at the gate murmur against me,*
    and the drunkards make songs about me.

14 But as for me, this is my prayer to you,*
    at the time you have set, O Lord:

15 'In your great mercy, O God,*
    answer me with your unfailing help.

16 'Save me from the mire; do not let me sink;*
    let me be rescued from those who hate me
        and out of the deep waters.

17 'Let not the torrent of waters wash over me,
        neither let the deep swallow me up;*
    do not let the Pit shut its mouth upon me.

18 'Answer me, O Lord, for your love is kind;*
    in your great compassion, turn to me.

19 'Hide not your face from your servant;*
    be swift and answer me, for I am in distress.

20 'Draw near to me and redeem me;*
   because of my enemies deliver me.

21 'You know my reproach, my shame and my dishonour;*
   my adversaries are all in your sight.'

22 Reproach has broken my heart and it cannot be healed;*
   I looked for sympathy, but there was none,
      for comforters, but I could find no one.

23 They gave me gall to eat,*
   and when I was thirsty, they gave me vinegar to drink.

31 As for me, I am afflicted and in pain;*
   your help, O God, will lift me up on high.

32 I will praise the name of God in song;*
   I will proclaim his greatness with thanksgiving.

33 This will please the Lord more than an offering of oxen,*
   more than bullocks with horns and hoofs.

34 The afflicted shall see and be glad;*
   you who seek God, your heart shall live.

35 For the Lord listens to the needy,*
   and his prisoners he does not despise.

36 Let the heavens and the earth praise him,*
   the seas and all that moves in them;

37 For God will save Zion and rebuild the cities of Judah;*
   they shall live there and have it in possession.

38 The children of his servants will inherit it,*
   and those who love his name will dwell therein.

   Thirsting on the cross,
   your Son shared the reproach of the oppressed
   and carried the sins of all:
   in him, O God, may the despairing find you,
   the afflicted gain life
   and the whole creation know its true king. **Amen.** 19

1 Lord, you have been our refuge*
  from one generation to another.

2 Before the mountains were brought forth,
    or the land and the earth were born,*
  from age to age you are God.

3 You turn us back to the dust and say,*
  'Go back, O child of earth.'

4 For a thousand years in your sight
    are like yesterday when it is past*
  and like a watch in the night.

5 You sweep us away like a dream;*
  we fade away suddenly like the grass.

6 In the morning it is green and flourishes;*
  in the evening it is dried up and withered.

7 For we consume away in your displeasure;*
  we are afraid because of your wrathful indignation.

8 Our iniquities you have set before you,*
  and our secret sins in the light of your countenance.

9 When you are angry, all our days are gone;*
  we bring our years to an end like a sigh.

10 The span of our life is seventy years,
    perhaps in strength even eighty;*
  yet the sum of them is but labour and sorrow,
    for they pass away quickly and we are gone.

11 Who regards the power of your wrath?*
  who rightly fears your indignation?

12 So teach us to number our days*
  that we may apply our hearts to wisdom.

13 Return, O Lord; how long will you tarry?*
  be gracious to your servants.

14 Satisfy us by your loving-kindness in the morning;*
  so shall we rejoice and be glad all the days of our life.

15 Make us glad by the measure of the days
    that you afflicted us*
  and the years in which we suffered adversity.

16 Show your servants your works*
   and your splendour to their children.

17 May the graciousness of the Lord our God be upon us;*
   prosper the work of our hands;
      prosper our handiwork.

Eternal Father,
our refuge from generation to generation,
in Christ your salvation has dawned for your people:
prosper the work of our hands
that the promise of your glorious kingdom
may be fulfilled in our midst;
through Jesus Christ our Lord. **Amen.** 18

THE NEW TESTAMENT CANTICLE

Either: THE SONG OF CHRIST'S GLORY

1   Christ Jesus was in the form of God,*
    but he did not cling to equality with God.

2   He emptied himself, taking the form of a servant,*
    and was born in our human likeness.

3   Being found in human form, he humbled himself,*
    and became obedient unto death,
        even death on a cross;

4   Therefore, God has highly exalted him,*
    and bestowed on him the name above every name,

5   That at the name of Jesus, every knee shall bow,*
    in heaven and on earth and under the earth.

6   And every tongue confess that Jesus Christ is Lord,*
    to the glory of God the Father. *Philippians 2. 5b-11*

    Glory to the Father, and to the Son,
        and to the Holy Spirit:*
    as it was in the beginning, is now,
        and shall be for ever. Amen.

Or: A SONG OF CHRIST THE SERVANT

1   Christ suffered for you, leaving you an example,*
    that you should follow in his steps.

2   He committed no sin, no guile was found on his lips,*
    when he was reviled, he did not revile in turn.

3   When he suffered, he did not threaten,*
    but he trusted in God who judges justly.

4   Christ himself bore our sins in his body on the tree,*
    that we might die to sin and live to righteousness.

5   By his wounds, you have been healed,
        for you were straying like sheep,*
    but have now returned
        to the Shepherd and Guardian of your souls.
                                                    1 Peter 2. 21-25

    Glory to the Father, and to the Son,
        and to the Holy Spirit:*
    as it was in the beginning, is now,
        and shall be for ever. Amen.

THE SCRIPTURE READING

Week 1 & Sundays in Lent

When it was noon, darkness came over the whole land until three in the afternoon. Then Jesus cried out with a loud voice, 'Eloi, Eloi, lema sabachthani?' which means, 'My God, my God, why have you forsaken me?' Then Jesus gave a loud cry and breathed his last. Now when the centurion, who stood facing him, saw that in this way he breathed his last, he said, 'Truly this man was the Son of God!' *Mark 15. 33-34, 37, 39*

Week 2 & Mondays in Lent

Is it nothing to you, all you who pass by? Look and see if there is any sorrow like my sorrow, which was brought upon me, which the Lord inflicted on the day of his fierce anger. For these things I weep; my eyes flow with tears; for a comforter is far from me, one to revive my courage; my children are desolate, for the enemy has prevailed. *Lamentations 1. 12, 16*

Week 3 & Tuesdays in Lent

Jesus said, 'Come to me, all you that are weary and are carrying heavy burdens, and I will give you rest. Take my yoke upon you and learn from me; for I am gentle and humble in heart and you will find rest for your souls. For my yoke is easy and my burden is light.' *Matthew 11. 28-30*

Week 4 & Wednesdays in Lent

The love of Christ urges us on, because we are convinced that one has died for all; therefore all have died. And he died for all so that those who live might live no longer for themselves but for him who died and was raised for them. *2 Corinthians 5. 14-15*

Week 5 & Thursdays in Lent

When the younger son came to himself he said, 'How many of my father's hired servants have bread enough and to spare, but I perish here with hunger! I will arise and go to my father and I will say to him, "Father, I have sinned against heaven and before you; I am no longer worthy to be called your son; treat me as one of your hired servants." ' And he arose and came to his father. But while he was still far off, his father saw him and had compassion and ran and embraced him and kissed him.

Luke 15. 17-20

Week 6 & Fridays in Lent

He was despised and rejected, a man of sorrows and acquainted with grief; and as one from whom others hide their faces he was despised, and we held him of no account. Surely he has borne our griefs and carried our sorrows; yet we accounted him stricken, struck down by God, and afflicted. But he was wounded for our transgressions, bruised for our iniquities; and upon him was the chastisement that made us whole, and by his stripes we are healed.

Isaiah 53. 3-5

Week 7 & Saturdays in Lent

Jesus said, 'I am the good shepherd. The good shepherd lays down his life for the sheep. The hired hand, who is not the shepherd and does not own the sheep, sees the wolf coming and leaves the sheep and runs away – and the wolf snatches them and scatters them. I am the good shepherd. I know my own and my own know me, just as the Father knows me and I know the Father. And I lay down my life for the sheep.'

John 10. 11-15

* * *

This RESPONSE to the reading may be used:

O Lord, do not forsake me;
Be not far from me, O my God.

THE GOSPEL CANTICLE: THE MAGNIFICAT

1   My soul proclaims the greatness of the Lord,*
    my spirit rejoices in God my Saviour,

2   For you, Lord, have looked with favour
        on your lowly servant.*
    From this day all generations will call me blessèd:

3   You, the Almighty, have done great things for me*
    and holy is your name.

4   You have mercy on those who fear you,*
    from generation to generation.

5   You have shown strength with your arm*
    and scattered the proud in their conceit,

6   Casting down the mighty from their thrones*
    and lifting up the lowly.

7   You have filled the hungry with good things*
    and sent the rich away empty.

8   You have come to the aid of your servant, Israel,*
    to remember the promise of mercy,

9   The promise made to our forebears,*
    to Abraham and his children for ever.   *Luke 1. 46-55*

    **Glory to the Father, and to the Son,
        and to the Holy Spirit:***
    **as it was in the beginning, is now,
        and shall be for ever.   Amen.**

THE PRAYERS

Intercession and thanksgiving are offered in free prayer or in silence, ending with the following:

Show us your mercy, O Lord,
and grant us your salvation.
Lord, have mercy.

The earth is full of violence:
look, O Lord, upon your covenant.
Christ, have mercy.

O God, do not be silent;
do not keep still, nor hold your peace, O God.
Lord, have mercy.

THE COLLECT for Fridays:

Lighten our darkness,
Lord, we pray,
and in your great mercy
defend us from all perils
  and dangers of this night;
for the love of your only Son,
our Saviour Jesus Christ . . .   3

Or for Lent & Passiontide:

Almighty and everlasting God,
who in your tender love towards the human race
sent your Son our Saviour Jesus Christ
to take upon him our flesh
and to suffer death upon the cross:
grant that we may follow the example
  of his patience and humility
and also be made partakers of his resurrection;
through Jesus Christ our Lord . . .   3/5

THE LORD'S PRAYER may be said.

Let us bless the Lord.
Thanks be to God.

Morning Prayer – Form 7

Saturday and daily in the Kingdom Season

THE PREPARATION

O Lord, open our lips
And our mouth shall proclaim your praise.

Blessèd are you, Sovereign God, ruler and judge of all,
to you be praise and glory for ever!
In the darkness of this age that is passing away,
may the glory of your kingdom which the saints enjoy
surround our steps as we journey on.
May we reflect the light of your glory this day
and so be made ready to come into your presence,
Father, Son and Holy Spirit:
Blessèd be God for ever!

THE WORD OF GOD

Week 1 & Sundays in the Kingdom – from Psalm 63

1   O God, you are my God; eagerly I seek you;*
       my soul thirsts for you, my flesh faints for you,
          as in a barren and dry land where there is no water;

2   Therefore I have gazed upon you in your holy place,*
       that I might behold your power and your glory.

3   For your loving-kindness is better than life itself;*
       my lips shall give you praise.

4   So will I bless you as long as I live*
       and lift up my hands in your name.

5   My soul is content, as with marrow and fatness,*
       and my mouth praises you with joyful lips,

6   When I remember you upon my bed,*
       and meditate on you in the night watches.

7   For you have been my helper,*
       and under the shadow of your wings I will rejoice.

8   My soul clings to you;*
       your right hand holds me fast.

To you we come, O Lord,
the true goal of all human desiring,
beyond all earthly beauty,
gentle protector, strong deliverer;
in the night you are our confidence:
from first light be our joy. **Amen.**   19

Week 2 & Mondays in the Kingdom − Psalm 125

1   Those who trust in the Lord are like Mount Zion,*
     which cannot be moved, but stands fast for ever.

2   The hills stand about Jerusalem;*
     so does the Lord stand round about his people,
        from this time forth for evermore.

3   The sceptre of the wicked shall not hold sway
        over the land allotted to the just,*
     so that the just shall not put their hands to evil.

4   Show your goodness, O Lord, to those who are good*
     and to those who are true of heart.

5   As for those who turn aside to crooked ways,
        the Lord will lead them away with the evildoers;*
     but peace be upon Israel.

God of power,
you are strong to save
and you never fail those who trust in you:
keep us under your protection
and spread abroad your reign of peace;
through Jesus Christ our Lord. **Amen.**   16

Week 3 & Tuesdays in the Kingdom – Psalm 124

1   If the Lord had not been on our side,*
    let Israel now say;

2   If the Lord had not been on our side,*
    when enemies rose up against us;

3   Then would they have swallowed us up alive*
    in their fierce anger towards us;

4   Then would the waters have overwhelmed us*
    and the torrent gone over us;

5   Then would the raging waters*
    have gone right over us.

6   Blessèd be the Lord!*
    he has not given us over to be a prey for their teeth.

7   We have escaped like a bird
    from the snare of the fowler;*
    the snare is broken and we have escaped.

8   Our help is in the name of the Lord,*
    the maker of heaven and earth.

God, maker of heaven and earth,
you save us in the water of baptism
and by the suffering of your Son you set us free:
help us to put our trust in his victory
and to know that there is salvation
only in the name of Jesus Christ our Lord. **Amen.**   16

Week 4 & Wednesdays in the Kingdom – Psalm 92

1   It is a good thing to give thanks to the Lord,*
    and to sing praises to your name, O Most High;

2   To tell of your loving-kindness early in the morning*
    and of your faithfulness in the night season;

3   On the psaltery and on the lyre*
    and to the melody of the harp.

4   For you have made me glad by your acts, O Lord;*
    and I shout for joy because of the works of your hands.

5   Lord, how great are your works!*
    your thoughts are very deep.

6   The dullard does not know,
       nor does the fool understand,*
    that though the wicked grow like weeds,
       and all the workers of iniquity flourish,

7   They flourish only to be destroyed for ever;*
    but you, O Lord, are exalted for evermore.

8   For lo, your enemies, O Lord,
       lo, your enemies shall perish,*
    and all the workers of iniquity shall be scattered.

9   But my horn you have exalted
       like the horns of wild bulls;*
    I am anointed with fresh oil.

10 My eyes also gloat over my enemies,*
    and my ears rejoice to hear the doom of the wicked
       who rise up against me.

11 The righteous shall flourish like a palm tree,*
    and shall spread abroad like a cedar of Lebanon.

12 Those who are planted in the house of the Lord*
    shall flourish in the courts of our God;

13 They shall still bear fruit in old age;*
    they shall be green and succulent;

14 That they may show how upright the Lord is,*
    my rock, in whom there is no fault.

Establish your people, O Lord,
in the way that leads to righteousness,
so that we may with confidence
come into your presence and sing your praise;
through Jesus Christ our Lord. **Amen.**   18

Week 5 & Thursdays in the Kingdom – Psalm 145

1 I will exalt you, O God my King,*
   and bless your name for ever and ever.

2 Every day will I bless you*
   and praise your name for ever and ever.

3 Great is the Lord and greatly to be praised;*
   there is no end to his greatness.

4 One generation shall praise your works to another*
   and shall declare your power.

5 I will ponder the glorious splendour of your majesty*
   and all your marvellous works.

6 They shall speak of the might of your wondrous acts,*
   and I will tell of your greatness.

7 They shall publish the remembrance
      of your great goodness;*
   they shall sing of your righteous deeds.

8 The Lord is gracious and full of compassion,*
   slow to anger and of great kindness.

9 The Lord is loving to everyone*
   and his compassion is over all his works.

10 All your works praise you, O Lord,*
   and your faithful servants bless you.

11 They make known the glory of your kingdom*
   and speak of your power;

12 That the peoples may know of your power*
   and the glorious splendour of your kingdom.

13 Your kingdom is an everlasting kingdom;*
   your dominion endures throughout all ages.

14 The Lord is faithful in all his words*
   and merciful in all his deeds.

15 The Lord upholds all those who fall;*
   he lifts up those who are bowed down.

16 The eyes of all wait upon you, O Lord,*
   and you give them their food in due season.

17 You open wide your hand*
   and satisfy the needs of every living creature.

18 The Lord is righteous in all his ways*
   and loving in all his works.

19 The Lord is near to those who call upon him,*
   to all who call upon him faithfully.

20 He fulfils the desire of those who fear him,*
   he hears their cry and helps them.

21 The Lord preserves all those who love him,*
   but he destroys all the wicked.

22 My mouth shall speak the praise of the Lord;*
   let all flesh bless his holy name for ever and ever.

*Lord God, King of the Universe,
you show the bright glory of your reign
in acts of mercy and enduring love:
raise the spirits of the downcast
and restore those who have fallen away,
that your Church may continually sing of your saving help;
through Jesus Christ our Lord.* **Amen.**   13

1   The Lord is my shepherd;*
       I shall not be in want.

2   He makes me lie down in green pastures*
       and leads me beside still waters.

3   He revives my soul*
       and guides me along right pathways for his name's sake.

4   Though I walk through the valley of the shadow of death,
          I shall fear no evil;*
       for you are with me;
          your rod and your staff, they comfort me.

5   You spread a table before me
          in the presence of those who trouble me;*
       you have anointed my head with oil,
          and my cup is running over.

6   Surely your goodness and mercy shall follow me
          all the days of my life,*
       and I will dwell in the house of the Lord for ever.

*For your Name's sake, O God,
lead us in the paths of righteousness
and let your mercy follow us
that we may dwell with you for ever.* **Amen.**   7

1 Alleluia!
     Sing to the Lord a new song;*
   sing his praise in the congregation of the faithful.

2 Let Israel rejoice in his maker;*
   let the children of Zion be joyful in their king.

3 Let them praise his name in the dance;*
   let them sing praise to him with timbrel and harp.

4 For the Lord takes pleasure in his people*
   and adorns the poor with victory.

5 Let the faithful rejoice in triumph;*
   let them be joyful on their beds.

6 Let the praises of God be in their throat*
   and a two-edged sword in their hand;

7 To wreak vengeance on the nations*
   and punishment on the peoples;

8 To bind their kings in chains*
   and their nobles with links of iron;

9 To inflict on them the judgement decreed;*
   this is glory for all his faithful people.
     Alleluia!

*Lord God, our maker and our king,
you judge all peoples according to your justice:
inspire and strengthen us with your Spirit,
that we may expose the pretence of worldly power
and ever witness to your truth;
through Jesus Christ our Lord.* **Amen.**   13

THE OLD TESTAMENT CANTICLE

Either: A SONG OF THE BRIDE

1   I will greatly rejoice in the Lord,*
     my soul shall exult in my God;

2   Who has clothed me with the garments of salvation,*
     and has covered me with the cloak of integrity,

3   As a bridegroom decks himself with a garland,*
     and as a bride adorns herself with her jewels.

4   For as the earth puts forth her blossom,*
     and as seeds in the garden spring up,

5   So shall God make righteousness and praise*
     blossom before all the nations.

6   For Zion's sake, I will not keep silent,*
     and for Jerusalem's sake, I will not rest,

7   Until her deliverance shines out like the dawn,*
     and her salvation as a burning torch.

8   The nations shall see your deliverance,*
     and all rulers shall see your glory;

9   Then you shall be called by a new name*
     which the mouth of God will give.

10 You shall be a crown of glory
     in the hand of the Lord,*
   a royal diadem in the hand of your God. *From Isaiah 61 &*

   **Glory to the Father, and to the Son,
     and to the Holy Spirit:***
   **as it was in the beginning, is now,
     and shall be for ever. Amen.**

Or: A SONG OF THE NEW CREATION

1   'I am the Lord, your Holy One,*
     the Creator of Israel, whom I have chosen.'

2   Thus says the Lord, who makes a way in the sea,*
     a path in the mighty waters,

3   'Remember not the former things,*
     nor consider the things of old.

4   'Behold, I make all things new;*
     now it springs forth, do you not perceive it?

5   'I will make a way in the wilderness
         and rivers in the desert,*
     to give drink to my chosen people,

6   'The people whom I formed for myself,*
     that they might declare my praise.'   *Isaiah 43. 15-21*

     Glory to the Father, and to the Son,
         and to the Holy Spirit:*
     as it was in the beginning, is now,
         and shall be for ever. Amen.

*A SONG OF THE RIGHTEOUS (page 240) is a particularly
appropriate alternative Canticle on All Saints' Day and
All Souls' Day.*

THE SCRIPTURE READING

Week 1 & Sundays in the Kingdom Season

Jacob dreamed that there was a ladder set up on the earth, the top of it reaching to heaven; and the angels of God were ascending and descending on it. And the Lord stood beside him and said, 'I am the Lord, the God of Abraham your father and the God of Isaac; the land on which you lie I will give to you and to your offspring.' Then Jacob woke from his sleep and said, 'Surely the Lord is in this place, and I did not know it!' And he was afraid and said, 'How awesome is this place! This is none other than the house of God, and this is the gate of heaven.'

Genesis 28. 12-13, 16-17

Week 2 & Mondays in the Kingdom Season

Do you not know that all of us who have been baptised into Christ Jesus were baptised into his death? Therefore we have been buried with him by baptism into death so that, as Christ was raised from the dead by the glory of the Father, we too might walk in newness of life.

Romans 6. 3-4

Week 3 & Tuesdays in the Kingdom Season

The angel of God who went before the host of Israel army moved and went behind them; and the pillar of cloud moved from in front of them and stood behind them. It came between the host of Egypt and the host of Israel. And there was the cloud and the darkness one did not come near the other all night.

Exodus 14. 19-20

Week 4 & Wednesdays in the Kingdom Season

God said to Moses, 'I will take you for my people and I will be your God: you shall know that I am the Lord your God, who has brought you out from under the burdens of the Egyptians. I will bring you into the land which I swore to give to Abraham, to Isaac and to Jacob; I will give it to you for a possession. I am the Lord.' But Moses said to the Lord, 'Behold, the people of Israel have not listened to me: how then shall Pharaoh listen to me, who am a man of uncircumcised lips?' But the Lord spoke to Moses and Aaron and gave them a charge to the people of Israel and to Pharaoh King of Egypt to bring the people out of the land of Egypt.

Exodus 6. 7-8, 12-13

Week 5 & Thursdays in the Kingdom Season

Therefore, since we are surrounded by so great a cloud of witnesses, let us also lay aside every weight and the sin that clings so closely, and let us run with perseverance the race that is set before us, looking to Jesus the pioneer and perfecter of our faith, who for the sake of the joy that was set before him endured the cross, despising the shame, and is seated at the right hand of the throne of God. Consider him who endured such hostility against himself from sinners, so that you may not grow weary or lose heart. In your struggle against sin you have not yet resisted to the point of shedding your blood. *Hebrews 12. 1-4*

Week 6 & Fridays in the Kingdom Season

Not that I have already obtained this or have already reached the goal, but I press on to make it my own, because Christ Jesus has made me his own. Belovèd, I do not consider that I have made it my own, but this one thing I do: forgetting what lies behind and straining forward to what lies ahead, I press on toward the goal for the prize of the upward call of God in Christ Jesus.

Philippians 3. 12-14

Week 7 & Saturdays in the Kingdom Season

Job said, 'Where shall wisdom be found, and where is the place of understanding? Mortals do not know the way to it and it is not found in the land of the living. God understands the way of it and he knows its place. For he looks to the ends of the earth and sees everything under the heavens. And he said, "Truly, the fear of the Lord, that is wisdom; and to depart from evil is understanding." ' *Job 28. 12-13, 23-24, 28*

*   *   *

This RESPONSE to the reading may be used:
I will sing for ever of your love, O Lord;
My lips shall proclaim your faithfulness.

THE GOSPEL CANTICLE: THE BENEDICTUS

1 Blessèd are you, Lord, the God of Israel,*
   you have come to your people and set them free.

2 You have raised up for us a mighty Saviour,*
   born of the house of your servant, David.

3 Through your holy prophets, you promised of old*
   to save us from our enemies,
      from the hands of all who hate us,

4 To show mercy to our forebears,*
   and to remember your holy covenant.

5 This was the oath you swore to our father, Abraham,*
   to set us free from the hands of our enemies,

6 Free to worship you without fear,*
   holy and righteous before you,
      all the days of our life.

7 And you, child,
      shall be called the prophet of the Most High,*
   for you will go before the Lord to prepare the way,

8 To give God's people knowledge of salvation*
   by the forgiveness of their sins.

9 In the tender compassion of our God*
   the dawn from on high shall break upon us,

10 To shine on those who dwell in darkness
      and the shadow of death,*
   and to guide our feet into the way of peace. *Luke 1. 68-79*

   **Glory to the Father, and to the Son,
      and to the Holy Spirit:***
   **as it was in the beginning, is now,
      and shall be for ever. Amen.**

THE PRAYERS

Intercession and thanksgiving are offered in free prayer or in silence, ending with the following:

Exalt yourself, O God, above the heavens,
and your glory over all the earth.
Lord, have mercy.

May the fields of the wilderness be rich pasture
and the hills be clothed with joy.
Christ, have mercy.

Send out your light and your truth, that they may lead us,
and bring us to your holy hill and to your dwelling.
Lord, have mercy.

THE COLLECT for Saturdays:

Merciful God, you have prepared for those who love you
such good things as pass our understanding:
pour into our hearts such love towards you
that we, loving you above all things,
may obtain your promises, which exceed all that we can desire;
through Jesus Christ our Lord . . .   3/5

Or for the Kingdom Season:

Almighty God, you have knit together your elect
into one communion and fellowship
in the mystical body of your Son Christ our Lord:
give us grace so to follow your blessèd saints
in all virtuous and godly living
that we may come to those inexpressible joys
which you have prepared for those who truly love you;
through Jesus Christ our Lord . . .   1⟩

THE LORD'S PRAYER may be said.

Let us bless the Lord.
Thanks be to God.

Evening Prayer - Form 7

Saturday and daily in the Kingdom Season

THE BLESSING OF THE LIGHT

Let us give thanks to our God, who has delivered us
from the dominion of darkness and made us partakers
in the inheritance of the saints in light.

The light and peace of Jesus Christ be with you all
And also with you.

Let us give thanks to the Lord our God
Who is worthy of all thanksgiving and praise.

Blessèd are you, Sovereign God, our light and our salvation,
eternal Creator of day and night,
to you be glory and praise for ever!
As we look for your coming in glory,
wash away our transgressions,
cleanse us by your refining fire
and make us temples of your Holy Spirit.
By the light of Christ, dispel the darkness of our hearts
and make us ready to enter your kingdom,
where songs of praise for ever sound,
Father, Son and Holy Spirit:
Blessèd be God for ever!

A SONG OF THE LIGHT

1   Hail, gladdening Light, of his pure glory poured,
    Who is the immortal Father, heavenly, blest,
    Holiest of Holies, Jesus Christ our Lord.

2   Now we are come to the Sun's hour of rest,
    The lights of evening round us shine;
    We hymn the Father, Son and Holy Spirit divine.

3   Worthy are you at all times to be sung
    With undefilèd tongue,
    Son of our God, giver of life, alone;
    Therefore in all the world your glories, Lord, they own.

THE WORD OF GOD

Week 1 & Sundays in the Kingdom – Psalm 17

1   Hear my plea of innocence, O Lord;
        give heed to my cry;*
    listen to my prayer,
        which does not come from lying lips.

2   Let my vindication come forth from your presence;*
    let your eyes be fixed on justice.

3   Weigh my heart, summon me by night,*
    melt me down; you will find no impurity in me.

4   I give no offence with my mouth as others do;*
    I have heeded the words of your lips.

5   My footsteps hold fast to the ways of your law;*
    in your paths my feet shall not stumble.

6   I call upon you, O God, for you will answer me;*
    incline your ear to me and hear my words.

7   Show me your marvellous loving-kindness,*
    O Saviour of those who take refuge at your right hand
        from those who rise up against them.

8   Keep me as the apple of your eye;*
    hide me under the shadow of your wings,

9   From the wicked who assault me,*
    from my deadly enemies who surround me.

10 They have closed their heart to pity,*
    and their mouth speaks proud things.

11 They press me hard, now they surround me,*
    watching how they may cast me to the ground,

12 Like a lion, greedy for its prey,*
    and like a young lion lurking in secret places.

13 Arise, O Lord; confront them and bring them down;*
    deliver me from the wicked by your sword.

14 Deliver me, O Lord, by your hand*
    from those whose portion in life is this world;

15 Whose bellies you fill with your treasure,*
   who are well supplied with children
     and leave their wealth to their little ones.

16 But at my vindication I shall see your face;*
   when I awake, I shall be satisfied,
     beholding your likeness.

Cast your eyes upon us, O Lord,
and hide us under the shadow of your wings,
that, trusting not to our own works
but in the refining fire of your compassion,
we may come to see you face to face;
through Jesus Christ our Lord. **Amen.**   14

Week 2 & Mondays in the Kingdom – Psalm 15

1 Lord, who may dwell in your tabernacle?*
   who may abide upon your holy hill?

2 Whoever leads a blameless life and does what is right,*
   who speaks the truth from his heart.

3 There is no guile upon his tongue;
   he does no evil to his friend;*
   he does not heap contempt upon his neighbour.

4 In his sight the wicked is rejected,*
   but he honours those who fear the Lord.

5 He has sworn to do no wrong*
   and does not take back his word.

6 He does not give his money in hope of gain,*
   nor does he take a bribe against the innocent.

7 Whoever does these things*
   shall never be overthrown.

Establish, O Christ, your kingdom in our hearts
and keep us untainted by this earthly life;
that in your Father's house we may be received
   into the eternal habitations;
where you are alive and reign,
now and for ever. **Amen.**   14

Week 3 & Tuesdays in the Kingdom – from Psalm 73

1   Truly, God is good to Israel,*
    to those who are pure in heart.

2   But as for me, my feet had nearly slipped;*
    I had almost tripped and fallen;

3   Because I envied the proud*
    and saw the prosperity of the wicked:

13 In vain have I kept my heart clean,*
    and washed my hands in innocence.

14 I have been afflicted all day long,*
    and punished every morning.

15 Had I gone on speaking this way,*
    I should have betrayed the generation of your children.

16 When I tried to understand these things,*
    it was too hard for me;

17 Until I entered the sanctuary of God*
    and discerned the end of the wicked.

18 Surely, you set them in slippery places;*
    you cast them down in ruin.

19 O how suddenly do they come to destruction,*
    come to an end and perish from terror!

20 Like a dream when one awakens, O Lord,*
    when you arise you will make their image vanish.

21 When my mind became embittered,*
    I was sorely wounded in my heart.

22 I was stupid and had no understanding;*
    I was like a brute beast in your presence.

23 Yet I am always with you;*
    you hold me by my right hand.

24 You will guide me by your counsel,*
    and afterwards receive me with glory.

25 Whom have I in heaven but you?*
    and having you I desire nothing upon earth.

26 Though my flesh and my heart should waste away,*
    God is the strength of my heart and my portion for ever.

27 Truly, those who forsake you will perish;*
   you destroy all who are unfaithful.

28 But it is good for me to be near God;*
   I have made the Lord God my refuge.

29 I will speak of all your works*
   in the gates of the city of Zion.

   Holy God, to whom our love rightly belongs,
   may we find true wisdom in your presence
   and set our hope not on uncertain riches
   but on the love that will hold us to the end,
   on Jesus Christ our Lord. **Amen.**   19

Week 4 & Wednesdays in the Kingdom – Psalm 77

1 I will cry aloud to God;*
   I will cry aloud and he will hear me.

2 In the day of my trouble I sought the Lord;*
   my hands were stretched out by night and did not tire;
      I refused to be comforted.

3 I think of God, I am restless,*
   I ponder and my spirit faints.

4 You will not let my eyelids close;*
   I am troubled and I cannot speak.

5 I consider the days of old;*
   I remember the years long past;

6 I commune with my heart in the night;*
   I ponder and search my mind.

7 Will the Lord cast me off for ever?*
   will he no more show his favour?

8 Has his loving-kindness come to an end for ever?*
   has his promise failed for evermore?

9 Has God forgotten to be gracious?*
   has he, in his anger, withheld his compassion?

10 And I said, 'My grief is this:*
   the right hand of the Most High has lost its power.'

11 I will remember the works of the Lord,*
    and call to mind your wonders of old time.

12 I will meditate on all your acts*
    and ponder your mighty deeds.

13 Your way, O God, is holy;*
    who is so great a god as our God?

14 You are the God who works wonders*
    and have declared your power among the peoples.

15 By your strength you have redeemed your people,*
    the children of Jacob and Joseph.

16 The waters saw you, O God;
        the waters saw you and trembled;*
    the very depths were shaken.

17 The clouds poured out water; the skies thundered;*
    your arrows flashed to and fro;

18 The sound of your thunder was in the whirlwind;
        your lightnings lit up the world;*
    the earth trembled and shook.

19 Your way was in the sea,
        and your paths in the great waters,*
    yet your footsteps were not seen.

20 You led your people like a flock*
    by the hand of Moses and Aaron.

Majestic God,
you led your people like a flock
and delivered them by your mighty power
    in times of old:
do not forget your people in their troubles
and raise up your power
to sustain the poor and helpless,
for the honour of your Name. **Amen.**   18

1   I will bless the Lord at all times;*
      his praise shall ever be in my mouth.

2   I will glory in the Lord;*
      let the humble hear and rejoice.

3   Proclaim with me the greatness of the Lord;*
      let us exalt his name together.

4   I sought the Lord and he answered me*
      and delivered me out of all my terror.

5   Look upon him and be radiant,*
      and let not your faces be ashamed.

6   I called in my affliction and the Lord heard me*
      and saved me from all my troubles.

7   The angel of the Lord
      encompasses those who fear him,*
      and he will deliver them.

8   Taste and see that the Lord is good;*
      happy are they who trust in him!

9   Fear the Lord, you that are his saints,*
      for those who fear him lack nothing.

10   The young lions lack and suffer hunger,*
      but those who seek the Lord
      lack nothing that is good.

11   Come, children, and listen to me;*
      I will teach you the fear of the Lord.

12   Who among you loves life*
      and desires long life to enjoy prosperity?

13   Keep your tongue from evil speaking*
      and your lips from lying words.

14   Turn from evil and do good;*
      seek peace and pursue it.

15   The eyes of the Lord are upon the righteous,*
      and his ears are open to their cry.

16   The face of the Lord is against those who do evil,*
      to root out the remembrance of them from the earth.

17 The righteous cry and the Lord hears them*
   and delivers them from all their troubles.

18 The Lord is near to the brokenhearted*
   and will save those whose spirits are crushed.

19 Many are the troubles of the righteous,*
   but the Lord will deliver him out of them all.

20 He will keep safe all his bones;*
   not one of them shall be broken.

21 Evil shall slay the wicked,*
   and those who hate the righteous will be punished.

22 The Lord ransoms the life of his servants,*
   and none will be punished who trust in him.

Send your holy angels to watch over us,
O loving God,
that on our lips will be found your truth
and in our hearts your love;
for his sake who died for love of our love,
even Jesus Christ our Saviour. **Amen.**   7

1   Give judgement for me, O God,
        and defend my cause against an ungodly people;*
    deliver me from the deceitful and the wicked.

2   For you are the God of my strength;
        why have you put me from you?*
    and why do I go so heavily
        while the enemy oppresses me?

3   Send out your light and your truth,
        that they may lead me,*
    and bring me to your holy hill
        and to your dwelling;

4   That I may go to the altar of God,
        to the God of my joy and gladness;*
    and on the harp I will give thanks to you,
        O God my God.

5   Why are you so full of heaviness, O my soul?*
    and why are you so disquieted within me?

6   Put your trust in God;*
    for I will yet give thanks to him,
        who is the help of my countenance, and my God.

Receive at your heavenly altar, O God,
the supplication of your people;
lead us into the way of truth and purify our hearts
that we may come before you,
who are our joy and our gladness;
through Jesus Christ our Lord. **Amen.**   14

Week 7 & Saturdays in the Kingdom – Psalm 16

1   Protect me, O God, for I take refuge in you;*
    I have said to the Lord, 'You are my Lord,
      my good above all other.'

2   All my delight is upon the godly that are in the land,*
    upon those who are noble among the people.

3   But those who run after other gods*
    shall have their troubles multiplied.

4   Their libations of blood I will not offer,*
    nor take the names of their gods upon my lips.

5   O Lord, you are my portion and my cup;*
    it is you who uphold my lot.

6   My boundaries enclose a pleasant land;*
    indeed, I have a goodly heritage.

7   I will bless the Lord who gives me counsel;*
    my heart teaches me, night after night.

8   I have set the Lord always before me;*
    because he is at my right hand I shall not fall.

9   My heart, therefore, is glad and my spirit rejoices;*
    my body also shall rest in hope.

10 For you will not abandon me to the grave,*
    nor let your holy one see the Pit.

11 You will show me the path of life;*
    in your presence there is fullness of joy,
    and in your right hand are pleasures for evermore.

O Lord, who did not abandon your Faithful One in the Pit
but raised him victorious from the grave:
show the path of life
    to those redeemed as his own possession,
that they may attain to the fullness of joy;
through Jesus Christ our Lord. **Amen.**   14

THE NEW TESTAMENT CANTICLE
Either: A SONG OF THE BLESSED

1   Blessèd are the poor in spirit,*
      for theirs is the kingdom of heaven.

2   Blessèd are those who mourn,*
      for they shall be comforted.

3   Blessèd are the meek,*
      for they shall inherit the earth.

4   Blessèd are those who hunger
        and thirst for what is right,*
      for they shall be satisfied.

5   Blessèd are the merciful,*
      for mercy shall be shown to them.

6   Blessèd are the pure in heart,*
      for they shall see God.

7   Blessèd are the peacemakers,*
      for they shall be called the children of God.

8   Blessèd are those who are persecuted
        for righteousness' sake,*
      for theirs is the kingdom of heaven.   *Matthew 5. 3-10*

   **Glory to the Father, and to the Son,
      and to the Holy Spirit:***
   **as it was in the beginning, is now,
      and shall be for ever. Amen.**

Or: A SONG OF THE REDEEMED

1   Behold, a great multitude*
    which no one could number,

2   From every nation,
        from all tribes and peoples and tongues,*
    standing before the throne and the Lamb.

3   They were clothed in white robes
        and had palms in their hands,*
    and they cried with a loud voice, saying,

4   'Salvation belongs to our God*
    who sits on the throne,
        and to the Lamb.'

5   These are they
        who have come out of the great tribulation,*
    they have washed their robes
        and made them white in the blood of the Lamb;

6   Therefore they stand before the throne of God,*
    whom they serve day and night within the temple.

7   And the One who sits upon the throne*
    will shelter them with his presence.

8   They shall never again feel hunger or thirst,*
    the sun shall not strike them,
        nor any scorching heat.

9   For the Lamb at the heart of the throne*
    will be their Shepherd,

10 He will guide them to springs of living water,*
    and God will wipe away every tear from their eyes.

    To the One who sits on the throne and to the Lamb*
    be blessing and honour and glory and might,
        for ever and ever. Amen.   *From Revelation 7*

THE SCRIPTURE READING

Week 1 & Sundays in the Kingdom Season

When evening had come, and since it was the day of Preparation, that is, the day before the sabbath, Joseph of Arimathea, a respected member of the council, who was also himself waiting expectantly for the kingdom of God, went boldly to Pilate and asked for the body of Jesus. Then Joseph brought a linen cloth and, taking down the body, wrapped it in the linen cloth and laid it in a tomb that had been hewn out of the rock. He then rolled a stone against the door of the tomb. *Mark 15. 42-43, 46*

Week 2 & Mondays in the Kingdom Season

This is the covenant that I will make with the house of Israel after those days, says the Lord: I will put my law within them and I will write it on their hearts. I will be their God and they shall be my people. No longer shall they teach one another or say to each other, 'Know the Lord', for they shall all know me, from the least of them to the greatest, says the Lord; for I will forgive their iniquity and remember their sin no more.
Jeremiah 31. 33-34

Week 3 & Tuesdays in the Kingdom Season

Jesus said, 'When the Son of Man comes in his glory, and all the angels with him, then he will sit on the throne of his glory. The king will say to those at his right hand, "Come, O blessèd of my Father, inherit the kingdom prepared for you from the foundation of the world; for I was hungry and you gave me food, was thirsty and you gave me drink, I was a stranger and you welcomed me, I was naked and you clothed me, I was sick and you visited me, I was in prison and you came to me." '
Matthew 25. 31, 34-36

Week 4 & Wednesdays in the Kingdom Season

So we do not lose heart. Though our outer nature is wasting away, our inner nature is being renewed every day. For this slight momentary affliction is preparing for us an eternal weight of glory beyond all comparison, because we look not to the things that are seen but to the things that are unseen; for the things that are seen are transient, but the things that are unseen are eternal.

2 Corinthians 4. 16-18

Week 5 & Thursdays in the Kingdom Season

One of the criminals who were hanged there kept deriding Jesus and saying, 'Are you not the Messiah? Save yourself and us!' But the other rebuked him, saying, 'Do you not fear God, since you are under the same sentence of condemnation? And we indeed have been condemned justly, for we are getting what we deserve for our deeds, but this man has done nothing wrong.' Then he said, 'Jesus, remember me when you come into your kingdom.' He replied, 'Truly I tell you, today you will be with me in Paradise.'

Luke 23. 39-43

Week 6 & Fridays in the Kingdom Season

I will recount the gracious deeds of the Lord, the praiseworthy acts of the Lord, because of all that the Lord has done for us and the great favour to the house of Israel that he has shown them according to his mercy, according to the abundance of his steadfast love. For he said, 'Surely they are my people, children who will not deal falsely'; and he became their saviour in all their distress. It was no messenger or angel but his presence that saved them; in his love and in his pity he redeemed them; he lifted them up and carried them all the days of old.

Isaiah 63. 7-9

Week 7 & Saturdays in the Kingdom Season

Jesus said to Thomas, 'I am the way and the truth and the life. No one comes to the Father except through me. If you know me, you will know my Father also. From now on you do know him and have seen him.'

John 14. 6

*　　　*　　　*

This RESPONSE to the reading may be used:
Lord, you will guide me by your counsel
And afterwards receive me with glory.

THE GOSPEL CANTICLE: THE MAGNIFICAT

1   My soul proclaims the greatness of the Lord,*
    my spirit rejoices in God my Saviour,

2   For you, Lord, have looked with favour
        on your lowly servant.*
    From this day all generations will call me blessèd:

3   You, the Almighty, have done great things for me*
    and holy is your name.

4   You have mercy on those who fear you,*
    from generation to generation.

5   You have shown strength with your arm*
    and scattered the proud in their conceit,

6   Casting down the mighty from their thrones*
    and lifting up the lowly.

7   You have filled the hungry with good things*
    and sent the rich away empty.

8   You have come to the aid of your servant, Israel,*
    to remember the promise of mercy,

9   The promise made to our forebears,*
    to Abraham and his children for ever.   *Luke 1. 46-55*

    **Glory to the Father, and to the Son,
        and to the Holy Spirit:***
    **as it was in the beginning, is now,
        and shall be for ever. Amen.**

THE PRAYERS

Intercession and thanksgiving are offered in free prayer or in silence, ending with the following:

Remember, O Lord, your compassion and love,
for they are from everlasting.
Lord, have mercy.

Let the sorrowful sighing of the prisoners come before you;
and by your great might, spare those who are condemned to die.
Christ, have mercy.

Lord, give strength to your people,
and give us your blessing of peace.
Lord, have mercy.

THE COLLECT for Saturdays:

Grant, Lord,
that we who are baptised into the death
  of your Son our Saviour Jesus Christ
may continually put to death our evil desires
  and be buried with him;
that through the grave and gate of death
we may pass to our joyful resurrection;
through his merits, who died and was buried
  and rose again for us,
your Son Jesus Christ our Lord. **Amen.**   3

Or for the Kingdom Season:

O God,
who in the work of creation
commanded the light to shine out of darkness:
we pray that the light of the glorious gospel of Christ
may shine into the hearts of all your people,
dispelling the darkness of ignorance and unbelief
and revealing to them the knowledge of your glory
in the face of Jesus Christ our Lord . . .   17

THE LORD'S PRAYER may be said.

Let us bless the Lord.
Thanks be to God.

Night Prayer

THE PREPARATION

The Lord almighty grant us a quiet night and a perfect end.
Amen.

Our help is in the name of the Lord
Who made heaven and earth.

A period of silence follows, for reflection on the past day.
Words of penitence may be used; the following or some other.

Most merciful God,
we confess to you,
before the whole company of heaven
and one another,
that we have sinned in thought, word and deed,
and in what we have failed to do.
Forgive us our sins,
heal us by your Spirit
and raise us to new life in Christ. Amen.

Or:

Holy God,
holy and strong,
holy and immortal:
have mercy on us.

O God, make speed to save us.
O Lord, make haste to help us.

Glory to the Father, and to the Son,
and to the Holy Spirit:*
as it was in the beginning, is now,
and shall be for ever. Amen.

Alleluia!

A HYMN may be sung, the following or some other.

Before the ending of the day,
Creator of the world, we pray
That you, with steadfast love, would keep
Your watch around us while we sleep.

From evil dreams defend our sight,
From fears and terrors of the night;
Tread under foot our deadly foe
That we no sinful thought may know.

O Father, that we ask be done
Through Jesus Christ, your only Son;
And Holy Spirit, by whose breath
Our souls are raised to life from death. Amen.

THE WORD OF GOD

THE PSALMODY
One or more of the following psalms may be used.

PSALM 4

1 Answer me when I call, O God, defender of my cause;*
   you set me free when I am hard-pressed;
      have mercy on me and hear my prayer.

2 'You mortals, how long will you dishonour my glory;*
   how long will you worship dumb idols
      and run after false gods?'

3 Know that the Lord does wonders for the faithful;*
   when I call upon the Lord, he will hear me.

4 Tremble, then, and do not sin;*
   speak to your heart in silence upon your bed.

5 Offer the appointed sacrifices*
   and put your trust in the Lord.

6 Many are saying,
      'O that we might see better times!'*
   lift up the light of your countenance upon us, O Lord.

7 You have put gladness in my heart*
   more than when grain and wine and oil increase.

8 I lie down in peace; at once I fall asleep;*
   for only you, Lord, make me dwell in safety.

PSALM 91

1 He who dwells in the shelter of the Most High,*
   abides under the shadow of the Almighty.

2   He shall say to the Lord,
      'You are my refuge and my stronghold,*
  my God in whom I put my trust.'

3   He shall deliver you from the snare of the hunter*
  and from the deadly pestilence.

4   He shall cover you with his pinions
      and you shall find refuge under his wings;*
  his faithfulness shall be a shield and buckler.

5   You shall not be afraid of any terror by night,*
  nor of the arrow that flies by day;

6   Of the plague that stalks in the darkness,*
  nor of the sickness that lays waste at midday.

7   A thousand shall fall at your side
      and ten thousand at your right hand,*
  but it shall not come near you.

8   Your eyes have only to behold*
  to see the reward of the wicked.

9   Because you have made the Lord your refuge,*
  and the Most High your habitation,

10 There shall no evil happen to you,*
  neither shall any plague come near your dwelling.

11 For he shall give his angels charge over you,*
  to keep you in all your ways.

12 They shall bear you in their hands,*
  lest you dash your foot against a stone.

13 You shall tread upon the lion and adder;*
  you shall trample the young lion and the serpent
      under your feet.

14 'Because he is bound to me in love
      therefore will I deliver him;*
  I will protect him, because he knows my name.

15 'He shall call upon me and I will answer him;*
  I am with him in trouble;
      I will rescue him and bring him to honour.

16 'With long life will I satisfy him,*
  and show him my salvation.'

PSALM 134

1   Behold now, bless the Lord,
     all you servants of the Lord,*
   you that stand by night in the house of the Lord.

2   Lift up your hands in the holy place and bless the Lord;*
     the Lord who made heaven and earth
     bless you out of Zion.

Each psalm, or the group of psalms, may end with:

   **Glory to the Father, and to the Son,
     and to the Holy Spirit:***
   **as it was in the beginning, is now,
     and shall be for ever. Amen.**

THE SCRIPTURE READING: the following or some other
                              (see page 232).

You, Lord, are in the midst of us and we are called by your
name; leave us not, O Lord our God.   *Jeremiah 14. 9*

Or:

You will keep them in perfect peace, whose minds are stayed on
you; because they trust in you.   *Isaiah 26. 3*

THE RESPONSORY may be said.

Into your hands, O Lord,
  I commend my spirit. (Alleluia! Alleluia!)
Into your hands, O Lord,
  I commend my spirit. (Alleluia! Alleluia!)

For you have redeemed me, Lord God of truth.
I commend my spirit. (*Or:* Alleluia! Alleluia!)

Glory to the Father, and to the Son,
  and to the Holy Spirit:
Into your hands, O Lord,
  I commend my spirit. (Alleluia! Alleluia!)

Keep me as the apple of your eye.
Hide me under the shadow of your wings.

THE GOSPEL CANTICLE: THE NUNC DIMITTIS

Refrain: **Save us,* O Lord, while waking,**
and guard us while sleeping,
that awake we may watch with Christ,
and asleep may rest in peace.

Or, on feasts:

Grant us your light, O Lord,*
that the darkness of our hearts being overcome,
we may receive the true light,
even Christ our Saviour.

1   Now, Lord, you let your servant go in peace:*
your word has been fulfilled.

2   My own eyes have seen the salvation*
which you have prepared in the sight of every people;

3   A light to reveal you to the nations*
and the glory of your people Israel.

Glory to the Father, and to the Son,
and to the Holy Spirit:*
as it was in the beginning, is now,
and shall be for ever. Amen.

The refrain is repeated after the canticle.

THE PRAYERS

Intercessions and thanksgivings are offered here.

THE COLLECT: the following or some other (see page 233).
Lighten our darkness,
Lord, we pray;
and in your mercy defend us
from all perils and dangers of this night;
for the love of your only Son,
our Saviour Jesus Christ. **Amen.**   3

THE LORD'S PRAYER may be said.

A devotional ANTHEM may be sung here, or after the blessing.

THE BLESSING

In peace, we will lie down and sleep;
For you alone, Lord, make us dwell in safety.

Abide with us, Lord Jesus,
For the night is at hand and the day is now past.

As the night-watch looks for the morning,
So do we look for you, O Christ.

[Come with the dawning of the day
**And make yourself known
  in the breaking of the bread.]**

The Lord bless us and watch over us;
the Lord make his face shine upon us
   and be gracious to us;
the Lord look kindly on us
   and give us peace. **Amen.**

ALTERNATIVE SCRIPTURE READINGS

SUNDAYS

The servants of the Lamb shall see the face of God, whose name will be on their foreheads. There will be no more night: they will not need the light of a lamp or the light of the sun, for God will be their light; and they will reign for ever and ever.

Revelation 22. 4-5

MONDAYS

In returning and rest, you shall be saved; in quietness and trust shall be your strength. *Isaiah 30. 15*

TUESDAYS

Watch, therefore – for you do not know when the master of the house will come, in the evening, or at midnight, or at cockcrow, or in the morning – lest he come suddenly and find you asleep. And what I say to you I say to all: Watch.

Mark 13. 35-end

WEDNESDAYS

In him was life, and the life was the light of all. The light shines in the darkness and the darkness has not overcome it.

John 1. 4-5

THURSDAYS

Be sober, be vigilant, because your adversary the devil is prowling round like a roaring lion, seeking whom he may devour. Resist him, strong in the faith. *1 Peter 5. 8, 9*

FRIDAYS

God has not destined us to the terrors of judgement but to the full attainment of salvation through our Lord Jesus Christ, who died for us, so that whether we wake or sleep, we might live with him. *1 Thessalonians 5. 9-10*

SATURDAYS

There remains a sabbath rest for the people of God; for those who enter God's rest also cease from their labours, as God did. Let us, therefore, strive to enter that rest. *Hebrews 4. 9-11*

ALTERNATIVE COLLECTS

Be present, O merciful God,
and protect us through the silent hours of this night,
so that we who are wearied by the changes
    and chances of this fleeting world,
may rest upon your eternal changelessness;
through Jesus Christ our Lord. **Amen.**   6›

Look down, O God,
from your heavenly throne,
illuminate the darkness of this night
with your celestial brightness,
and from the children of light
banish the deeds of darkness;
through Jesus Christ our Saviour. **Amen.**   6›

Visit this place, O Lord, we pray,
and drive far from it all the snares of the enemy;
may your holy angels dwell with us
    and guard us in peace
and may your blessing be always upon us;
through Jesus Christ our Lord. **Amen.**   6›

Keep watch, dear Lord,
with those who wake, or watch or weep this night,
and give your angels charge over those who sleep.
Tend the sick,
give rest to the weary,
sustain the dying, calm the suffering,
and pity the distressed;
all for your love's sake,
O Christ our Redeemer. **Amen.**   *St Augustine*

SUNDAYS & EASTER

Almighty God,
by triumphing over the powers of darkness
Christ has prepared a place for us
  in the new Jerusalem:
may we, who have this day given thanks
  for his resurrection,
praise him in the eternal city
of which he is the light;
through Jesus Christ our Lord . . .   17

MONDAYS & PENTECOST

Come, O Spirit of God,
and make within us your dwelling place and home.
May our darkness be dispelled by your light,
and our troubles calmed by your peace;
may all evil be redeemed by your love,
all pain transformed through the suffering of Christ,
and all dying glorified in his risen life. **Amen.**   6›

TUESDAYS & ADVENT

Stir up your power, O God,
and come among us.
Heal our wounds,
calm our fears
and give us peace;
through Jesus our Redeemer. **Amen.**   7

WEDNESDAYS & CHRISTMAS

We give you thanks, O God,
for the gift to the world of our Redeemer;
as we sing your glory at the close of this day,
so may we know his presence in our hearts,
who is our Saviour and our Lord,
now and for ever. **Amen.**   7

THURSDAYS & EPIPHANY

King of kings and Lord of lords,
making the true light to shine:
lighten our darkness now and evermore
that with our lips
   and in our lives
we may praise you;
for you are our God, now and for ever. **Amen.**   7

FRIDAYS

Lord Jesus Christ, Son of the living God,
who at this evening hour lay in the tomb
and so hallowed the grave
to be a bed of hope
for all who put their trust in you:
give us such sorrow for our sins,
which were the cause of your passion,
that, when our bodies lie in the dust,
our souls may live with you for ever. **Amen.**   6›

LENT

Almighty God,
may we, by the prayer and discipline of Lent,
enter into the mystery of Christ's sufferings;
that by following in the Way,
we may come to share in the glory;
through Jesus Christ our Lord. **Amen.**   7

PASSIONTIDE

Almighty God,
as we stand at the foot of the cross of your Son,
help us to see and know your love for us,
so that in humility, love and joy
we may place at his feet
all that we have and all that we are;
through Jesus Christ our Saviour. **Amen.**   7

SATURDAYS

Come to visit us, O God, this night,
so that by your strength
we may rise with the new day
to rejoice in the resurrection of your Son,
Jesus Christ our Saviour. **Amen.**   7

A LATIN HYMN BEFORE SLEEP – *SALVE REGINA*

*Traditionally, this anthem is sung at the end of Night Prayer
from after Pentecost to Advent, or it may be the unchanging
final anthem at Night Prayer. This loose English translation
can be made to fit the same plainsong music.*

Salve, Regina, mater misericordiæ;
Hail, Holy Queen, Mother of mercy;

vita, dulcedo, et spes nostra, salve.
Hail, our life, our sweetness and our hope.

Ad te clamamus, exsules, filii Evæ,
To you do we cry, the banished children of Eve;

ad te suspiramus,
to you do we send up our sighs,

gementes et flentes in hac lacrimarum valle;
mourning and weeping in this vale of tears;

eia, ergo, advocata nostra,
turn then, most gracious advocate,

illos tuos misericordes oculos ad nos converte,
your eyes of mercy towards us,

Et Iesum, benedictum fructum ventris tui,
and, after this our exile, show unto us

nobis post hoc exsilium ostende,
the blessèd fruit of your womb, Jesus,

O clemens, O pia, O dulcis Virgo Maria.
O tender, O loving, O sweet Virgin Mary.

Additional Canticles

1 *A SONG OF SOLOMON*

1 Set me as a seal upon your heart,*
    as a seal upon your arm;

2 For love is strong as death
    passion fierce as the grave;*
 its flashes are flashes of fire,
    a raging flame.

3 Many waters cannot quench love,*
 neither can the floods drown it.

4 If all the wealth of our house
    were offered for love,*
 it would be utterly scorned. *Song of Songs 8. 7-8*

   **Glory to the Father, and to the Son,
    and to the Holy Spirit:***
 **as it was in the beginning, is now,
    and shall be for ever. Amen.**

2 *A SONG OF PEACE*

1 Come, let us go up to the mountain of God,*
 to the house of the God of Jacob;

2 That God may teach us his ways,*
 and that we may walk in his paths.

3 For the law shall go out from Zion,*
 and the word of the Lord from Jerusalem.

4 God shall mediate between the nations,*
 and shall judge for many peoples.

5 They shall beat their swords into ploughshares,*
 and their spears into pruning hooks.

6 Nation shall not lift up sword against nation,*
 neither shall they learn war any more.

7 O people of Jacob, come:*
 let us walk in the light of the Lord. *Isaiah 2. 3-5*

   **Glory to the Father, and to the Son,
    and to the Holy Spirit:***
 **as it was in the beginning, is now,
    and shall be for ever. Amen.**

3   *A SONG OF JERUSALEM OUR MOTHER*

1   'Rejoice with Jerusalem and be glad for her*
    all you who love her', says the Lord.

2   'Rejoice with her in joy,*
    all you who mourn over her,

3   'That you may drink deeply with delight*
    from her consoling breast.'

4   For thus says our God,*
    'You shall be nursed and carried on her arm.

5   'As a mother comforts her children,*
    so I will comfort you;

6   'You shall see and your heart shall rejoice;*
    you shall flourish like the grass of the fields.' *From Isaiah 66*

**Glory to the Father, and to the Son,
    and to the Holy Spirit:***
**as it was in the beginning, is now,
    and shall be for ever. Amen.**

4   *A SONG OF LAMENTATION*

1   Is it nothing to you, all you who pass by?*
    Look and see if there is any sorrow like my sorrow;

2   Which was brought upon me,*
    which the Lord inflicted
        on the day of his fierce anger.

3   For these things I weep;
        my eyes flow with tears;*
    for a comforter is far from me,
        one to revive my courage;

4   Remember my affliction and my bitterness,*
    the wormwood and the gall!

5   The steadfast love of the Lord never ceases,*
    his mercies never come to an end;

6   They are new every morning;*
    great is thy faithfulness.

7   'The Lord is my portion', says my soul,*
    'therefore I will hope in him.'

8   The Lord is good to those who wait for him,*
    to the soul that seeks him.

9   It is good that we should wait quietly*
    for the salvation of the Lord.

10 It is good to bear the yoke in our youth;*
    to sit alone in silence when it is laid upon us.

11 For the Lord will not reject for ever,*
    though he causes grief, he will have compassion,

12 According to the abundance of his steadfast love;*
    for he does not willingly afflict or grieve anyone.
                                    From Lamentations 1 & 3

    Glory to the Father, and to the Son,
      and to the Holy Spirit:*
    as it was in the beginning, is now,
      and shall be for ever. Amen.

5   *A SONG OF NEW LIFE*

1   I called to you, O God, out of my distress
      and you answered me;*
    out of the belly of Sheol I cried,
      and you heard my voice.

2   You cast me into the deep,
      into the heart of the seas,*
    and the flood surrounded me,
      all your waves and billows passed over me.

3   Then I said, I am driven away from your sight;*
    how shall I ever look again upon your holy temple?

4   The waters closed in over me,
      the deep was round about me;*
    weeds were wrapped around my head
      at the roots of the mountains.

5   I went down to the land beneath the earth,*
    yet you brought up my life from the depths, O God.

6   As my life was ebbing away, I remembered you, O God,*
    and my prayer came to you, into your holy temple.

7   With the voice of thanksgiving, I will sacrifice to you;*
    what I have vowed I will pay,
      for deliverance belongs to the Lord!   *Jonah 2. 2-9*

    Glory to the Father, and to the Son,
      and to the Holy Spirit:*
    as it was in the beginning, is now,
      and shall be for ever. Amen.

6   *A SONG OF THE RIGHTEOUS*

1   The souls of the righteous are in the hand of God*
    and no torment will ever touch them.

2   In the eyes of the foolish, they seem to have died;*
    but they are at peace.

3   For though, in the sight of others, they were punished,*
    their hope is of immortality.

4   Having been disciplined a little,
      they will receive great good,*
    because God tested them and found them worthy.

5   Like gold in the furnace, God tried them*
    and, like a sacrificial burnt offering, accepted them.

6   In the time of their visitation, they will shine forth*
    and will run like sparks through the stubble.

7   They will govern nations and rule over peoples*
    and God will reign over them for ever.   *Wisdom 3. 1-8*

    Glory to the Father, and to the Son,
      and to the Holy Spirit:*
    as it was in the beginning, is now,
      and shall be for ever. Amen.

7   *THE SONG OF THE THREE*

1   Blessèd are you, the God of our forebears,*
    worthy to be praised and exalted for ever.

2   Blessèd is your holy and glorious name,*
    worthy to be praised and exalted for ever.

3   Blessèd are you, glorious in your holy temple,*
    worthy to be praised and exalted for ever.

4   Blessèd are you who behold the depths,*
     worthy to be praised and exalted for ever.

5   Blessèd are you, enthroned on the cherubim,*
     worthy to be praised and exalted for ever.

6   Blessèd are you on the throne of your kingdom,*
     worthy to be praised and exalted for ever.

7   Blessèd are you in the heights of heaven,*
     worthy to be praised and exalted for ever.

Bless the Father, the Son and the Holy Spirit,*
worthy to be praised and exalted for ever.

Song of the Three 29-34

8   *THE EASTER ANTHEMS*

1   Christ our passover has been sacrificed for us,*
     so let us celebrate the feast,

2   Not with the old leaven of corruption and wickedness*
     but with the unleavened bread of sincerity and truth.

3   Christ once raised from the dead dies no more;*
     death has no more dominion over him.

4   In dying, he died to sin once for all;*
     in living, he lives to God.

5   See yourselves, therefore, as dead to sin*
     and alive to God in Jesus Christ our Lord.

6   Christ has been raised from the dead;*
     the first fruits of those who sleep.

7   For since by one man came death,*
     by another has come also the resurrection of the dead,

8   For as in Adam all die,*
     even so in Christ shall all be made alive.

From 1 Cor 6, Rom 6 & 2 Cor 15

Glory to the Father, and to the Son,
  and to the Holy Spirit:*
as it was in the beginning, is now,
  and shall be for ever. Amen.

9   *A SONG OF CREATION - BENEDICITE*
     This canticle should be recited without pause.

1   Bless the Lord all created things:
     who is worthy to be praised and exalted for ever.

2   Bless the Lord you heavens:
     who is worthy to be praised and exalted for ever.

3   Bless the Lord you angels of the Lord,
     bless the Lord all you his hosts:
     bless the Lord you waters above the heavens,
     who is worthy to be praised and exalted for ever.

4   Bless the Lord sun and moon,
     bless the Lord you stars of heaven:
     bless the Lord all rain and dew,
     who is worthy to be praised and exalted for ever.

5   Bless the Lord all winds that blow,
     bless the Lord you fire and heat:
     bless the Lord scorching wind and bitter cold,
     who is worthy to be praised and exalted for ever.

6   Bless the Lord dews and falling snows,
     bless the Lord you nights and days:
     bless the Lord light and darkness,
     who is worthy to be praised and exalted for ever.

7   Bless the Lord frost and cold,
     bless the Lord you ice and snow:
     bless the Lord lightning and clouds,
     who is worthy to be praised and exalted for ever.

8   O let the earth bless the Lord;
     bless the Lord you mountains and hills:
     bless the Lord all that grows in the ground,
     who is worthy to be praised and exalted for ever.

9   Bless the Lord you springs,
     bless the Lord you seas and rivers:
     bless the Lord you whales
         and all that swim in the waters,
     who is worthy to be praised and exalted for ever.

10 Bless the Lord all birds of the air,
   bless the Lord you beasts and cattle:
   bless the Lord all people of the earth,
   who is worthy to be praised and exalted for ever.

11 O People of God bless the Lord;
   bless the Lord you priests of the Lord:
   bless the Lord you servants of the Lord,
   who is worthy to be praised and exalted for ever.

12 **Bless the Lord all you of upright spirit,**
   bless the Lord you that are holy and humble in heart:
   bless the Father, the Son and the Holy Spirit,
   who is worthy to be praised and exalted for ever.
   The Song of the Three 35-65

10 *A SONG OF THE CHURCH - TE DEUM*
   This canticle should be recited without pause.

1 We praise you, O God:
   we acclaim you as the Lord;

2 All creation worships you:
   the Father everlasting.

3 To you all angels, all the powers of heaven:
   the cherubim and seraphim, sing in endless praise,

4   Holy, holy, holy Lord, God of power and might:
       heaven and earth are full of your glory.

5 The glorious company of apostles praise you:
   the noble fellowship of prophets praise you.

6 The white-robed army of martyrs praise you:
   throughout the world, the holy Church acclaims you.

7   Father, of majesty unbounded:
       your true and only Son, worthy of all praise,
       the Holy Spirit, advocate and guide.

8 You, Christ, are the King of glory:
   the eternal Son of the Father.

9 When you took our flesh to set us free:
   you humbly chose the Virgin's womb.

10 You overcame the sting of death:
  and opened the kingdom of heaven to all believers.

11 You are seated at God's right hand in glory:
  we believe that you will come to be our judge.

12   Come then, Lord, and help your people,
    bought with the price of your own blood:
    and bring us with your saints
    to glory everlasting.

10 A SONG OF CHRIST'S GOODNESS

1 Jesus, as a mother you gather your people to you;*
  you are gentle with us as a mother with her children.

2 Often you weep over our sins and our pride,*
  tenderly you draw us from hatred and judgement.

3 You comfort us in sorrow and bind up our wounds,*
  in sickness you nurse us
    and with pure milk you feed us.

4 Jesus, by your dying,
    we are born to new life;*
  by your anguish and labour
    we come forth in joy.

5 Despair turns to hope through your sweet goodness;*
  through your gentleness, we find comfort in fear.

6 Your warmth gives life to the dead,*
  your touch makes sinners righteous.

7 Lord Jesus, in your mercy, heal us;*
  in your love and tenderness, remake us.

8 In your compassion, bring grace and forgiveness,*
  for the beauty of heaven, may your love prepare us.
                    Anselm of Canterbury/Trans: 19

  **Glory to the Father, and to the Son,
    and to the Holy Spirit:***
  **as it was in the beginning, is now,
    and shall be for ever. Amen.**

Prayers and Praises
for Various Occasions

A GENERAL PRAYERS

1 THE COLLECT FOR PURITY

Almighty God,
to whom all hearts are open,
all desires known
and from whom no secrets are hidden,
cleanse the thoughts of our hearts
that by the inspiration of your Holy Spirit,
we may perfectly love you
and worthily magnify your holy name;
through Jesus Christ our Lord. **Amen.**   3

2 A PRAYER OF ST BENEDICT

O gracious and holy Father,
give us wisdom to perceive you,
diligence to seek you,
patience to wait for you,
eyes to behold you,
a heart to meditate upon you
and a life to proclaim you;
through the power of the Spirit
  of Jesus Christ our Lord. **Amen.**

3 A PRAYER OF ST RICHARD OF CHICHESTER

Thanks be to you, O Lord Jesus Christ,
for all the benefits that you have given us,
for all the pains and insults
  which you have borne for us.
O most merciful Redeemer, Friend and Brother,
may we know you more clearly,
love you more dearly
and follow you more nearly,
now and for evermore. **Amen.**

4 A PRAYER OF ST ALCUIN

Eternal Light, shine into our hearts.
Eternal Goodness, deliver us from evil.
Eternal Power, be our support.
Eternal Darkness, scatter the darkness of ignorance.
Eternal Pity, have mercy upon us.
Grant that,
   with all our hearts and minds and strength,
we may evermore seek your face;
and finally bring us, in your infinite mercy,
to your holy presence.
So strengthen our weakness that,
following in the footsteps of your blessèd Son,
we may obtain your mercy
and enter into your promised joy. **Amen.**

5 A PRAYER OF ST FRANCIS

May the power of your love, Lord Christ,
fiery and sweet as honey,
so absorb our hearts
as to withdraw them from all that is under heaven.
Grant that we may be ready
   to die for love of your love,
as you died for love of our love. **Amen.**

6 A PRAYER FOR THE CHURCH

Most gracious Father,
we pray for your holy catholic Church:
fill it with all truth
and in all truth with all peace;
where it is corrupt, purge it;
where it is in error, direct it;
where anything is amiss, reform it;
where it is right, strengthen and confirm it;
where it is in want, furnish it;
where it is divided, heal it
   and unite it in your love;
through Jesus Christ our Lord. **Amen.** *William Laud*

7 A PRAYER TO BE AN INSTRUMENT OF PEACE

Lord, make me an instrument of your peace.
Where there is hatred, let me sow love;
where there is injury, pardon;
where there is doubt, faith;
where there is despair, hope;
where there is darkness, light;
where there is sadness, joy.
O Divine Master, grant that I may not so much
seek to be consoled as to console,
to be understood as to understand,
to be loved as to love.
For it is in giving that we receive,
it is in pardoning that we are pardoned,
and it is in dying that we are born to
eternal life. **Amen.** *19th Century French Prayer*

8 A PRAYER FOR MISSION & EVANGELISM

Give to your Church, O God,
a bold vision and a daring charity,
a refreshed wisdom and a courteous understanding,
that the eternal message of your Son
may be acclaimed as the good news of the age;
through him who makes all things new,
even Jesus Christ our Lord. **Amen.**

9 A PRAYER FOR QUIET AND RETREAT

Grant us, O merciful God,
the will to seek you, whom we desire above all,
that we may find you and be found in you;
may your love and wisdom
   guide words spoken in your name;
may we find faith and hope
in the still small voice
which tells us of your presence;
may we be one with you
   in Jesus our Redeemer. **Amen.**

10 A PRAYER FOR MEETING

Almighty God,
you have given your Holy Spirit to the Church
to lead us into all truth:
bless with your grace and presence
the members of *this meeting*;
keep *us* steadfast in faith and united in love,
that *we* may reveal your glory
and prepare the way of your kingdom;
through Jesus Christ our Lord . . .   3

11 THE GENERAL THANKSGIVING

Almighty God, Father of all mercies,
we your unworthy servants
give you most humble and hearty thanks
for all your goodness and loving-kindness.
We bless you for our creation, preservation,
    and all the blessings of this life;
but above all for your immeasurable love
in the redemption of the world
by our Lord Jesus Christ,
for the means of grace and for the hope of glory.
And give us, we pray,
such a sense of all your mercies
that our hearts may be unfeignèdly thankful,
and that we show forth your praise,
not only with our lips but in our lives,
by giving up ourselves to your service,
and by walking before you
    in holiness and righteousness all our days;
through Jesus Christ our Lord,
to whom with you and the Holy Spirit,
    be all honour and glory,
for ever and ever. **Amen.**   *Edward Reynolds 1›*

B LITANIES

*Only a limited number of litanies can be included in this book
but, as only the Officiant normally requires a full copy, it is
suggested that the many other sources available be used, such as*
Patterns for Worship *and* The Promise of His Glory.

1 THE GREAT LITANY

*Sections I and VI are always used, but a selection of
appropriate suffrages may be made from Sections II, III, IV and V.*

I

Let us pray.

God the Father,
have mercy on us.

God the Son,
have mercy on us.

God the Holy Spirit,
have mercy on us.

II

From all evil and mischief;
from pride, vanity and hypocrisy;
from envy, hatred and malice;
and from all evil intent,
Good Lord, deliver us.

From sloth, worldliness and love of money;
from hardness of heart
  and contempt for your word and your laws,
Good Lord, deliver us.

From sins of body and mind;
from deceits of the world, the flesh and the devil,
Good Lord, deliver us.

From famine and disaster;
from violence, murder and dying unprepared,
Good Lord, deliver us.

In all times of sorrow;
in all times of joy;
in the hour of our death and at the day of judgement,
Good Lord, deliver us.

By the mystery of your holy incarnation;
by your birth, childhood and obedience;
by your baptism, fasting and temptation,
Good Lord, deliver us.

By your ministry in word and work;
by your mighty acts of power;
and by your preaching of the kingdom,
Good Lord, deliver us.

By your agony and trial;
by your cross and passion;
and by your precious death and burial,
Good Lord, deliver us.

By your mighty resurrection;
by your glorious ascension;
and by your sending of the Holy Spirit,
Good Lord, deliver us.

III

Hear our prayers, O Lord our God.
Hear us, good Lord.

Govern and direct your holy Church;
fill it with love and truth;
and grant it that unity which is your will.
Hear us, good Lord.

Give us boldness to preach the gospel in all the world,
and to make disciples of all the nations.
Hear us, good Lord.

Enlighten your ministers with knowledge and understanding,
that by their teaching and their lives
they may proclaim your word.
Hear us, good Lord.

Give your people grace to hear and receive your word,
and to bring forth the fruit of the Spirit.
Hear us, good Lord.

Bring into the way of truth
all who have erred and are deceived.
Hear us, good Lord.

Strengthen those who stand;
comfort and help the fainthearted;
raise up the fallen;
and finally beat down Satan under our feet.
Hear us, good Lord.

IV

Guide the leaders of the nations
into the ways of peace and justice.
Hear us, good Lord.

Guard and strengthen your servant Elizabeth our Queen,
that she may put her trust in you
and seek your honour and glory.
Hear us, good Lord.

Endue the High Court of Parliament
and all the Ministers of the Crown
with wisdom and understanding.
Hear us, good Lord.

Bless those who administer the law,
that they may uphold justice, honesty and truth.
Hear us, good Lord.

Give us the will to use the resources of the earth
   to your glory,
and for the good of all.
Hear us, good Lord.

Bless and keep all your people.
Hear us, good Lord.

V

Help and comfort the lonely, the bereaved,
  and the oppressed.
Lord, have mercy.

Keep in safety those who travel,
and all who are in danger.
Lord, have mercy.

Heal the sick in body and mind,
and provide for the homeless, the hungry
  and the destitute.
Lord, have mercy.

Show your pity on prisoners and refugees,
and all who are in trouble.
Lord, have mercy.

Forgive our enemies, persecutors and slanderers,
and turn their hearts.
Lord, have mercy.

Hear us as we remember those who have died
  in the peace of Christ,
both those who have confessed the faith
and those whose faith is known to you alone,
and grant us with them
a share in your eternal kingdom.
Lord, have mercy.

VI

Give us true repentance;
forgive us our sins of negligence and ignorance
  and our deliberate sins;
and grant us the grace of your Holy Spirit
to amend our lives according to your holy word.
Holy God,
holy and strong,
holy and immortal:
have mercy on us.   3/5›

When this litany is said instead of 'The Prayers' section in
the Office, the collect of the day is added here and the
Lord's Prayer follows the collect.

SOME SHORT LITANIES

These are some suitable responses to use with the following short litanies:

Lord, have mercy. **Lord, have mercy.**

Kyrie eleison. **Kyrie eleison.**

Domine, **Exaudi nos.**

Christ, have mercy. **Christ, have mercy.**

Christe eleison. **Christe eleison.**

Lord, hear us; **Lord, graciously hear us.**

Lord, in your mercy, **Hear our prayer.**

God of love, **Hear our prayer.**

Maranatha! **Come, Lord Jesus!**

2 *GENERAL*

In the love of God,
let us complete our evening sacrifice of praise.

For the unity and peace of the holy Church of God
throughout the world: **R.**

For the peace and stability of all peoples
and for those in authority: **R.**

For our own country and its national life
and for all who dwell among us: **R.**

For a blessing on our homes, for our relations and friends
and all whom we love: **R.**

For the sick and the suffering
and for all who minister to their needs: **R.**

For all who sleep in Christ,
that Christ will remember them in his heavenly kingdom: **R.**

Rejoicing in the fellowship of the blessèd Virgin Mary,
(*Saint N.*) and all the saints, let us commend ourselves
into the mighty hands of God: *Collect*

3 SUNDAYS & EASTERTIDE

On this day that the Lord has made, let us give God the glory
and pray for the people he has redeemed.

That we may live as those who believe
in the triumph of the cross: **R.**

That all people may receive the good news of his victory: **R.**

That those born to new life in the waters of baptism
may know the power of his resurrection: **R.**

That those who suffer pain and anguish may find healing and peace
in the wounds of Christ: **R.**

That in the undying love of Christ,
we may have union with all who have died: **R.**

Let us join our voices with the saints in proclaiming
that Christ has given us the victory: *Collect*

4 MONDAYS & PENTECOST

Through Christ, who ever lives to make intercession for us,
let us pray to the Lord.

Lift up our hearts to the heavenly places
and inspire us to serve you as a royal priesthood: **R.**

Let all peoples acknowledge your kingdom
and grant on earth the blessing of peace: **R.**

Send down upon us the gift of the Spirit
and renew your Church with power from on high: **R.**

May peace abound and righteousness flourish,
that we may tread underfoot injustice and wrong: **R.**

Help us to proclaim the good news of salvation,
and grant us the needful gifts of your grace: **R.**

Rejoicing in the fellowship of the Church on earth,
let us join our prayers with the saints in glory: *Collect*

5 TUESDAYS, ADVENT & KINGDOM SEASON

Watchful at all times,
let us pray for strength to stand with confidence
before our Maker and Redeemer.

That God may bring in his kingdom with judgement and mercy,
let us pray to the Lord: **R.**

That God may establish among the nations
his sceptre of righteousness, let us pray to the Lord: **R.**

That God may bind up the broken-hearted,
restore the sick and raise up all who have fallen,
let us pray to the Lord: **R.**

That the light of God's coming may dawn
on all who live in darkness and in the shadow of death,
let us pray to the Lord: **R.**

That with all the saints in light,
we may shine forth as lights of the world,
let us pray to the Lord: **R.**

So we commend ourselves and all for whom we pray
to the mercy and protection of our heavenly Father: *Collect*

6 WEDNESDAYS & CHRISTMASTIDE

Let us give glory to God on high,
who from his fullness have received grace upon grace.

For the holy Church of God throughout the world,
that with one heart we may rejoice in the Word made flesh,
let us pray to the Lord: **R.**

For good will in the hearts of all; and on earth, peace,
let us pray to the Lord: **R.**

For the poor, the outcast and the homeless; for the helpless,
the lonely and the unloved, let us pray to the Lord: **R.**

For all who have gone before us,
whose hope was in the Word made flesh,
let us pray to the Lord: **R.**

With the blessèd Virgin Mary,
Saint N. and all the host of heaven,
let our voices rise to praise God's glory: *Collect*

7 THURSDAYS & EPIPHANY

From the rising of the sun to its setting, let us pray to the Lord

That the people of God in all the world
may worship in spirit and in truth,
let us pray to the Lord: **R.**

That the Church may discover again that unity which is your gi
let us pray to the Lord: **R.**

That the nations of the earth
may seek after the ways that make for peace,
let us pray to the Lord: **R.**

That the whole creation, groaning in travail,
may be set free to enjoy the glorious liberty
of the children of God,
let us pray to the Lord: **R.**

That all who with Christ have entered the shadow of death
may find the fulfilment of life and peace,
let us pray to the Lord: **R.**

With all the saints in light,
let us offer eternal praise to the Lord made manifest: *Collect*

8 FRIDAYS, LENT & PASSIONTIDE

With faith and love and in union with Christ,
let us offer our prayer before the throne of grace.

Have mercy on your people,
for whom your Son laid down his life. **R.**

Bring healing and wholeness to people and nations,
and have pity on those torn apart by division. **R.**

Strengthen all who are persecuted for your name's sake,
and deliver them from evil. **R.**

Bring comfort to the dying,
and gladden their hearts with the power of your glory. **R.**

Give rest to the departed and bring them, with your saints,
to glory everlasting. **R.**

As we rejoice in the triumph of the cross,
we pray that the whole of creation may find fulfilment
in the eternal kingdom of God: *Collect*

9 SATURDAYS & PENTECOST

In the power of the Spirit and in union with Christ,
let us pray to the Father.

You guide your Church in the way of truth:
stir up among us the gifts of your grace. **R.**

Holy Wisdom fills the whole of creation:
by your Spirit, renew the face of the earth. **R.**

We are temples of the Spirit:
confirm our lives in the service of the gospel. **R.**

Your anointing restores wholeness to a broken world:
give healing to the sick, freedom to captives
and hope to the dying. **R.**

Nothing in all creation can separate us from your love:
receive into your keeping
those who have departed this life. **R.**

As we rejoice in the power of his Spirit,
may God grant us today the faith of the apostles,
the boldness of the prophets
and the strength of the martyrs: *Collect*

10 AN ORTHODOX LITANY FOR THE EVENING

That this evening may be holy, good and peaceful:
We pray to you, O Lord.

That your holy angels may lead us
in the paths of peace and goodwill:
We pray to you, O Lord.

That we may be pardoned and forgiven
for our sins and offences:
We pray to you, O Lord.

That there may be peace in your Church
and for the whole world:
We pray to you, O Lord.

That we may be bound together by your Holy Spirit,
in communion with (N. and with) all your saints,
entrusting one another and all our life to Christ:
We pray to you, O Lord.

C TRADITIONAL ANTHEMS & PRAYERS
FROM THE CHURCHES

Anthems and prayers that are from both Anglican and other traditions may be used as appropriate.

1 *ANTHEM TO THE THEOTOKOS*

Into his joy, the Lord has received you,
Virgin God-bearer, Mother of Christ.

You have beheld the King in his beauty,
Mary, daughter of Israel.

You have made answer for the creation
To the redeeming will of God.

Light, fire and life, divine and immortal,
Joined to our nature you have brought forth,

That to the glory of God the Father,
Heaven and earth might be restored.

Greek Orthodox Hymn/Trans: West Malling

2 *INDIAN PRAYER BEFORE SLEEP – CHRISTARAKSHA*

May the cross of the Son of God,
which is mightier than all the hosts of Satan
and more glorious than all the hosts of heaven,
abide with you in your going out and your coming in.
By day and night, at morning and at evening,
at all times and in all places
  may it protect and defend you.
From the wrath of evildoers,
from the assaults of evil spirits,
from foes visible and invisible,
from the snares of the devil,
from all passions that beguile the soul and body:
may it guard, protect and deliver you. **Amen.**

3 JEWISH PRAYER ON THE EVE OF SABBATH

Father of mercy,
continue, we pray, your loving-kindness to us all.
Make us worthy to walk in the way of the righteous before you,
loyal to your Law and clinging to good deeds.
Keep far from us all manner of shame, grief and care;
and grant that peace, light and joy
ever abide in our home;
for with you is the fountain of life,
and in your light do we see light. **Amen.**

4 ARMENIAN ORTHODOX DISMISSAL

Keep us in peace, O Christ our God,
under the protection of your holy and venerable cross;
save us from our enemies, visible and invisible,
and count us worthy to glorify you with thanksgiving,
with the Father and the Holy Spirit,
now and for ever, world without end. **Amen.**

5 PRAYER AT THE TIME OF DEATH

May Christ give you rest in the land of the living
and open for you the gates of paradise;
may he receive you as a citizen of the Kingdom,
and grant you forgiveness of your sins:
for you were his friend.   *Orthodox Funeral Rite*

6 THE RUSSIAN KONTAKION

Give rest, O Christ, to your servants, with your saints:
where sorrow and pain are no more,
neither sighing, but life everlasting.
You only are immortal, the creator and maker of all:
and we are mortal, formed of the earth,
And unto earth shall we return.
For so you did ordain when you created me, saying:
'Dust thou art and unto dust shalt thou return.'
All we go down to the dust;
and, weeping o'er the grave, we make our song:
Alleluia! Alleluia! Alleluia!
Give rest . . .

7 PRAYER OF A JEWISH MOURNER – KADDISH

The Kaddish is an affirmation of faith in the face of death,
said by the chief mourner, surrounded by the congregation.

Magnified and sanctified be the great name of God
in the world which he created according to his will.
May he establish his Kingdom in your life and in your days,
and in the lifetime of all his people:
quickly and speedily may it come; and let us say Amen!

Blessèd be God for ever!

Blessed, praised and glorified,
exalted, extolled and honoured,
magnified and lauded be the name of the Holy One;
blessèd be God!
Though he be high above all the blessings and hymns,
praises and consolations,
which are uttered in the world; and let us say Amen!

Blessèd be God for ever!

May there be abundant peace from heaven
and life for us and for all people; let us say Amen!

Blessèd be God for ever!

8 WORLD PRAYER FOR PEACE

O God, lead us from death to life,
from falsehood to truth.
Lead us from despair to hope,
from fear to trust.
Lead us from hate to love, from war to peace.
Let peace fill our hearts, our world, our universe. **Amen.**

Satish Kumar›

9 A FRANCISCAN ENDING TO THE OFFICE

May our blessèd Lady pray for us.
May Saints N. & N. pray for us.
May all the saints of God pray for us.
May the angels of God befriend us
   and watch around us to protect us.
May the Lord Jesus give us his blessing of peace. **Amen.**

Occasional Services

The following brief rites may be used at the conclusion of Morning or Evening Prayer, in order to focus on an aspect of the Church's prayer in Christ, particularly appropriate to the day or season, e.g. the 'Prayers at the Foot of the Cross', page 271, are suitable on Fridays as a weekly reminder of the crucifixion.

Alternatively, they might stand on their own as short services focused on a theme or ministry, e.g.:
'Thanksgiving for Baptism', page 262, might be used on the anniversary of a baptism or for use with parents and godparents the evening before a baptism;
'The Oil of Gladness', page 264, when remembering someone in particular sickness or distress, and can used by one person or with a group, with or without anointing or the laying on of hands;
'Watching and Waiting', page 267, at a late night vigil for a particular intention;
'A Celebration of the Word', page 269, at a Bible Study or where there is to be a sharing of testimonies;
'Unity in Christ', page 270, at the start of an ecumenical meeting;
'Prayers at the Foot of the Cross', page 271, when thinking about the sufferings of others;
'The Gospel Proclamation', page 272, as a way of marking, the previous evening, Sundays and important feast days of the Church.

Equally, some might be used by those who wanted a regular time of prayer in the middle of the day.

These are just a few examples of how they might be used: the daily attribution from Celebrating Common Prayer *is still given, with some new material ('The Oil of Gladness', 'Watching and Waiting', 'Grace at Meals' and 'Prayers for Travellers'), some previously found only in the Franciscan Supplement ('Praying Farewell'), and some from other parts of* Celebrating Common Prayer *but felt to be appropriate in this new situation ('At the Time of Death').*

1 THANKSGIVING FOR BAPTISM *(Sundays)*

If possible, it should be celebrated at the font; or a bowl of water may be used.

I saw water flowing from the threshold of the Temple.
Wherever the river flows
everything will spring to life. Alleluia.

On the banks of the river grow trees
  bearing every kind of fruit.
Their leaves will not wither nor their fruit fall.

Their fruit will serve for food,
their leaves for the healing of the nations.
For the river of the water of life
flows from the throne of God and of the Lamb.

Water may be poured into a font or bowl.

God in Christ gives us water welling up for eternal life.
With joy you will draw water from the wells of salvation.
Lord, give us this water and we shall thirst no more.

Let us give thanks to the Lord our God
Who is worthy of all thanksgiving and praise.

Blessèd are you, Sovereign God of all,
to you be glory and praise for ever!
You are our light and our salvation.
From the deep waters of death
you have raised your Son to life in triumph.
Accept our sacrifice of praise, we pray,
and sanctify these waters of your new creation,
that we, with all who have been born anew
  by water and the Spirit,
may be renewed in your image,
walk by the light of faith,
and serve you in newness of life;
through your anointed Son, Jesus Christ,
to whom with you and the Holy Spirit
we lift our voices of praise,
Father, Son and Holy Spirit.
Blessèd be God for ever!

The thanksgiving over the water may be followed by

THE APOSTLES' CREED

I believe in God, the Father almighty,
creator of heaven and earth.

I believe in Jesus Christ, God's only Son, our Lord,
who was conceived by the Holy Spirit,
born of the Virgin Mary,
suffered under Pontius Pilate,
was crucified, died, and was buried;
he descended to the dead.
On the third day he rose again;
he ascended into heaven,
he is seated at the right hand of the Father,
and he will come to judge the living and the dead.

I believe in the Holy Spirit,
the holy catholic Church,
the communion of saints,
the forgiveness of sins,
the resurrection of the body,
and the life everlasting. Amen.

Almighty God,
in our baptism you have consecrated us
to be temples of your Holy Spirit.
May we, whom you have counted worthy,
nurture this gift of your in-dwelling Spirit
  with a lively faith,
and worship you with upright lives;
through Jesus Christ. Amen.

*Water may be sprinkled over the people or they may be invited
to use it to sign themselves with the cross.*

THE PEACE

God has made us one in Christ.
He has set his seal upon us
and, as a pledge of what is to come,
has given the Spirit to dwell in our hearts.

The peace of the Lord be always with you
And also with you.

THE BLESSING

May God, who in Christ gives us a spring of water
   welling up to eternal life,
perfect in us the image of his glory;
and may the blessing of God almighty,
the Father, the Son and the Holy Spirit,
be upon us and remain with us always. **Amen.**

Let us bless the Lord. (Alleluia! Alleluia!)
Thanks be to God! (Alleluia! Alleluia!)

2   'THE OIL OF GLADNESS' –
PRAYERS FOR HEALING   *(Mondays)*

The love of God has been poured into our hearts,
through the Holy Spirit who has been given to us.
We dwell in him and he in us.

Give thanks to the Lord and call upon his name:
Make known his deeds among the peoples.

Sing to him, sing praises to him:
And speak of all his marvellous works.

Holy, holy, holy is the Lord God almighty:
Who was and is and is to come.

Heavenly Father,
you anointed your Son Jesus Christ
with the Holy Spirit and with power
to bring to us all the blessings of your kingdom:
anoint your Church with the same Holy Spirit,
that we who share in his suffering and victory
may bear witness to the gospel of salvation;
through Jesus Christ our Lord. **Amen.**

If anointing is to take place, the oil is brought forward.

Our help is in the name of the Lord
Who made heaven and earth.
Blessèd be the name of the Lord,
Now and for ever. Amen.

Blessèd are you, Sovereign God, gentle and merciful,
creator of heaven and earth.
Your Word brought light out of darkness
and daily your Spirit renews the face of the earth.
You anointed your Son, Jesus Christ, with power
and pour out your Spirit on us in our baptism,
that we may become a holy people
in the royal priesthood of your new covenant.

The apostles anointed the sick in your name,
bringing wholeness and joy to a broken world;
and by your grace renewed each day
your Church continues the gifts of healing,
giving your people new life and health
that they may bless your name for ever.

Hear the prayer we offer for all your people,
and remember in your mercy those for whom we pray:
heal the sick, raise the fallen,
strengthen the fainthearted,
bring light to those in darkness
and enfold in your mercy
   the fearful and those who have no hope.

In the fullness of time,
reconcile all things in Christ and make them new,
that we may be restored in your image,
renewed in your love
and serve you as sons and daughters in your kingdom.

Through your anointed Son, Jesus Christ, our Lord,
to whom with you and the Holy Spirit
we lift our voices of thanks and praise:
**Blessèd be God, our strength and our salvation,
now and for ever. Amen!**

There may be a time of silence for remembering the sick.

At the laying on of hands:
In the name of Jesus Christ
and in full trust in his power to make you whole,
we lay our hands upon you.
May he bring you healing and salvation,
deliver you from every evil
and confirm and strengthen in you all that is good.

At the anointing:
As with this sign of oil your body is outwardly anointed,
so inwardly may you be anointed with the Holy Spirit,
and may the Father of our Lord Jesus Christ
grant you the riches of his grace,
his healing and his peace.

The Peace
God has made us one in Christ.
He has set his seal upon us
and as a pledge of what is to come
has given the Spirit to dwell in our hearts.

The peace of the Lord be always with you
And also with you.
The peace may be exchanged.

Let us bless the Lord.
Thanks be to God!

3 WATCHING AND WAITING (*Tuesdays & Advent*)

All present light candles from the Paschal Candle or some other central light.

May almighty God come among us in power
and reveal in our midst the promise of his kingdom. **Amen.**

Hear the words of the gospel according to Saint Luke.
Glory to Christ our Saviour!

Let your loins be girded and your lamps burning, and be like
those who are waiting for their master to come home from the
marriage feast, so that they may open to him at once when he
comes and knocks. Blessèd are those servants whom the master
finds awake when he comes; truly I say to you, he will gird
himself and have them sit at table and he will come and serve
them. If he comes in the second watch, or in the third, and
finds them so, blessèd are those servants! But know this, that
if the householder had known at what hour the thief was coming,
he would have been awake and would not have left his house to
be broken into. You also must be ready; for the Son of Man is
coming at an hour you do not expect.   *Luke 12. 35-40*

This is the gospel of Christ.
Praise to Christ our Lord!

After a short silence, the RESPONSORY is said:

Your salvation is near those who fear you,
   that glory may dwell in our land.
Your salvation is near those who fear you,
   that glory may dwell in our land.

Mercy and truth have met together,
   righteousness and peace have kissed each other,
That glory may dwell in our land.

Glory to the Father, and to the Son, and to the Holy Spirit.
Your salvation is near those who fear you,
   that glory may dwell in our land.

Keep us, O Lord,
while we tarry on this earth,
in a serious seeking after you
and in an affectionate walking with you,
every day of our lives;
that when you come
we may be found not hiding our talent,
nor serving the flesh,
nor yet asleep with our lamp unfurnished,
but waiting and longing for our Lord,
our glorious God for ever. **Amen.**

Individual candles are put out and all wait in silent vigil.

And the end of the vigil, all say:
Our Father . . .

Awake, O sleeper, and arise from the dead
And Christ shall give you light!

Let us bless the Lord.
Thanks be to God!

4 A CELEBRATION OF THE WORD (Wednesdays)

A Bible may be carried in and placed on the altar table or lectern.

Your word is a lantern to my feet
And a light upon our path.

Almighty God,
we thank you for the gift of your holy word.
May it be a lantern to our feet,
a light to our paths,
and a strength to our lives.
Take us and use us
to love and serve all your people
in the power of the holy Spirit
and in the name of your Son,
Jesus Christ our Lord. **Amen.**   3›

The Officiant may invite those present to share their testimonies.

After a suitable period, the Officiant says:

The Word of life which was from the beginning
We proclaim to you.

The darkness is passing away
and the true light is already shining.
The Word of life which was from the beginning.

That which we heard, which we saw with our eyes,
and touched with our own hands,
We proclaim to you.

For our fellowship is with the Father,
and with his Son, Jesus Christ our Lord.
**The Word of life, which was from the beginning,
we proclaim to you.**

O God, by whose command
  the order of time runs its course:
forgive our restlessness, perfect our faith
and, while we await the fulfilment of your promise,
grant us to have a good hope through the Word made flesh,
even Jesus Christ our Lord . . .   17

May the grace of Christ, the incarnate Word, be with us all.
Amen.

Let us bless the Lord.
Thanks be to God!

5 UNITY IN CHRIST *(Thursdays)*

Christ is our peace, who has made us one,
He has broken down the barriers which divided us.

O God, the Father of our Lord Jesus Christ,
our only Saviour, the Prince of Peace:
give us grace seriously to lay to heart
the great dangers we are in by our unhappy divisions.
Take away all hatred and prejudice,
and whatever else may hinder us
   from godly union and concord;
that, as there is but one Body and one Spirit
and one hope of our calling,
one Lord, one faith, one baptism,
one God and Father of us all,
so we may henceforth be all of one heart and of one soul,
united in one holy bond of truth and peace, of faith and charity
and may with one mind and one mouth glorify you;
through Jesus Christ our Lord. **Amen.**   *1*

I am the vine and you are the branches.
Abide in us, that we may abide in you.

This is my commandment,
   that you love one another as I have loved you.
Abide in us, that we may abide in you.

Greater love has no one than this,
that a man lay down his life for his friends.
Abide in us, that we may abide in you.

You are my friends if you do what I command you;
love one another as I have loved you.
Abide in us, that we may abide in you.

Lord Jesus Christ,
who said to your apostles,
Peace I leave with you, my peace I give to you;
look not on our sins but on the faith of your Church
and grant us the peace and unity of your kingdom,
where you live and reign, now and for ever. **Amen.**

The peace of the Lord be always with you.
And also with you.

'The kiss of peace' may be exchanged.

6   PRAYERS AT THE FOOT OF THE CROSS   *(Fridays)*

A cross or crucifix is appropriate as the central symbol and lights may be burning before it.   It may be mounted or laid on the ground.

On the cross, our Lord offered himself to the Father for the whole world. So, at the foot of his cross, we join our prayers with his.

Either:

We adore you, O Christ, and we bless you
Because by your holy cross you have redeemed the world.

Holy God,
Holy and strong,
Holy and immortal,
have mercy on us.

Or:

We glory in your cross, O Lord,
and praise and glorify your holy resurrection;
For by virtue of the cross,
joy has come to the whole world.

God, be merciful to us and bless us,
and show us the light of your countenance
and be merciful to us
That your ways may be known upon earth,
your saving health among all nations.

We glory in your cross, O Lord,
and praise and glorify your holy resurrection;
For by virtue of the cross,
joy has come to the whole world.

Whilst silence is kept, or appropriate hymns or chants are sung, anyone may come forward to touch the cross, for example by placing their forehead on it, as a sign of entrusting to God, in union with Christ and his suffering, their own burdens as well as those of others, especially those who are oppressed or persecuted, prisoners of conscience, the sick or the suffering.

Almighty Father,
look with mercy on this your family
for which our Lord Jesus Christ
was content to be betrayed
and was given up into the hands of the wicked
and to suffer death upon the cross;
who is alive and glorified
with you and the Holy Spirit,
one God, now and for ever. **Amen.**   3/5

THE BLESSING

May the life-giving cross
be the source of all our joy and peace. **Amen.**

Let us bless the Lord.
Thanks be to God.

7   THE GOSPEL PROCLAMATION   *(Saturdays)*

*The gospel reading for the following day may be introduced
by this acclamation:*

We proclaim not ourselves, but Christ Jesus as Lord
And ourselves as your servants for Jesus' sake.

For the God who said, Let light shine out of darkness,
Has caused the light to shine within us.

To give the light of the knowledge of the glory of God
In the face of Jesus Christ.

THE GOSPEL

Hear the good news of our Lord Jesus Christ
  in the gospel according to . . .
Glory to Christ our Saviour.

After the gospel reading:

This is the gospel of Christ.
Praise to Christ our Lord.

Then may be said THE SONG OF TIMOTHY

Here are words you can trust:
Remember Jesus Christ, risen from the dead.
He is our salvation, our eternal glory.

If we have died with him, we shall also live with him;
If we endure, we shall also reign with him.

If we are faithless, he keeps faith;
**For he has broken the power of death
and brought life and immortality to light
through the gospel.**

Or another suitable hymn or canticle.

THE COLLECT of the following day is said.

THE BLESSING

Let us bless the living God:
He was born of the Virgin Mary,
Revealed in his glory,

Worshipped by angels,
Proclaimed among the nations,

Believed in throughout the world,
Exalted to the highest heavens.

Blessèd be God, our strength and our salvation,
Now and for ever. Amen.

8 GRACE BEFORE MEALS

The eyes of all wait upon you, O God,
And you give them their food in due season.

You open wide your hand
And fill all things living with plenteousness.

Bless, O Lord, these gifts to our use
 and us in your service;
relieve the needs of those in want
 and give us thankful hearts;
for Christ's sake. **Amen.**

Or:

Bless us, O Lord, who bless your holy name
and by this food, feed us for your service. **Amen.**

9 GRACE AFTER MEALS

All your works praise you, O God,
And your faithful servants bless you.

They make known the glory of your kingdom
And speak of your power.

For these and all God's gifts and graces,
let us bless the Lord.
Thanks be to God.

Or:

Bless the Lord, O my soul,
And all that is within me, bless his holy name.

Bless the Lord, O my soul,
And forget not all his benefits.

Blessèd be God, eternal king,
for these and all his good gifts to us. **Amen.**

Thy soul was like a star, and dwelt apart;
Thou hadst a voice whose sound was like the sea:
Pure as the naked heavens, majestic, free,
So didst thou travel on life's common way
In cheerful godliness; and yet thy heart
The lowliest duties on herself did lay.   *William Wordsworth*

The following may be said by one person or more, and may be changed to suit the circumstances:

O Lord, save your servants,
Who put *their* trust in you.

Send *them* help from your holy sanctuary,
And ever more mightily defend *them*.

Be unto *them*, O Lord, a strong tower
From the face of the enemy.

Show *them* your ways, O Lord,
And teach *them* your paths.

O God, give your angels charge over *them*,
To keep *them* in all our ways.

Every day will I bless the Lord
**And may the God of the journey make the way
straight and fair.**

Merciful God, giver of life and health,
guide, we pray, with your wisdom
all who are striving to protect travellers
from injury and harm;
grant to those who travel consideration for others,
and to those who walk and play
a thoughtful caution and care;
so that without fear or misfortune
we may all come safely to our journey's end,
by your mercy, who care for each one of us;
through Jesus Christ, our Saviour. **Amen.**   *Douglas Crick*

Let us go in peace
In the name of Christ. Amen!

11 PRAYING FAREWELL

This may be used when anyone is departing from the local community. It may be adapted according to circumstances, including the absence of the person leaving.
To symbolise unending love, the group may gather in a circle.

The Officiant begins:
God of our beginnings and endings,
we celebrate all we have shared with *N. & N.*
and ask your blessing as *they* continues on *their* journey.
May the love that is in our hearts
be a bond that unites us forever,
wherever we may be.
May the power of your presence
bless this moment of our leave-taking;
for the sake of Jesus Christ, our Redeemer. **Amen.**

Then may follow either the following PSALMODY or some other.

1   **You, O God, will guard us from all evil:**
    you will protect our lives.

2   **You will protect our going out and our coming in:**
    both now and for ever.

3   **Where can I flee from your Spirit:**
    or where can I flee from your presence?

4   **If I climb to heaven, you are there:**
    if I lie in the grave, you are there also.

5   **If I take the wings of the morning:**
    and dwell in the depths of the sea,

6   **Even there, your hand shall lead me:**
    your hand shall hold me fast.   *From Psalms 121 & 139*

Come to our help, comfort us and give us life,
in your merciful goodness, O God,
for we are yours;
keep our feet from the evil path
and save us through Jesus Christ,
your Word and Wisdom. **Amen.**   16

Any of the following READINGS may be used.

I thank my God, every time I remember you, constantly praying with joy for all of you, because of your sharing in the gospel. And this is my prayer, that love may overflow more and more with knowledge and full insight to help to determine what is best, so that in the day of Christ we may be pure and blameless, having produced the harvest of righteousness that comes through Jesus Christ for the glory and praise of God.   *Philippians 1. 3, 4, 9*

Or: Exodus 13. 21-22; John 3. 5-8; John 16. 21-24;
2 Corinthians 4. 7-9.

The following RESPONSE may be said. The local community (LC) may say their words together or individuals take a particular part.

LC (1)	**As you journey onward,** **we ask forgiveness where we have failed you;** **we give thanks for all you have given us;** **we assure you of our love and prayers.**
Those leaving	As I leave, I ask forgiveness where I have failed you; I give thanks for all that you have given to me; I assure you of my love and prayers.
LC (2)	**As you experience the pain of change,** **and the insecurity of moving on,** **we pray that you may also experience** **the blessing of inner growth.**
Those leaving	I know that God goes with me.
LC (3)	**As you meet the poor, the pained,** **and the stranger on the Way,** **we pray that you may see in each one** **the face of Christ.**
Those leaving	I know that God goes with me.
LC (4)	**As you walk through the good times and the bad,** **we pray that you may never lose sight** **of the shelter of God's loving arms.**
Those leaving	I know that God goes with me.

LC (5)   **As you ponder your decisions**
          and wonder over the fruits of your choice,
          we pray that the peace of Christ
          may reign in your heart.

Those   I know that God goes with me.
leaving

The Officiant then says,

We praise and thank you, God of the journey,
for our *brothers and sisters* who *are* soon to leave us.
We entrust *them* into your loving care,
knowing that you are always the faithful traveller
    and companion on the Way.
Shelter and protect *them* from all harm and anxiety.
Grant *them* the courage to meet the future,
and grace to let go into new life;
through Jesus Christ our Saviour. **Amen.**

N. & N., may God bless you. **Amen.**

Then each person present may make the sign of the cross
on the forehead of those leaving, saying,

Go in peace, for our God goes with you.
and 'the kiss of peace' may be exchanged.

This service may be used on hearing the news of a death, or on the day of the funeral by those not able to be present or on any such suitable occasion.   If it seems appropriate, they might be adapted to be used with a person who is very close to death.

We shall not all die
But we shall be changed.

The trumpet shall sound and the dead will rise immortal
And we shall be changed.

The perishable must be clothed with the imperishable
and the mortal must be clothed with immortality.

We shall not all die
But we shall be changed.

An appropriate HYMN may be sung, such as the 'Dies Irae', or the 'Kontakion' (page 259), or 'Jesus, remember me when you come into your kingdom'.

Any of the following PSALMS may be said: Ps 23 (page 202), Ps 42 (page 105), Ps 43 (page 218), Ps 121 (page 59), Ps 130 (page 106), Ps 139 (page 28).

Any of the following READINGS may be used, or some other:
Jesus said, 'Do not let your hearts be troubled.   Believe in God, believe also in me.   In my Father's house are many dwelling places.   If it were not so, would I have told you that I go to prepare a place for you?   And if I go and prepare a place for you, I will come again and will take you to myself, so that where I am, there you may be also.   I am the way, and the truth, and the life.   No one comes to the Father except through me.   If you know me, you will know my Father also. From now on, you do know him and have seen him.'   *John 14. 1-3, 6-7*
Or: Isaiah 25. 6-9; Hosea 6. 1-3; John 11. 21-27;
Romans 6. 3-9; 2 Corinthians 4.16 - 5.5; Philippians 1. 20-26;
1 Thessalonians 4. 13-18.

MEMORIES OF THE DEPARTED may be shared, ending with the following prayer:

O God,
who brought us to birth
and in whose arms we die:
in our grief and shock
contain and comfort us,
embrace us with your love,
give us hope in our confusion
and grace to let go into new life;
through Jesus Christ. **Amen.**   15

Then may be said A SONG OF FAITH AND HOPE

1   Now that we have been justified through faith,*
       we are at peace with God
            through Jesus Christ our Lord.

2   And so we exult in our hope of the splendour of God*
       and we even exult in the sufferings we endure.

3   For our hope is not in vain,*
       because God's love has flooded our inmost hearts
            through the Holy Spirit which has been given to us.

4   When we were still powerless, Christ died for the ungodly;*
       he died for us while we were still sinners,
            and so God's love for us is revealed.

5   We are more than conquerors through Christ who loved us,
       for nothing can separate us from the love of God
            which is ours, through Jesus Christ. *From Romans 5 & 8*

       **Glory to the Father, and to the Son,
            and to the Holy Spirit:***
       **as it was in the beginning, is now,
            and shall be for ever. Amen.**

INTERCESSION may be offered.

Lord, have mercy. **Lord, have mercy.**
Christ, have mercy. **Christ, have mercy.**
Lord, have mercy. **Lord, have mercy.**

We commend *N.* to you, O God,
as *s/he* journeys beyond our sight.

God of all consolation,
in your unending love and mercy
you turn the darkness of death
into the dawn of new life.
Your Son, by dying for us, conquered death
and by rising again,
restored to us eternal life:
may we then go forward eagerly to meet our Redeemer
and, after our life on earth,
be reunited with all our brothers and sisters
in that place where every tear is wiped away
and all things are made new;
through Jesus Christ our Saviour. **Amen.**

Or

Heavenly Father,
into whose hands Jesus Christ
commended his spirit at the last hour:
into those same hands we now commend your servant *N.*,
that death may be for *her/him*
the gate to life and to eternal fellowship with you;
through Jesus Christ our Lord. **Amen.**

Lord Jesus, remember us in your kingdom and teach us to pray:
Our Father . . .

Then is said:

Go forth upon your journey from this world, O Christian
soul; in the name of God the Father who created you.
Amen.
In the name of Jesus Christ who suffered for you.
Amen.
In the name of the Holy Spirit who strengthens you.
Amen.
In communion with (the blessèd Virgin Mary,
Saint *N.* and with) all the blessèd saints;
with the angels and archangels and all the heavenly host.
Amen.

May your portion this day be in peace
and your dwelling in the city of God.
Amen.

And/or:

N., our companion in faith and *brother/sister* in Christ,
we entrust you to God who created you.
May you return to the Most High who formed you
    from the dust of the earth.
May the angels and the saints come to meet you
    as you go forth from this life.
May Christ, who was crucified for you,
    take you into his Kingdom.
May Christ the Good Shepherd
give you a place within his flock.
May Christ forgive you your sins
    and keep you among his people.
May you see your Redeemer face to face
    and delight in the vision of God for ever. **Amen.**

And/or:

N., may Christ give you rest in the land of the living
and open for you the gates of paradise;
may he receive you as a citizen of the Kingdom,
and grant you forgiveness of your sins:
for you were his friend.

Then is said THE BLESSING:

We remember the living and the departed.
Now to the One who is able to keep us from falling
and set us in the presence of the divine glory,
to the only God our Saviour
be glory and majesty, dominion and praise,
now and for ever. **Amen.**

Or the 'Kaddish' may be said, page 260.

A time of silence may be kept.

The Christian Year

THE NAMING AND CIRCUMCISION
OF JESUS THE CHRIST (1 January)

Reading
Peter, filled with the Holy Spirit, said, 'This Jesus is "the stone that was rejected by you, the builders; it has become the cornerstone." There is salvation in no one else, for there is no other name under heaven given among mortals by which we must be saved.' *Acts 4. 11, 12*

Response
To us a child is born, to us a Son is given,
And he shall be called The Prince of Peace!

Collect
Almighty God, whose blessèd Son was circumcised
in obedience to the law for our sake
and given the Name that is above every name:
give us grace faithfully to bear his Name,
to worship him in the freedom of the Spirit,
and to proclaim him as the Saviour of the world;
who is alive and reigns with you and the Holy Spirit,
one God, now and for ever. **Amen.**   3

EPIPHANY (6 January)

Reading
We do not proclaim ourselves, we proclaim Jesus Christ as Lord and ourselves as your servants for Jesus' sake. For it is the God who said, 'Let light shine out of darkness' who has shone in our hearts to give the light of the knowledge of the glory of God in the face of Jesus Christ. *2 Corinthians 4. 5, 6*

Response
The Lord has manifested his glory,
He has revealed himself to the nations.

Collect
O God, by the leading of a star
you manifested your only Son
   to the peoples of the earth.
Lead us, who know you now by faith,
to your holy presence,
where we may see your glory face to face;
through Jesus Christ our Lord . . .   10

THE BAPTISM OF CHRIST
THE FIRST SUNDAY OF EPIPHANY

Reading
John testified, 'I saw the Spirit descending from heaven like a
dove, and it remained on him. I myself did not know him but
the one who sent me to baptise with water said to me, "He on
whom you see the Spirit descend and remain is the one who
baptises with the Holy Spirit." '   *John 1. 32, 33*

Response
Behold my Chosen, in whom my soul delights;
The Anointed One, on whom my Spirit rests.

Collect
Almighty God,
who anointed Jesus at his baptism with the Holy Spirit
and revealed him as your belovèd Son:
inspire us, your children,
who are born of water and the Spirit,
to surrender our lives to your service,
that we may rejoice to be called the sons and daughters of God;
through Jesus Christ our Lord . . .   3/5

CONVERSION OF PAUL (25 January)

Reading
For I want you to know that the gospel that was proclaimed by
me is not of human origin; for I did not receive it from a
human source, nor was I taught it, but I received it through a
revelation of Jesus Christ.   *Galatians 1. 11-12*

Response
Faith comes by hearing
And hearing by the word of Christ.

Collect
Almighty God,
who caused the light of the gospel
   to shine throughout the world
through the preaching of your servant Saint Paul:
grant that we who celebrate his wonderful conversion
may follow him in bearing witness to your truth;
through Jesus Christ our Lord . . .   3

PRESENTATION OF CHRIST – CANDLEMAS (2 February)

Reading
Christ became like us in every respect, so that he might be a
merciful and faithful high priest in the service of God, to make
a sacrifice of atonement for the sins of the people.

Hebrews 2. 17

Response
We wait for your loving-kindness, O God,
In the midst of your temple.

Collect
Almighty and everliving God,
clothed in majesty,
we pray that as your only-begotten Son
  was this day presented in the Temple,
in substance of our mortal nature,
so we may be presented to you
with pure and clean hearts,
by your Son Jesus Christ our Lord . . .   1›

ASH WEDNESDAY

Reading
Jesus said, 'When you fast, anoint your head and wash your face,
so that your fasting may be seen not by others but by your
Father who is in secret.'   *Matthew 6. 17, 18*

Response
Create in us a clean heart, O God,
And renew a right spirit within us.

Collect
Almighty and everlasting God,
you hate nothing that you have made
and forgive the sins of all those who are penitent:
create and make in us new and contrite hearts
that we, worthily lamenting our sins
  and acknowledging our wretchedness,
may receive from you, the God of all mercy,
perfect remission and forgiveness;
through Jesus Christ our Lord . . .   1›

JOSEPH, HUSBAND OF THE BVM (19 March)

Reading
Jacob was the father of Joseph the husband of Mary, of whom
Jesus was born, who is called Messiah.   *Matthew 1. 16*

Response
Behold the faithful and wise servant
Whom the Master placed over his household.

Collect
O God,
who from the family of your servant David
raised up Joseph
to be the guardian of your only Son
and spouse of the Virgin Mary, his mother:
give us grace to follow him
in faithful obedience to your commands;
through Jesus Christ our Lord . . .   16

ANNUNCIATION OF OUR LORD TO THE BVM (25 March)

Reading
The Holy Spirit will come upon you, Mary, and the power of the
Most High will overshadow you; therefore the child to be born
will be holy, and will be called the Son of God.   *Luke 1. 35*

Response
Behold, the handmaid of the Lord,
Let it be to me according to your word.

Collect
We beseech you, O Lord,
to pour your grace into our hearts;
that as we have known the incarnation
   of your Son Jesus Christ
by the message of an angel,
so by his cross and passion
we may be brought to the glory of his resurrection;
through Jesus Christ our Lord . . .   3

PALM SUNDAY

Reading

The crowds that went ahead of Jesus and that followed were shouting, 'Hosanna to the Son of David! Blessèd is the one who comes in the name of the Lord! Hosanna in the highest heaven!' When he entered Jerusalem, the whole city was in turmoil, asking, 'Who is this?'   *Matthew 21. 9-10*

Response

God's love for us is revealed in this:
That while we were yet sinners, Christ died for us.

Collect

Everlasting God,
who in your tender love towards the human race
   sent your Son our Saviour Jesus Christ
to take upon him our flesh
and to suffer death upon the cross:
grant that we may follow the example
   of his patience and humility,
and also be made partakers of his resurrection;
through Jesus Christ our Lord . . .   3/5

MAUNDY THURSDAY

Reading

Jesus said, 'If I, your Lord and Teacher, have washed your feet, you also ought to wash one another's feet. For I have set you an example, that you also should do as I have done to you.'
                                        John 13. 14-15

Response

Christ loved those who were his
And showed them how deep was his love for them.

Collect

Almighty Father,
whose Son Jesus Christ has taught us
that what we do for the least
   of our brothers and sisters
we do also for him:
give us the will to be the servant of others
   as he was the servant of all,
who gave up his life and died for us,
yet is alive and reigns with you and the Holy Spirit,
one God, now and for ever. **Amen**   3/5

GOOD FRIDAY

Reading

Christ Jesus emptied himself, taking the form of a servant,
being born in human likeness; and being found in human form, he
humbled himself and became obedient to the point of death, even
death on a cross. *Philippians 2. 7-8*

Response

We adore you, O Christ, and we bless you,
For by your holy cross, you have redeemed the world.

Collect

Almighty Father,
look with mercy on this your family
for which our Lord Jesus Christ
  was content to be betrayed
  and given up into the hands of the wicked
  and to suffer death upon the cross;
who is alive and glorified
  with you and the Holy Spirit,
one God, now and for ever. **Amen.**   *3/5*

EASTER EVE

Reading

Jesus said, 'Destroy this temple, and in three days I will
raise it up.' This he said of the temple that was his body.
John 2. 19, 21

Response

Return to the Lord, who will have mercy,
To our God, who will richly pardon.

Collect

Grant, Lord,
that we who are baptised into the death
  of your Son our Saviour Jesus Christ
may continually put to death our evil desires
  and be buried with him;
that through the grave and gate of death
we may pass to our joyful resurrection;
through his merits, who died and was buried
  and rose again for us,
your Son Jesus Christ our Lord. **Amen**   *3*

EASTER DAY

Reading

Christ our Passover has been sacrificed for us: therefore let us keep the feast with the unleavened bread of sincerity and truth.

1 Corinthians 5. 7-8

Response

This is the day that the Lord has made. Alleluia!
Let us rejoice and be glad in it. Alleluia!

Collect

Lord of all life and power,
who through the mighty resurrection of your Son
overcame the old order of sin and death
to make all things new in him:
grant that we, being dead to sin
and alive to you in Jesus Christ,
may reign with him in glory;
to whom with you and the Holy Spirit
be praise and honour, glory and might,
now and in all eternity. **Amen.**

3

ASCENSION DAY

Reading

Why do you stand looking up toward heaven? This Jesus, who has been taken up from you into heaven, will come in the same way as you saw him go into heaven.

Acts 1. 11

Response

I am ascending to my Father and to your Father,
To my God and your God.

Collect

Grant, we pray, Almighty God,
that as we believe your only-begotten Son
  our Lord Jesus Christ
to have ascended into the heavens,
so we may also in heart and mind thither ascend
and with him continually dwell;
who is alive and reigns with you and the Holy Spirit,
one God, now and for ever. **Amen.**

1›

THE DAY OF PENTECOST

Reading
Jesus said, 'I will ask the Father and he will give you another
advocate, to be with you for ever, the Spirit of truth.'

John 14. 16-17a

Response
The Spirit searches all things,
Even the depths of God.

Collect
Almighty God,
who at this time
taught the hearts of your faithful people
by sending to them the light of your Holy Spirit:
grant us by the same Spirit
to have a right judgement in all things
and evermore to rejoice in his holy comfort;
through the merits of Christ Jesus our Saviour,
who is alive and reigns with you in the unity of the Spirit,
one God, now and for ever. **Amen.**   3

VISIT OF THE BVM TO ELIZABETH (31 May)

Reading
Elizabeth heard Mary's greeting and her child leapt in her womb.
Elizabeth exclaimed with a loud cry: 'Blessèd are you among
women, and blessèd is the fruit of your womb.'   *Luke 1. 41, 42*

Response
God has looked with favour on his lowly servant,
From this day, all generations shall call her blessèd.

Collect
Almighty God,
by whose grace Elizabeth rejoiced with Mary
and hailed her as the mother of the Lord:
fill us with your grace
that we may acclaim her Son as our Saviour
and rejoice to be called his brothers and sisters;
through Jesus Christ our Lord . . .   3/5

PENTECOST 1 – TRINITY SUNDAY

Reading
Jesus said to the disciples, 'Go, therefore, and make disciples of all nations, baptising them in the name of the Father and of the Son and of the Holy Spirit.'   *Matthew 28. 19*

Response
Holy, holy, holy is the Lord of hosts,
Who was, and is, and who is to come.

Collect
Almighty and everlasting God,
you have given us your servants grace,
by the confession of a true faith,
to acknowledge the glory of the eternal Trinity
and in the power of the divine Majesty to worship the Unity.
Keep us steadfast in this faith,
that we may evermore be defended from all adversities;
through Jesus Christ our Lord . . .   3

THURSDAY AFTER PENTECOST 1
DAY OF THANKSGIVING FOR THE EUCHARIST –
CORPUS CHRISTI

Reading
Jesus said, 'Those who eat my flesh and drink my blood abide in me and I in them.'   *John 6. 56*

Response
Mortals ate the food of angels,
You gave them bread from heaven.

Collect
Lord Jesus Christ,
we thank you that in this wonderful sacrament
you have given us the memorial of your passion:
grant us so to reverence the sacred mysteries
   of your body and blood
that we may know within ourselves
and show forth in our lives the fruits of your redemption;
for you live and reign with the Father and the Holy Spirit,
one God, now and for ever. **Amen**   3›

BIRTH OF JOHN THE BAPTIST (24 June)

Reading

'Truly I tell you', said Jesus, 'among those born of women, no one has arisen greater than John the Baptist.'   *Matthew 11. 11*

Response

'See, I am sending my messenger ahead of me,
To prepare my way before me.'

Collect

Almighty God,
whose servant John the Baptist
was wonderfully born to fulfil your purpose
by preparing the way for the advent of your Son:
lead us to repent according to his preaching
and, after his example,
constantly to speak the truth, boldly rebuke vice,
and patiently suffer for the truth's sake;
through Jesus Christ our Lord . . .   3

PETER & PAUL Apostles (29 June)

Reading

God, who worked through Peter, making him an apostle to the circumcised, also worked through me, in sending me to the Gentiles.   *Galatians 1. 8*

Response

Their voice has gone out to all the earth
And their words to the ends of the world.

Collect

Almighty God,
whose apostles Peter and Paul glorified you
in their death as in their life:
grant that your Church,
inspired by their teaching and example,
may ever stand firm on the one foundation
which is your Son, Jesus Christ our Lord . . .   3›

MARY MAGDALEN Apostle to the Apostles (22 July)

Reading

'Woman, why are you weeping? Whom are you looking for?'
Supposing him to be the gardener, she said to him, 'Sir, if you
have carried him away, tell me where you have laid him, and I
will take him away.' Jesus said to her, 'Mary!' She turned
and said to him in Hebrew, 'Rabbouni!', which means Teacher.

John 20. 13-16

Response

Mary came and told the disciples:
'I have seen the Lord!'

Collect

Almighty God, whose Son restored Mary Magdalen
  to health of mind and body
and called her to be a witness to his resurrection:
forgive us and heal us by your grace,
that we may serve you in the power of his risen life;
who is alive and reigns with you and the Holy Spirit,
one God, now and for ever. **Amen.**   3

TRANSFIGURATION OF CHRIST (6 August)

Reading

Jesus said, 'Father, glorify your name.' Then a voice came from
heaven, 'I have glorified it and I will glorify it again.'

John 12. 28

Response

It is good that we are here
To behold the glory that is Christ.

Collect

Almighty Father,
whose Son was revealed in majesty
before he suffered death upon the cross:
give us faith to perceive his glory
that we may be strengthened to suffer with him
and be changed into his likeness, from glory to glory;
who is alive and reigns with you and the Holy Spirit,
one God, now and for ever. **Amen.**   3

THE BLESSED VIRGIN MARY,
MOTHER OF OUR LORD (15 August)

Reading

Jesus went with his parents and came to Nazareth, and was obedient to them. His mother treasured all these things in her heart. And Jesus increased in wisdom and in years, and in divine and human favour.   *Luke 2. 51-52*

Response

Blessèd are you, Mary, the Lord is with you.
Through you we received our Redeemer,
   the Lord Jesus Christ!

Collect

Almighty God,
who chose the blessèd Virgin Mary
to be the mother of your only Son:
grant that we who are redeemed by his blood
may share with her
in the glory of your eternal kingdom;
through Jesus Christ our Lord . . .   3

BIRTH OF THE BVM (8 September)

Reading

When the time had fully come, God sent forth his Son, born of a woman, born under the law, to redeem those who were under the law, so that we might receive adoption as children.
                                                    Galatians 4. 4-5

Response

Blessèd are you, O Virgin Mary,
For you believed that what was said to you by the Lord
   would be fulfilled.

Collect

Almighty God,
who with special grace made the blessèd Virgin Mary
to be the mother of your only Son:
by the same grace make us holy in body and soul
and ever preserve in us your gifts of humility and love;
through Jesus Christ our Lord . . .   11›

HOLY CROSS DAY (14 September)

Reading
Christ abolished the law with its commandments and ordinances,
that he might create in himself one new humanity in place of
the two, thus making peace, and might reconcile both to God in
one body through the cross. *Ephesians 2. 15, 16*

Response
Far be it from me to glory
Save in the cross of our Lord Jesus Christ.

Collect
Almighty God,
who in the passion of your blessèd Son
made an instrument of painful death
to be for us the means of life:
grant us so to glory in the cross of Christ
that we may gladly suffer for his sake;
who is alive and reigns with you and the Holy Spirit,
one God, now and for ever. **Amen.** 3

MICHAEL & ALL ANGELS (29 September)

Reading
Jesus said, 'Truly, I say to you, you will see heaven opened,
and the angels of God ascending and descending upon the Son of
man.' *John 1. 51*

Response
The Lord commanded his angels
To keep you in all your ways.

Collect
Eternal Lord God,
you have drawn us together with the angels
in a wonderful order to serve you:
grant that as your holy angels
  always minister to you in heaven,
so, by your appointment,
they may help and defend us on earth;
through Jesus Christ our Lord . . . 3/5

ALL SAINTS' DAY (1 November)

Reading

There was a great multitude, which no one could number, from every nation, from all tribes and peoples and languages, standing before the throne and before the Lamb, robed in white, with palm branches in their hands. They cried out in a loud voice saying: 'Salvation belongs to our God, who is seated on the throne, and to the Lamb!' *Revelation* 7. 9, 10

Response

The righteous will shine like the sun
In the kingdom of the Father.

Collect

Almighty God, you have knit together your elect
into one communion and fellowship
  in the mystical body of your Son Christ our Lord.
Give us grace so to follow your blessèd saints
in all virtuous and godly living,
that we may come to those inexpressible joys
which you have prepared for those who truly love you;
through Jesus Christ our Lord . . .   3›

COMMEMORATION OF THE FAITHFUL DEPARTED
known as **ALL SOULS' DAY** (2 November)

Reading

Jesus said, 'Very truly, I tell you, anyone who hears my word and believes him who sent me has eternal life, and does not come under judgement, but has passed from death to life.' *John* 5. 24

Response

I am the resurrection and the life;
Whoever believe in me, though they die,
  yet shall they live.

Collect

O God, the maker and redeemer of all:
grant us, with all the faithful departed,
the sure benefits of your Son's saving passion
  and glorious resurrection
that, in the last day,
when you gather up all things in Christ,
we may with them enjoy the fullness of your promises;
through Jesus Christ our Lord . . .   11›

THE KINGSHIP OF CHRIST
THE SUNDAY NEXT BEFORE ADVENT

Reading
God raised Christ from the dead and enthroned him at his right
hand in the heavenly realms, far above all government and
authority, all power and dominion.　　　　*Ephesians 1. 20-21*

Response
God raised Christ from the dead
And enthroned him at his right hand in heaven.

Collect
Eternal Father,
whose Son Jesus Christ ascended to the throne of heaven
that he might rule over all things as Lord:
keep the Church in the unity of the Spirit
and in the bond of his peace
and bring the whole created order to worship at his feet;
who is alive and reigns with you and the Holy Spirit,
one God, now and for ever. **Amen.**　　　　3

ADVENT SUNDAY

Reading
Now it is time for you to wake out of sleep, for salvation is
nearer to us now than when we first became believers.
　　　　Romans 13. 11

Response
Lord Jesus, you are the one who is to come,
The one whom we await with longing hearts.

Collect
Almighty God,
give us grace to cast away the works of darkness
and to put on the armour of light,
now in the time of this mortal life,
in which your Son Jesus Christ
　　came to us in great humility:
so that on the last day,
when he shall come again in his glorious majesty
　　to judge the living and the dead,
we may rise to the life immortal;
through him who is alive and reigns
　　with you and the Holy Spirit,
one God, now and for ever. **Amen.**　　　　3

CONCEPTION OF THE BVM (8 December)

Reading

The Lord himself will give you a sign: look, the virgin is with child and shall bear a son, and shall name him Emmanuel, God is with us.   *Isaiah 7. 14*

Response

The Almighty has done great things for her
And holy is his name!

Collect

Eternal God,
who prepared the blessèd Virgin Mary
to be the mother of your Son:
grant that, as we rejoice in his coming as our Saviour,
so we may be ready to greet him
when he comes as our Judge;
for he is alive and reigns with you and the Holy Spirit,
one God, now and for ever. **Amen.**   1

CHRISTMAS DAY (25 December)

Reading

Belovèd, let us love one another, because love is from God;
everyone who loves is born of God and knows God. Whoever does
not love does not know God, for God is love. God's love was
revealed among us in this way: God sent his only Son into the
world so that we might live through him.   *1 John 4. 7-9*

Response

Glory to God in the Highest!
And on earth, peace!

Collect

Almighty God,
you have given us your only-begotten Son
to take our nature upon him
and as at this time to be born of a pure virgin:
grant that we, who have been born again
and made your children by adoption and grace,
may daily be renewed by your Holy Spirit;
through Jesus Christ our Lord . . .   1›

ST STEPHEN THE FIRST MARTYR (26 December)

Reading

As they were stoning Stephen, he prayed, 'Lord Jesus, receive my spirit.' And he knelt down and cried with a loud voice, 'Lord, do not hold this sin against them.' And when he had said this, he fell asleep. *Acts 8. 59-60*

Response

God is love, and those who abide in love abide in God.
God abides in those who confess that Jesus
  is the Son of God.

Collect

Heavenly Father,
give us grace in all our sufferings for the truth
to follow the example of your martyr, Saint Stephen:
that we also may look to him who was crucified
and pray for those who persecute us;
through Jesus Christ our Lord . . .   3

JOHN THE EVANGELIST (27 December)

Reading

Peter turned and saw following them the disciple whom Jesus loved, who had lain close to his breast at the supper. Peter said, 'Lord, what about this man?' Jesus said to him, 'If it is my will that he remain until I come, what is that to you? Follow me!' *John 21. 20-22*

Response

The Word became flesh and dwelt among us,
Full of grace and truth.

Collect

Merciful Father,
whose Son is the light of the world:
so guide your Church by the teaching
  of your apostle and evangelist Saint John
that we may walk by the light that has come among us
and finally know him as the light of everlasting life;
who is alive and reigns with you and the Holy Spirit,
one God, now and for ever. **Amen.**   3

THE HOLY INNOCENTS (28 December)

Reading

Jesus called a child, whom he put among his disciples, and
said, 'Truly I tell you, unless you change and become like
children, you will never enter the kingdom of heaven. Whoever
welcomes one such child in my name welcomes me.' *Matthew 18. 3*

Response

To all who received him, who believed in his name,
He gave power to become the children of God.

Collect

Heavenly Father,
whose children suffered at the hands of Herod,
though they had done no wrong:
give us grace neither to act cruelly
nor to stand indifferently by,
but to defend the weak from the tyranny of the strong;
in the name of Jesus Christ who suffered for us,
but who is alive and reigns with you and the Holy Spirit,
one God, now and for ever. **Amen.** 3

NEW YEAR'S EVE (31 December)

Reading

In the beginning, Lord, you founded the earth, and the heavens
are the work of your hands; they will perish but you remain;
they will all grow old like a garment, like a cloak you will
roll them up, and they will be changed. But you are the same,
and your years will never end. *Hebrews 1. 10-12*

Response

In the beginning was the Word,
And the Word was God.

Collect

God and Father of our Lord Jesus Christ,
whose years never fail
and whose mercies are new each returning day:
let the radiance of your Spirit renew our lives,
warming our hearts and giving light to our minds;
that we may pass the coming year
   in joyful obedience and firm faith;
through him who is the beginning and the end,
your Son Christ our Lord. **Amen.** 6

The Common of Holy Days

OF THE BLESSED VIRGIN MARY

Reading
Mary said, 'Behold, the handmaid of the Lord; let it be to me
according to your word.' *Luke 1. 38*

Response
Hail, Mary, full of grace, the Lord is with you.
Because God has blessed you for ever.

Collect
Almighty God,
with grace you have made the blessèd Virgin Mary
to be the mother of your only Son:
by the same grace,
hallow our bodies in chastity
and our souls in humility and love;
through Jesus Christ our Lord . . .   9›

OF APOSTLES & EVANGELISTS

Reading
Preach the word, be urgent in season and out of season,
convince, rebuke and exhort; be unfailing in patience and
teaching. Always be steady, enduring suffering; do the work of
an evangelist, fulfil your ministry. *2 Timothy 4. 1-2, 4-5*

Response
You did not choose me, but I chose you,
I appointed you to go out and bear fruit,
   the fruit that shall last.

Collect
Almighty God,
who built your Church upon the foundation
   of the apostles and prophets
with Jesus Christ himself as the chief corner-stone:
so join us together in unity of spirit by their doctrine,
that we may be made a holy temple acceptable to you;
through Jesus Christ our Lord . . .   3

OF MARTYRS

Reading

When the Lamb opened the fifth seal, I saw under the altar the souls of those who had been slaughtered for the word of God and for the testimony they had given.   *Revelation 6. 9*

Response

Blessèd are those who are persecuted for the cause of right,
The kingdom of heaven is theirs!

Collect

Almighty God,
by whose grace and power your holy *martyr N.*
triumphed over suffering and *was* faithful unto death:
strengthen us with your grace,
that we may endure reproach and persecution,
and faithfully bear witness to the name
   of Jesus Christ our Lord . . .   3

OF TEACHERS OF THE FAITH OR CONFESSORS

Reading

Wisdom guided them in straight paths; she showed them God's kingdom and gave them knowledge of holy things.   *Wisdom 10. 10*

Response

Those who keep the commandments and teach them
Shall be considered great in the kingdom of heaven.

Collect

Almighty God,
who enlightened your Church
   by the teaching of your servant *N.*:
enrich it evermore with your heavenly grace,
and raise up faithful witnesses,
who by their life and teaching
may proclaim the truth of your salvation;
through Jesus Christ our Lord . . .   3›

OF BISHOPS

Reading

Remember your leaders, who preached the word of God to you; and reflecting on the outcome of their life and work, follow the example of their faith.   *Hebrews 13. 7*

Response

I will give you shepherds after my own heart,
Who will feed you with knowledge and understanding.

Collect

Almighty God,
the light of the faithful
and shepherd of souls,
who set your servant *N.* to be a bishop in the Church,
to feed your sheep by the word of Christ
and to guide them by good example:
give us grace to keep the faith of the Church
and to follow in the footsteps
of Jesus Christ our Lord . . .   3›

OF RELIGIOUS

Reading

A young man said to Jesus, 'I have kept all the commandments from my youth; what do I still lack?' Jesus said to him, 'If you wish to be perfect, go, sell your possessions, give the money to the poor, and you will have treasure in heaven; then come, follow me.'   *Matthew 19. 20-21*

Response

Blessèd are the pure in heart,
For they shall see God.

Collect

Almighty God,
by whose grace *N.*,
kindled by the fire of your love,
became a burning and a shining light in your Church:
inflame us with the same spirit of discipline and love,
that we may ever walk before you as children of light;
through Jesus Christ our Lord . . .   3

OF MISSIONARIES

Reading

How beautiful upon the mountains are the feet of the messenger
who announces peace, who brings good news, who announces
salvation, who says to Zion, 'Your God reigns!'   *Isaiah 52. 7*

Response

Give thanks to the Lord; call upon his name!
Tell the nations all that he has done!

Collect

Everlasting God,
whose *servants N. & N.* carried the good news of your Son
to the dark places of the world:
grant that we who commemorate *their* service
may know the hope of the gospel in our hearts
and manifest its light in all our ways;
through Jesus Christ our Lord . . .   3›

OF GROUP COMMEMORATIONS

Reading

In all these things, we are more than conquerors through him who
loved us. For I am convinced that neither death, nor life, nor
angels, nor rulers, nor things present, nor things to come, nor
powers, nor height, nor depth, nor anything in all creation,
will be able to separate us from the love of God in Christ Jesus
our Lord.   *Romans 8. 37-end*

Response

The Lord looks on those who revere him,
On those who trust in his merciful love.

Collect

Almighty God,
who call your witnesses from every nation
and reveal your glory in their lives:
make us thankful for the example of *N. & N.*
and strengthen us by their fellowship,
that we, like them, may be faithful
  in the service of your kingdom;
through Jesus Christ our Lord . . .   3›

OF ANY SAINT

Reading

Finally, beloved, whatever is true, whatever is honourable, whatever is just, whatever is pure, whatever is pleasing, whatever is commendable, if there is any excellence and if there is anything worthy of praise, think on these things.

Philippians 4. 8

Response

The righteous will be remembered for ever,
The memory of the righteous is a blessing.

Collect

Almighty God, who built your Church
   through the love and devotion of your saints,
we give thanks for your servants *N. & N.,*
whom we commemorate today:
inspire us to follow *their* example
that we in our generation may rejoice with *them*
in the vision of your glory;
through Jesus Christ our Lord . . .   3›

FOR UNITY

Reading

Two are better than one, because they have a good reward for their toil. For if they fall, one will lift up the other; but woe to the one who is alone and falls and does not have another to help.   *Ecclesiastes 4. 9, 10*

Response

Christ is our peace, who had made us one,
Christ has broken down the barriers which divided us.

Collect

Heavenly Father,
who called us in the Body of your Son Jesus Christ
to continue his work of reconciliation
and reveal you to all the world:
forgive us the sins which tear us apart,
give us the courage to overcome our fears
and to seek that unity
which is your gift and your will;
through Jesus Christ our Lord . . .   3

FOR PEACE

Reading

Jesus said, 'I have said this to you that you may have peace.
In the world, you face persecution. But take courage; I have
overcome the world!'   *John 17. 33*

Response

Live with one another in peace
And the God of peace will be with you.

Collect

Almighty Father,
whose will is to restore all things
in your belovèd Son, Jesus Christ:
govern the hearts and minds of those in authority,
and bring the families of the nations,
divided and torn apart by the ravages of sin,
to be subject to his just and gentle rule;
who is alive and reigns with you and the Holy Spirit,
one God, now and for ever. **Amen.**   3

THE DEPARTED

Reading

We do not live to ourselves and we do not die to ourselves.
If we live, we live to the Lord; if we die, we die to the Lord.
So then, whether we live or whether we die, we are the Lord's.
For to this end, Christ died and lived again, so that he might
be Lord of both the dead and the living.   *Romans 14. 7-9*

Response

I am the resurrection and the life, said the Lord,
**Whoever believe in me, though they die,
    yet shall they live.**

Collect

Merciful God,
whose Son Jesus Christ is the resurrection
    and the life of all the faithful:
raise us from the death of sin
to the life of righteousness,
that at the last, we (*with our brother/sister N.,*)
may come to your eternal joy;
through Jesus Christ our Lord . . .   3

Table of Moveable Feasts

YEAR	SUNDAYS BEFORE LENT	ASH WED	EASTER DAY	ASC. DAY	PENTECOST	1ST SUNDAY OF THE K'DOM	ADVENT SUNDAY	YEAR
1994	6 Feb : 2 Before Lent	16 Feb	3 Apr	12 May	22 May	6 Nov ⊕	27 Nov	1994
1995	5 Feb : 4 Before Lent	1 Mar	16 Apr	25 May	4 Jun	5 Nov	3 Dec	1995
1996 [LV]	4 Feb : 3 Before Lent	21 Feb	7 Apr	16 May	26 May	3 Nov	1 Dec	1996 [LV]
1997	9 Feb : 1 Before Lent	12 Feb	30 Mar	8 May	18 May	2 Nov	30 Nov	1997
1998	8 Feb : 3 Before Lent	25 Feb	12 Apr	21 May	31 May	1 Nov	29 Nov	1998
1999	7 Feb : 2 Before Lent	17 Feb	4 Apr	13 May	23 May	7 Nov ⊕	28 Nov	1999
2000 [LV]	6 Feb : 5 Before Lent	8 Mar	23 Apr	1 Jun	11 Jun	5 Nov	3 Dec	2000 [LV]
2001	4 Feb : 4 Before Lent	28 Feb	15 Apr	24 May	3 Jun	4 Nov	2 Dec	2001
2002	3 Feb : 2 Before Lent	13 Feb	31 Mar	9 May	19 May	3 Nov	1 Dec	2002
2003	9 Feb : 4 Before Lent	5 Mar	20 Apr	29 May	8 Jun	2 Nov	30 Nov	2003
2004 [LV]	8 Feb : 3 Before Lent	25 Feb	11 Apr	20 May	30 May	7 Nov ⊕	28 Nov	2004 [LV]
2005	6 Feb : 1 Before Lent	9 Feb	27 Mar	5 May	15 May	6 Nov ⊕	27 Nov	2005
2006	5 Feb : 4 Before Lent	1 Mar	16 Apr	25 May	4 Jun	5 Nov	3 Dec	2006
2007	4 Feb : 3 Before Lent	21 Feb	8 Apr	17 May	27 May	4 Nov	2 Dec	2007
2008 [LV]	3 Feb : 1 Before Lent	6 Feb	23 Mar	1 May	11 May	2 Nov	30 Nov	2008 [LV]
2009	8 Feb : 3 Before Lent	25 Feb	12 Apr	21 May	31 May	1 Nov	29 Nov	2009
2010	7 Feb : 2 Before Lent	17 Feb	4 Apr	13 May	23 May	7 Nov ⊕	28 Nov	2010

Scripture Index

Psalm Index

General Index

Acknowledgements

Gratitude is expressed to Charles Mortimer Guilbert, Custodian of the Standard *Book of Common Prayer* (1979) of the Episcopal Church in the USA, for use of The Psalms and other material from that book, on which no copyright is claimed. The psalms have been adjusted to comply with British orthography and usage and inclusivised in most references to human beings.

Scriptural texts are a combination of as many as eleven different translations of the Bible, as well as reference to original texts, and it would be impossible to give a specific attribution each time; however, the *Revised Standard Version* and the *New Revised Standard Version* have probably made the most notable contribution to the texts finally chosen.

Gratitude is also expressed to the following for permission to reproduce material, some of which is copyright:

© The Division of Christian Education of the National Council of the Churches of Christ in the USA: scriptural texts from the *Revised Standard Version* (1946, 1952 & 1971) and the *New Revised Standard Version* (1989) of the Bible;

Prayers with the attribution 1, adapted from *The Book of Common Prayer*, the rights in which are vested in the Crown, are reproduced by permission of the Crown's Patentee, Cambridge University Press;

© The Central Board of Finance of the Church of England:

Prayers from *The Book of Common Prayer as proposed in 1928*, with the attribution 2;

Prayers and canticles from *The Alternative Service Book 1980 (ASB)*, prayers with the attribution 3; The Calendar;

Prayers from *Lent, Holy Week, Easter*, Church House Publishing, CUP & SPCK, 1984 & 1986, with the attribution 4;

Adaptation to prayers in *The Alternative Service Book 1980* made in *Making Women Visible*, Church House Publishing, 1988, with the additional attribution 5;

Prayers from *The Promise of His Glory*, Church House Publishing & Mowbray, 1991, with the attribution 6;

© The International Consultation on English Texts (ICET), 1970, 1971 & 1975; now known as The English Language Liturgical Consultation (ELLC) 1988: the English translations of *The Lord's Prayer* (adapted by ASB), *The Apostles' Creed, Benedictus, Te Deum, Magnificat* and *Nunc dimittis*;

© Janet Morley: a prayer from *All Desires Known*, SPCK, 1992, with the attribution 15;

© David Silk, Bishop of Ballarat: prayers from *Prayers for Use at the Alternative Services*, Mowbray, copyright © 1980 & 1986, with the attribution 17;

Portsmouth Cathedral: for the use of several of the 'prayers of light', which began life there.

Especial thanks are due to Ruth McCurry, Religious Publisher at Mowbray, for her invaluable assistance in ensuring that the advice offered is 'user friendly' and for gently persuading the Compilers to exclude religious verbiage.

The number which precedes each item in the list of sources or authors below is used throughout the book to ascribe the material to which permission relates or to which acknowledgement is made; such numbers in the text are slightly inset from the right margin. A number accompanied by the symbol › indicates that minor alterations have been made.

The Church of England

1   *The Book of Common Prayer*
2   *The Book of Common Prayer as proposed in 1928*
3   *The Alternative Service Book 1980*
4   *Lent, Holy Week & Easter*
5   *Making Women Visible*
6   *The Promise of His Glory*

The Anglican Communion

7   The Society of Saint Francis (SSF)
8   The Anglican Church of Canada, *Book of Alternative Services*
9   The Episcopal Church of Scotland, *Book of Common Prayer* (1929)
10 The Episcopal Church of the USA, *Book of Common Prayer* (1979)
11 The Church of the Province of Southern Africa, *Liturgy 75*

Individuals

12 The Revd Paul Gibson
13 The Revd Christopher Irvine
14 The Revd Charles MacDonnell
15 Dr Janet Morley
16 The Revd Canon Michael Perham
17 The Rt Revd David Silk
18 The Rt Revd David Stancliffe
19 The Revd Michael Vasey

If any copyright has been unwittingly transgressed, or a necessary gratitude gone unexpressed, the Society offers its apologies and will rectify any such oversight in any future edition.